DATE			

© THE BAKER & TAYLOR CO.

The Development of the Labour
Process in Capitalist Societies

The Development of the Labour Process in Capitalist Societies

A Comparative Study of the Transformation of Work Organization in Britain, Japan and the USA

Craig R. Littler

Imperial College,
London University

Heinemann Educational Books

For Gill

Heinemann Educational Books Ltd
22 Bedford Square, London WC1B 3HH

LONDON EDINBURGH MELBOURNE AUCKLAND
HONG KONG SINGAPORE KUALA LUMPUR
IBADAN NAIROBI JOHANNESBURG
EXETER (NH) KINGSTON PORT OF SPAIN

First published 1982

British Library Cataloguing in Publication Data

The development of the labour process in capitalist
societies
1. Industrial relations   2. Industrial sociology
I. Title
306'.36   HD6971
ISBN 0-435-82540-2
ISBN 0-435-82541-0 Pbk

Typeset by Inforum Ltd, Portsmouth
Printed by Biddles Ltd, Guildford, Surrey

Contents

List of Figures

List of Tables

Acknowledgements

This book would not have been possible without the willing co-operation of numerous people. I would like to thank the following for their help, criticism and comment: June Bayles, Bob Blackburn, V. M. A. Brownlow, Michael Burrage, David Dunkerley, Patrick Fridenson, Howard Gospel, Edwin Layton, David Lee, Martin Lockett, Joseph Melling, Horace Moulden, John Pleming and Stephen Wood. I am particularly grateful to Ronald Dore for his assistance on Japan and for the help and encouragement which I received from Sydney Pollard, Graeme Salaman, Stephen Hill and Gill Palmer.

Routledge & Kegan Paul, the Open University Press, and the British Sociological Association were kind enough to give permission to include in this book material originally published in the following:

Understanding Taylorism, *British Journal of Sociology*, **29**, 2, June, 1978

Social Sciences: A Second Level Course, D207, 'Power & Ideology in Work Organizations: Britain and Japan', Block 3, Study Section 22, 1981

Bravermania and Beyond: Recent Theories of the Labor Process, *Sociology*, **16**, 2, May 1982.

Grateful acknowledgement is made to the following for permission to reproduce tables in this book:

Table 6.2 from *Working Hours in British Industry: An Economic History*, M.A. Bienefeld, published by Weidenfeld and Nicolson.
Figure 8.1 from *The Rise of Corporate Economy*, L. Hannah, published by Methuen.
Table 11.1 from *Capital in the American Economy*, published by N.B.E.R./Princeton University Press.

Lastly, I am grateful to Elsie Palmer for undertaking the burdensome task of typing and re-typing.

1 Introduction: Basic Issues of The Labour Process Debate

Since the publication of Braverman's *Labor and Monopoly Capital* in 1974 there has been a continuing and widening labour process debate in sociology, economics and labour history. In essence this debate is about the nature, origins and processes of transformation of work organization. In this chapter I will outline the basic points of disagreement in terms of four broad areas: traditional modes of labour control; the processes of change under monopoly capitalism; employer strategies and patterns of opposition; and labour markets and the labour process.

Firstly there is the question of the conceptualization of nineteenth century modes of labour control. This links with the labour aristocracy debate (see Moorhouse, 1978). A number of historians have sought to explain nineteenth century labour/capital relationships in terms of a 'labour aristocracy', but the basis of this aristocracy (high wages or skill or authority at work) is the subject of disagreement. In particular it is not clear whether the skilled craft group is coincident with the labour aristocracy (contrast Foster, 1974; Stedman-Jones, 1975; Hinton, 1973). From our point of view the fundamental question is whether competitive capitalism can be identified with craft work such that rationalization really meant the displacement of craft control. Writers such as Braverman have provided an inadequate analysis of traditional forms of labour control such that it is difficult to locate the specific context and targets of rationalization. Frequently handicraft labour under petty commodity production is made the measure of all production processes. In so far as 'craft control' is not identified with petty commodity handicraft production, it tends to remain an unexamined concept (see Chapter 3). I shall argue that a simple model of craft deskilling is untenable and that an empirical investigation of the implementation of Taylorism in Britain leads to a different and more complex picture (see especially Chapter 9).

Understanding the social relations of craft production and traditional modes of management is connected with the thorny problem of conceptualizing 'skill'. This is discussed at length in Chapter 2.

The second broad area of debate relates to the conceptualization of the processes of change under advanced capitalism. This question breaks down into several subordinate questions. Is it possible to characterize changes in work organization in terms of a unilinear trend or has there been a combination of processes, some of which are in conflict and contradictory? Has there been a pattern of uneven development with significant differences among industries? If the latter has been the case, then this raises the problem of how we classify industries. Many of the current arguments about craft control and deskilling would be clarified if we had an adequate sociological classification of industries. The simple dichotomies on offer (science-based versus non-science based; monopolistic versus competitive; labour-intensive versus capital-intensive) are not adequate to the theoretical demands placed upon them. In Chapter 6 I attempt to work out an historically-based classification of industries.

Central to understanding the pattern of development of the capitalist labour process is the problem of periodization. As I will point out in Chapter 3, there is a significant disagreement between Braverman and Marx as to when the real subordination of labour (RSL) occurred. For Marx the real subordination of labour to capital occurred largely during the Industrial Revolution, whereas Braverman suggests that the organization of work and the structure of control carried the marks of a pre-industrial order for long after the Industrial Revolution. In addition, several writers (Edwards, 1979; Burgess, 1980) wish to identify 'crises of control' which constitute a watershed in the development of the labour process. But was the crucial period of transformation in Britain the Great Depression of 1873–96, or the First World War, or the inter-war years, or none of these? I will argue in this book that the crucial period of change was the inter-war period, though there was no simple, singular crisis of control.

Related to the problem of the timing and speed of change is the question of the links between the transformation of the labour process and the trajectory of the manufacturing firm, especially the development of monopoly capitalism. In particular, can we derive labour process dynamics from the logic of capital concentration and accumulation? In other words is the labour process deducible from the capitalist mode of production? It is at this point that there is the crucial divide between those theorists who emphasize teleological models of economic and industrial development, and those who insist that it is necessary to situate labour strategies within the particular circumstances of investment strategies, product markets, and the policies of trade unions and employers' federations. This exemplifies the perennial friction between 'iron law' theorists and conjunctural theorists, between global perspectives and detailed, empirical analysis.

Even if we adopt a global, theoretical perspective, there are still disagreements about the core features of the logic of capitalism. How much emphasis should be given to Taylorism, or the notion of de-skilling, or bureaucratization and bureaucratic control? Braverman, for example, insists on rejecting the concept of bureaucratization, a rejection which seems to be based on a fear of losing sight of Marxian fundamentals, including class antagonisms, by using Weberian concepts. In contrast Edwards (1979), Burawoy (1979) and Clawson (1980) argue that some notion of bureaucratic control is essential in order theoretically to grasp the nature of advanced capitalism. Some of the contradictory views about deskilling are discussed in Chapter 2, Weberian ideas on bureaucratization are dealt with in Chapter 4 and the sharp disagreements about the influence of Taylorism are discussed in Chapters 5 and 11.

The third general area of debate relates to the conceptualization of organizational forms and dominant managerial strategies. In other words, how are we to characterize the 'end-points' of the process of change? This raises the deeper problem of how far it is possible to be taxonomic about the labour process and labour strategies.[1]   It can be argued that the notion of 'management strategy' and typologies of strategy are impossible because there is a negotiative, learning process whereby workers react to managerial tactics and new strategies recede in importance, decay and blend with the old. As a result 'conflicting principles of labour-management may be woven into the structure of the firm' (Jones, 1978, p. 13.). A failure to appreciate this point leads to what may be called the 'panacea fallacy', which, for example, permeates Edwards's (1979) work. The fallacy here is the assumption that because welfarism or Taylorism did not provide a total solution to the so-called 'labour problem' but contained contradictions, *something else did provide a total solution*. This assumption in turn leads to a conceptual search in order to pin-point the magic strategy that successfully stabilized capital/labour relations. This fallacy ignores the obvious fact that all control strategies are developing in ways which involve combinations of management practices and which may involve perpetual contradictions.

The counter-argument here is that instead of simple dichotomies (such as those of Friedman, 1977), it is necessary to evolve more complex typologies and that the cost of not doing this is to give up theorizing entirely (see Chapter 4). But even if this is granted, then is it useful to start with labour control strategies as the basis of a taxonomy? There are two interwoven issues here. First, it may not be possible to isolate control because control and influence may be achieved by *non-*

control mechanisms. Managerial decisions concerning levels and areas of investment, types of product and raw materials, marketing strategies, accounting procedures and so on may have control implications. Thus the introduction of numerically-controlled machine tools in many plants was motivated by product criteria – the necessity for totally accurate machining of complex jobs for aerospace and nuclear work. Clearly however, the spread of numerically-controlled machine tools raises control issues, as much recent literature points out (e.g. Noble 1979; Jones, 1978).

Second, it is worth noting that employers' strategies can occur at several levels; that of the firm, employers' federation or indeed the state. The coherence of strategy often depends on ideological integration and the intermediate coordination provided by employers' associations. Thus there is the problem of the units of analysis and of disentangling firm-level control strategies from the wider economic or ideological framework.

What light do cross-cultural comparisons throw on the issue of alternative managerial strategies? The British experience has become the typical model of industrialization for social theory, particularly Marxist theory. This, of course, raises the question of whether the British case was an archetypal case. Briefly, the answer is no. As Kumar points out: 'Seen from the perspective of the present, a century and a half later, the British case stands out as unique in almost every important respect.' (Kumar, 1978, p. 126). It was unique in its gradualness, in its bourgeois nature, in its unplanned nature and the lack of state control, and in its freedom from foreign influences. In addition, Britain had no model to follow and there was a total lack of management or organization theory during the Industrial Revolution (see Chapter 6).

On the continent, the commercial class was a much more marginal group in society and, as a result, it was *not* the middle classes who promoted industrialization. The pattern in France, Germany and Italy was one of forced industrialization imposed, often on an unwilling society, by the state. Industrialization in these societies was from the start a political imperative. Moreover this was true of second-generation industrializers such as Japan as we shall see in Chapter 10. In general this book argues that cross-cultural analysis is essential in order to grasp the significance of British developments (see Chapters 10, 11 and 12).

Cross-cultural comparisons also illustrate the nature and effects of worker resistance to employer control strategies. What is crucial here is the composition and the changing composition of the working class. What is missing from some labour process writing (Braverman, Zimbalist, Clawson) is the notion that an industrial labour force must be

constituted by, for example, migration and by the internal differentiation of the workforce within one society. Clearly there are different
types of capitalist society in terms of the constitution of its labour force.
An obvious point in relation to the USA is that the waves of immigration created a labour process 'increasingly organized on the basis of
ethnically and linguistically segregated work groups' (Davis, 1980,
p. 37; also see Chapter 11). This splintered world of US labour clearly
affected the potential for worker resistance to labour rationalization. As
Braverman hardly mentions shopfloor resistance to the process that he
describes and provides no discussion of the trade union responses, he
robs himself of any opportunity to analyse the different patterns of
opposition. It will be a major contribution of this book to explore the
following questions. How much resistance to developing managerial
control systems occurred in Britain, especially in the crucial inter-war
period? Did more resistance occur in Britain than in other capitalist
societies, such as Japan and the USA? If so, why was this the case?
What were the sources and patterns of resistance? Answers to these
questions will enable us to fill in the lacunae in the labour process
debate.

The fourth general area of debate arises from the recent integration of
some economic and sociological analysis. As Lee (1981) has pointed out
it is only possible to analyse deskilling in relation to the total structure
of opportunities, which entails some notion of a labour market. This
raises the problem of what are the links and correspondence between
labour market structures and the labour process (see Edwards, 1979
and Chapter 2 of this work). Finally, the concept of labour markets and
segmented labour markets relates to the broad issues of class and the
reproduction of class differences within the labour process, issues
which overlap with the link between waged and non-waged labour.

These, then, have been the basic issues of the labour process debate
and form the main concerns of the following chapters.[2]

Part One Theoretical Perspectives

2 The Division of Labour and Deskilling

The division of labour

The term 'division of labour' has been used in various ways and thus causes considerable confusion. As an essential preliminary, therefore, I will sort out these confusions and then go on to clarify the notion of 'skill' and processes of skill change in production. Broadly there are three types of division of labour under capitalism:

(1) Within the factory and firm organized by management;
(2) Between workers working for different units of capital, which is organized through the market in terms of commodity exchange;
(3) Between commodity production and non-commodity production within residual sectors or organized by the state or by the family.

Each form of the division of labour refers to different levels of abstraction and different historical processes are pertinent. Thus corresponding to (1), (2) and (3) above are the following processes:

(1) Skill changes, rationalization and struggles within production;
(2) The concentration and centralization of capital and the international division of labour;
(3) Capitalist expansion with respect to both other economic systems and domestic production, plus political struggles over the forms of state intervention. (Himmelweit, 1982).

The primary focus of this chapter is on the division of labour within the factory and the associated historical skill changes. This has been the typical level of analysis in the labour process debate, but as I will point out in the final section of this chapter in relation to the labour market, hypotheses about the directions of change in the labour process entail a detailed consideration of the second level of the division of labour, because competition among firms affects the total opportunity structure for skills (Lee, 1981). In sum, in order to establish aggregate skill movements the level of analysis should be, but usually has not been, societal.

Conceptions of skill

All debate about changes in the skill-content of jobs under capitalism turns upon some conception of skill. One approach to skill is to regard it as an objective characteristic of work routines and job knowledge such that it can be defined in terms of job-learning time or the type of knowledge-base of the occupation.

In considering objective notions of skill it is useful to go back to the work of Georges Friedmann who was one of the first modern theorists to attempt some analytic distinctions. Essentially he distinguished between the specialist and the specialized (semi-skilled) worker. There are three bases for this distinction. Firstly, the specialist's sphere of activity stems from a previous professional training, whereas the specialized worker has not received 'any general training such as would form a background explaining or illuminating his "unit of work" by connecting it with the whole process'. Secondly, the specialist still has a recognized trade or profession, whilst the specialized worker does simple repetitive jobs which no longer form part of any basic trade. Thirdly, there is a distinction in terms of the relation between the self and the role: 'In the one the whole person is involved in the job: in the other . . . there is no such involvement at all, still less any development of personality.' (Friedmann, 1961, pp. 85–88).

Though Friedmann's distinction in terms of general versus specific job knowledge and routinized versus non-routinized work procedures has been generally accepted and indeed forms the common currency of most academic discussions on skill, it nevertheless does not readily apply to manual work variation. Fox, also noting the incompleteness of Friedmann's categories, suggests a two-dimensional model of work roles. Starting with Jacques's distinction between prescribed and discretionary work, he proposes a dimension of 'discretionary-content' such that 'the behaviours called for by the role may be either specifically defined, thereby offering little choice, or diffusely defined, thereby requiring the exercise of discretion'. And this is combined with a dimension of 'task-range' (Fox, 1974, pp. 16 and 24–5; Jacques, 1961). These distinctions are best shown by means of a diagram (Figure 2.1).

Using the categories in Figure 2.1, it is clear that Friedmann's 'specialist' falls into Box B, whilst the 'specialized worker' corresponds to A. Moreover, we can say that a shift from D to B is best termed 'specialization', whilst a shift from D to A is best called 'fragmentation'. Thus some types of change in the labour process, namely specialization, can create high status specialists with considerable discretion. In

Figure 2.1   Dimensions of work roles

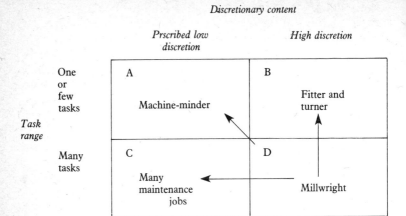

Discretionary content

considering Figure 2.1, it is important not to confuse the specific examples in the boxes with the basic concepts. The millwright for example is a limited starting-point. Capitalism largely created this job-category and expanded it through the latter years of the eighteenth century and the early years of the nineteenth. The point of Figure 2.1 is to summarize two dimensions of skill and to locate the different processes of change in the labour process.

The dimension of discretionary content relates to a second widespread conception of 'skill', namely skill as job autonomy. In a recent comprehensive survey of jobs in a local labour market, Blackburn and Mann concluded that:

A relatively skilled position was one of trust, where the worker was granted a sphere of competence within which decisions, *whether routine or complex*, could be taken by the worker himself. This 'guaranteed autonomy' is the essence of the traditional craft occupation within which the workers themselves control the productive process . . . Psychologically it is an encouragement to self-direction . . . It is social, not technical. The centre of the technique is not complexity, but autonomy and freedom.

(Blackburn and Mann, 1979, p. 292, emphasis added)

Similarly Hinton, in discussing engineering craftsmen in the 1900s, stresses the tradition and centrality of job-autonomy. Inside every engineering worker, according to Hinton, lay an image of the traditional millwright, a worker who could do a job from start to finish without interference or intervention from the employer (Hinton, 1973, pp. 96–7). This structural notion clearly links 'skill', and changes in skill levels, to the modes of control in the work organization. It means that it is not possible to define 'skill' independently of organizational control and control processes.

Both skill as job-learning time and skill as job-autonomy have an apparently objective basis. However, in practice it proves difficult to find an objective basis for the labour quality of jobs. When asked how many skilled employees he has, the typical employer will state the number of people who are paid the 'skilled rate'. However, this allows the possibility that the vast majority of workers who are paid the skilled rate do jobs that can be learned in months, weeks or even days. For example, at present skilled engineering jobs require four years' apprenticeship, but few would pretend that this is a measure of the necessary training time. Indeed in 1978 the Engineering Industry Training Board argued for an end to so-called time-served apprenticeships and the substitution of 'training to standard', which could have meant apprentices becoming full 'craftsmen' in two years. The reaction of employers and unions was illuminating. The employers, accustomed to apprentices as a cheap source of labour, were frightened of the prospect of having to pay adult wages to 18-year-olds, whilst the engineering unions opposed radical changes for fear of whittling away the divide between craft and general workers' unions.

What the above example illustrates is that there is a third conception of 'skill', namely skill as social status. It is theoretically possible for skill to be socially constructed through the artificial delimitation of certain work as skilled. This conception of skill traces its origins to the work of H.A. Turner who argued that workers are skilled or unskilled 'according to whether or not entry to the occupation is deliberately restricted and not in the first place according to the nature of the occupation itself' (Turner, 1962, p. 184). In this view, then, skill depends not on objective factors, but on custom and tradition plus collective organization. It is union organization, with or without the help of the employers, which seeks to control the supply of labour, access to jobs and job-training time, so that the training time is no more than a form of 'ritual servitude' (More, 1980; Lee, 1981).

This social construction theory of skill can come in two forms – a strong one or a weak one. The strong version asserts that it is possible to label certain work activities as skilled *whatever the technical content*, and that many jobs carry unnecessary skill labels. The corollary of this, presumably, is that most people can do most jobs on the labour market. Only entry barriers prevent them. The weak version of the theory is that nearly all skilled jobs have some objective skill content but that it is strategic position within the production process combined with collective organization which gains the occupation a skill label. According to this view, some so-called unskilled or semi-skilled jobs also have a significant skill content which goes unrecognized and unrewarded.

We can express the differences visually between the strong and weak versions of the theory in Figure 2.2. It is important to note from Figure 2.2 that even the strong version does not argue that there is no such thing as a technical basis to skill. It is accepted that there is a small core of jobs with a correspondence between skill labels and technical expertise.

The weak version of the social construction hypothesis does not change significantly the nature of the deskilling debate. Indeed it is an unsurprising assertion. All it says is that employers do not pay high wages for skilled workers unless they have to. Sometimes they do not have to, so they don't. The strong version of the social construction theory projects the deskilling debate onto a different level. If most skilled jobs have no technical basis of skill, and this typically has been

Figure 2.2   Social construction theories of skill

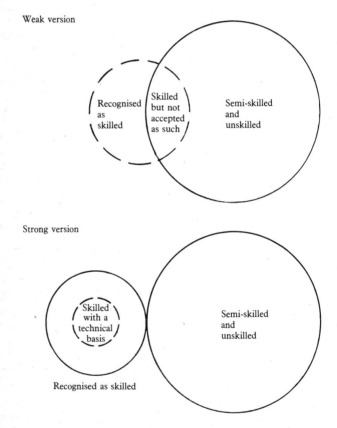

(The broken lines indicate the perimeter of the technical basis of skill.)

the case, then the deskilling hypothesis is largely irrelevant to the overall organization of production. Thus we are no longer concerned with the objective nature of work procedures and job-knowledge, but with the politics of the workplace and the labour market.

It is important to note that these politics are *intra*-class as well as class politics. For example the machine tool industry, because of the complexity and precision of its products and the small batches in which they are made, is peculiarly dependent on the skills of its workers. Because of the need for technically skilled men, employers are often prepared to pay more to get them, but are inhibited by the threat of claims for comparable rises from less skilled workers who want to reduce differentials (NIESR, 1980). What this example suggests is that 'deskilling' in the sense of compression of pay differentials is partly the result of the successful unionization and bargaining leverage of the unskilled and semi-skilled. In considering the shipbuilding industry, Reid suggests a parallel hypothesis: 'It seems then that the commonly used dichotomy between the skilled and the unskilled . . . derives more from long traditions of ideological conflict within the labour movement.' (Reid, 1980, pp. 201–2). We will return to these arguments in later chapters.

Though different writers emphasize different conceptions of skill, the first two notions – skill as job knowledge and skill as job autonomy – can come together as elements of an expanded model in the 'ideal of craftsmanship'. The model of craftsmanship is best presented by Mills. He argues that craftsmanship involves six major characteristics.

There is no ulterior motive in work other than the product being made and the processes of its creation. The details of daily work are meaningful because they are not detached in the worker's mind from the product of the work. The worker is free to control his own working action. The craftsman is thus able to learn from his work and to use and develop his capacities and skills in its prosecution. There is no split of work and play, or work and culture. The craftsman's very livelihood determines and infuses his entire mode of living.
(Mills, 1951, p. 220)

Mills traces the origins of the model of craftsmanship back to Ruskin who romanticized what he presumed was the work situation of the medieval artisan. Nevertheless this ideal of craftsmanship is the benchmark for Braverman with which he compares and analyses modern, capitalist work organization. In particular, Braverman's concept of skill emphasizes the unity of conception and execution, of planning and doing. This brings us onto the theories about the development of the labour process within capitalism.

Deskilling or upgrading?
There is a remarkable contrast between the views of Durkheim and Marx in relation to the effects of an increasing division of labour.

Though Durkheim recognized various forms of social disorganization, and indeed the possible dehumanization of work, he nevertheless argued that 'the division of labour does not produce these consquences because of a necessity of its own nature' (Durkheim, 1933, pp. 371–2). On the contrary, the whole thrust of Durkheim's work was that a complex division of labour created, potentially, a new form of social solidarity, and was the foundation of a new moral order (p. 400). For Marx on the other hand the division of labour in modern industry turned the worker into a 'crippled monstrosity', 'riveted to a single fractional task' and was a source of resentment, alienation and revolution.[1] These contrasting views have continued their careers since and are exemplified today by the technological theorists (Kerr *et al.*, 1973) plus the human capital theorists (e.g. Becker, 1964) as opposed to neo-Marxists like Braverman. We will look at Braverman and the deskilling thesis in more detail in Chapter 3. For the moment it is illuminating to clearly set out the contrary views.

Industrial society is seen as characterized by one of two contradictory processes. First, there is the view that industrialization requires high levels of skill and a wide variety of skills. As a result there is the continuous upgrading of skills and the continuous development of new skills. This has been paralleled by an enormous expansion of secondary and higher education. Second, in total or partial contradiction to the first interpretation, is the view that the fundamental and increasing problem of modern industry is that work has been subject to processes of rationalization and routinization which reduce workers to mindless robots. This process has been, and is being, experienced by widening circles of workers, including white-collar and administrative workers. Such a hypothesis is often associated with theories stressing the homogenization of the working class and the proletarianization of the middle class (Caplow, 1954, p. 27; Kerr *et al.*, 1973, pp. 43–4 and 47–8; Johnson, 1976, p. 44; Montagna, 1977, pp. 171–2; Dunkerley, 1980.)

Lee (1981, p. 57) most clearly summarizes the implicit contradictions of the two views in diagrammatic form:

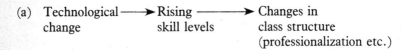

(a) Technological ——▶ Rising ———▶ Changes in
     change   skill levels   class structure
                                             (professionalization etc.)

(b) Exploitation ——▶ Falling ———▶ Changes in
     (realization of   skill levels   class structure
     surplus value   (proletarianization
     in the labour   etc.)
     process)

A first step in sorting out the contradictory assertions in relation to skill is to specify clearly the nature of the processes involved. Thus, if we look back at Figure 2.1, it is clear that some theorists, such as Durkheim, have had the process of specialization (D to B) in the forefront of their minds when discussing the division of labour and social interdependence. Other writers, such as Marx, have focused on job-fragmentation (D to A) with its apparent dehumanizing effect. Moreover, the conceptual distinctions of Figure 2.1 permit a clearer statement and understanding of more complex hypotheses. Thus Wright Mills suggested that the division of labour has typically shifted from D to B to A, i.e. that fragmentation is proceeded by a specialization stage.

In its early stages, a new division of labour may specialize men in such a way as to increase their levels of skill, but later, especially when whole operations are split and mechanized, such division develops certain faculties at the expense of others, and narrows all of them. And as it comes more fully under mechanization and centralized management, it levels men off again as automatons. Then there are few specialists and a mass of automatons; both integrated by the authority which makes them interdependent and keeps each in his own routine. Thus, in the division of labour, the open development and free exercise of skills are managed and closed.

(Mills, 1951, p. 227)

Though D to B to A may be a well-trodden path, this does not preclude the possibility of shifts from D to C. What would such a change represent in the real world? Essentially it indicates a transition from professional or craft work to flexible, multi-skilled work roles based on a core of technical knowledge. This type of transition process has been suggested by Alain Touraine. Arguing against a simple de-skilling hypothesis, Touraine distinguishes three phrases of industrial capitalism: phase 1 is the old system of work characterized by craft work with limited product specialization. Phase 2 is 'the period of transition characterized by the development of mechanization, or the feeding of machines by unskilled workmen'. Phase 3 is the phase of automation, where the worker has no direct role in the productive process; instead he controls, supervises and maintains (Touraine, 1962; cf. Marx, 1976, p. 618). Thus we have three possible hypotheses about the directions of change within the capitalist labour process.

(1) The human capital view of upgrading and increasing specialization;

(2) The Braverman deskilling hypothesis which supposes continued fragmentation of work;

(3) The Touraine hypothesis of a widespread transition to flexible multi-skilled, supervisory or maintenance job roles.

Finally we can add two more hypotheses. The first arises from the discussion of the social construction thesis in the previous section.

(4)   A technical process of deskilling has occurred but this has been overlain by the continued social construction and social maintenance of 'skills' such that a widespread proletarianization has not occurred.

The final hypothesis is complex. It foreshadows some of the arguments in Chapter 3, and recognizes that in order to discuss seriously the directions of change in the labour process it is necessary to consider the relations between units of capital. Underlying much labour process theory up to the present has been the assumption that the confrontation of capital and labour is the basic feature of the capitalist mode of production such that the basic dynamics of capitalism can be derived at this level of abstraction. On this basis it is assumed that there is an intrinsic tendency for labour-saving innovations to exceed capital-saving innovations. But it is not possible to analyse capitalism, let alone a social formation, through *one* essential relation. Class struggle is a crucial pressure towards labour-saving innovations, but this is not the only systemic pressure which capitalists face and on a day-to-day level it might not be the most pressing one. This dynamic is modified by competition between units of capital and in this competitive struggle it does not matter whether technological innovations are labour-saving or capital-saving (Wright, 1975).

Recognizing capital-saving innovations means recognizing that the development of technology and science has resulted in increased work complexity as well as the lodging of skills in machines. This means that the influences on skill can operate in two opposing directions and that the outcome is problematic. As Edwards (1978, p. 109) puts it:

(5)   'accumulation must be seen as simultaneously deskilling and reskilling the labour force. Rather than the simple one-way process that Braverman describes, we must recognize this more complicated, two-way process.'

This, then, is our last hypothesis concerning skill changes. It is partly the purpose of this book to investigate these alternative hypotheses by examining the changes in the labour process in Britain, the USA and Japan.[2]

Skill is not just an aspect of the labour process, but is part of the labour market and labour market processes. We will complete this chapter by a brief examination of the capitalist labour market.

Labour markets and the labour process

The labour market is an abstraction from numerous processes of allocating people to jobs: an abstraction from a multiplicity of organizational decisions concerning hiring, firing, promotions and job transfers. But the labour market is more than an abstraction, it has a palpable existence. For most people there is a vast difference between being *in* an organization, and being *in* the labour market, and for the school-leaver, the job-changer and the redundant the labour market does exist as a set of social institutions – the employment exchange, the newspaper job column, the personnel office and the grapevine. For many the return to the labour market comes as a sharp shock. As Allen puts it, 'People of all income levels and status are compelled to cart their skills around in varying forms when confronted by unemployment.' (Allen, 1977, p. 66). One does not need to see the shuffling queues of casual catering workers in the twilight London streets nor the undernourished building workers in Mexico City, each with a card proclaiming 'carpenter', 'bricklayer', 'labourer', to realize that the labour market is one part of economic theory which bears heavily on the individual.

It is in the labour market, then, that the buyer and seller of labour power meet, but the cards around the necks of the Mexican building workers tell us that buyer and seller meet in terms of skill. On the face of it labour power is obtained for its skill content (whether dexterity, job-knowledge or innovative abilities) and we have already noted that there are large variations among sellers in these respects. However, the concept of a labour market does not enable us to reject non-objective notions of skill *because there are different conceptions of labour market processes*. I will briefly set out three perspectives in tabular form (Table 2.1) and consider their relevance to deskilling.

The neoclassical model stems, of course, from Adam Smith and assumes that human beings interact more as isolated individuals than as group members. In general, labour has always proved to be a difficult factor to bring under the control of market theory. The inadequacies of the neoclassical view have often led to an alternative perspective – that of a carve up of the labour market by occupational groups. We can see here a correspondence to sociological theories of skill: the neoclassical model links with objective conceptions of skill, whilst the social construction theory of skill entails some notion of occupational regulation of the labour market. The theory which finds no counterpart from our survey of the literature on skill is that of dual labour markets. It is worth examining dual labour market theory in more detail.

Dual labour market theories have been developed by Doeringer and Piore (1971), Piore (1972) and Gordon (1972) to explain an assumed fundamental split in the labour market. According to these writers there are primary and secondary labour markets. The primary sector is composed of jobs in large, oligopolistic firms (IBM and ICI for example) in which the internal labour market plays a dominant role in job allocation. In this market there are 'jobs with relatively high wages, good working conditions, chances of advancement, equity and due process in the administration of work rules, and above all, employment stability'. In contrast, in the secondary sector:

Jobs tend to be low-paying with poorer working conditions, little chance of advancement, a highly personalized relationship between workers and supervisors which leaves wide latitude for favouritism and is conducive to harsh and capricious work discipline, and with considerable instability in jobs and a high turnover among the labour force.

(Piore, 1972, p. 3)

In the secondary sector the external labour market is the major job-allocator.

We can see from the above that labour economists have rediscovered Weber by means of the concept of an internal labour market. Essentially the concept refers to the incorporation of labour market functions within the body of the organization. Thus most jobs in an organization, especially the higher, better-paid jobs are shielded from the direct influence of competitive forces in the external labour market. Instead positions are filled by the promotion and transfer of workers who have already gained entry to the firm. The internal labour market connects to the external market by certain job positions that constitute points of entry into the organization.

If the dual labour market model is to make sense, then there must be some evidence of employers with primary and secondary orientations to the labour market. In other words, some employers must seek to recruit stable workers whilst other employers must actively seek unstable workers. Secondly, there must be evidence that potential discriminatory factors (sex, race, age, etc.) divide the labour force into non-competing segments. In Chapter 10 I will discuss the development of internal labour markets in Japan in terms of the permanent employment system. Whatever the relevance of the dual labour market model to Britain and the USA, it is clearly highly relevant to the Japanese experience.

What is the significance of dual labour market theories to processes of deskilling? Firstly, the concept of internal labour markets or bureaucratic career structures implies that the social construction of skill theoretically can be of two forms. We have seen that vulnerability to deskilling and the interchangeability of labour can result in defensive positions and artifical job rights, but there is the alternative argument: employers may erect artificial job structures and 'skill' distinctions as a means of reducing the power and cohesion of working class opposition by the creation of career consciousness. If people see their lives as a

Table 2.1   *Labour market theories*

	Neoclassical	*Occupational regulation*	*Dual labour market theory*
Type of market	A single labour market in which all employers and all workers operate	Fragmented market with occupational controls in relation to training, certification of competence and conditions of employment	Stratified labour market with a basic split between primary and secondary markets
Demand factors (i.e. employers' hiring practices)	All employers seek to recruit the most productive and cheapest labour	Employers are constrained by the occupational structuring of work and the reservation of certain job areas as 'skilled' or as 'professional'	Employers have primary or secondary orientations to the labour market and seek different categories of workers. Internal labour markets close off many jobs
Supply factors	Education, job knowledge and dexterity constitute 'human capital' and result in differences in wage rates. Workers flow into and out of jobs freely according to marginal differences in wages	Informal and formal job controls segment the market. Job skills are secondary	Sex, race, age, etc. stratify the labour force into non-competing groups. Job skills are secondary

succession of promotions then this squeezes the potential for collective action (see Chapter 4 and Stone, 1973, pp. 40–3).

Secondly, it should be emphasized that the economic basis of de-skilling is labour cheapening. According to Adam Smith the economic advantages of an increasing division of labour are threefold: increased specialized dexterity and skill, the minimization of changeover and work preparation time and the stimulus to the invention of specialized machinery (1970, p. 112). Charles Babbage considered this statement to be incomplete and added the well-known Babbage Principle. Essentially this involves stripping a skilled job to an essential core, and 'deskilling' all the surrounding tasks. This division is then linked to status and pay differences. Moreover Babbage was advocating, and envisaging a continual process, *a dynamic of deskilling* (Babbage, 1835). However, any deskilling and labour cheapening depends on existing and potential stratification amongst the population, especially in the absence of a large reserve army of labour. Thus a stratified labour market is the necessary condition for the dynamics of deskilling. The employer must be able to secure masses of cheap labour as substitutes for skilled workers.

Thirdly, the notion of segmented labour markets and of job areas within organizations (women's work versus men's work) suggests that any deskilling hypotheses may need more specification. It may be the case that the skill content of women's jobs has sharply decreased whilst the opportunities for men's jobs to be labelled 'skilled' have actually *increased*. On the face of it this type of process seems to have occurred within several industries (for example the insurance industry) and it complicates any assessment of the dynamics of work organization.

Summary and conclusions

The deskilling debate is beset by conceptual confusions. This chapter has attempted to clarify both the concepts of the division of labour and of skill. Thus, three conceptions of skill were distinguished, namely skill as work routines, skill as socially-constructed status and skill as control over process and product. In addition, it was suggested that there are two dimensions of an objective notion of skill – task range and discretionary content. Putting these dimensions together allowed us to distinguish between two different processes of change in the labour process: specialization and fragmentation. It was argued that specialization is not so much a deskilling process as one which concentrates skill onto a smaller task range, though the process of specialization can facilitate a later fragmentation process.

Having clarified some of the conceptual confusions, we were able to set out five different hypotheses about the directions of change in the capitalist labour process – the upgrading hypothesis, the Braverman deskilling thesis, the Touraine hypothesis, the argument that there has been a disjuncture of the technical and social aspects of skill, and, finally, the view that there has been a two-way process in which the influences on skill have been complex and, perhaps, indeterminate.

Finally, we considered some of the complex relations between the labour process and the labour market. Three models of the labour market were summarized, and it was suggested that the contemporary idea of internal labour markets is simply Weberian bureaucratic theory transcribed into a different jargon (see Chapter 4). The notion of internal labour markets or organizational career structures implies stratification of the labour market and such stratification is a necessary condition for the dynamic process of deskilling to occur.

3 Labour Process Theory

In this chapter I will briefly outline some key Marxian ideas about the labour process and then examine the recent neo-Marxist theories of the labour process, especially the contribution of Braverman.

Marx and the labour process

For Marx the labour process is at the centre of any analysis of society. Every mode of production is defined by the specific combination of two sets of relations:

(1) *The relation to nature.* The means of appropriating nature or producing useful things are called the forces of production. The organization of work or the specific relations that producers have with one another in the production process is also a productive force. An essential aspect of work organization is the *relations of possession*; in other words the extent of control over direct production exercised by the producers themselves.

(2) *Relations of economic ownership* or property relations. Property relations are defined as the basis of general relations of dominance and subordination, both within and beyond the sphere of production.

History is divided into a succession of dominant modes of production. Capitalism as a mode of production is defined as a structuring in which the direct producers are *legally* separated from the means of production and in which they no longer 'possess' the means of production. In order to understand the latter relation it is necessary to look at the Marxian distinction between the formal and real subsumption of labour under capital.

In its early stages capital acquired a formal domination over labour in terms of legal ownership which gave capitalists the right to the products including the right to realize a profit through the market. However, this formal control rested on a pre-existing labour process, and capitalists did not necessarily have the power to determine working methods or to train and supervise workers. 'The real subordination of labour to capital and with it the specifically capitalist mode of production only came into existence when capitalists transformed the organizational and technical basis of production itself.' (Stark, 1978, p. 4). In other words, capitalists had to seize hold of the labour process at the workshop level. In a sense, formal subordination takes place in the labour market with the meeting of capitalist and worker, whilst the development of real subordination takes place in the workshop.

In analysing the development of the capitalist labour process, Marx distinguished three phases: simple cooperation, manufacture and machinofacture. However, there is the problem of whether Marx was talking about *historical phases* or *analytic types* independent of historical forms. Essentially Marx was ambiguous about this problem and there is no general agreement about the nature of the stages of capitalist development. Thus Berg argues that 'The phases of manufacture and modern industry were abstractions and were not, therefore, meant to sum up any particular historical period.' (Berg, 1979, p. 5). In contrast Andrew Friedman, amongst others, associates each phase of development with an historical period (Friedman, 1977, pp. 15–17). This approach leads to a second level of disagreement about periodization. I will say more about this in later sections.

All three phases of capitalism are marked by the workers' lack of independent access to means of subsistence, the concentration of large numbers of workers under one roof, by the emergence of a direct authority or management, and by the manifestation of the production process as an 'externality' to the workers. Even in the case of simple cooperation

the interconnection between their various labours confronts them, in the realm of ideas as a plan drawn up by the capitalist, and in practice, as his authority, as the powerful will of a being outside them, who subjects their activity to their purpose.

(Marx, 1976, p. 450)

Beyond the common characteristics of each phase of capitalism were, however, significant differences. These are best summarized in a simple table (see Table 3.1).

There are three paths of change from traditional handicraft production to the phase of manufacture:[1]

(1) The combination in one workshop of different, previously independent craftsmen (e.g. the manufacture of carriages). This quickly passes beyond simple cooperation because the craftsmen become narrowed down to a particular product.

(2)   The assemblage into one workshop of craftsmen of the same type. The work is then subdivided between them, so that they become 'detail-workers' (e.g. needle manufacture or paper manufacture).

(3)   The combination of *disjecta membra*; of existing, domestic partial workers into one workshop (e.g. textiles, watch manufacture). In other words the transition process passes through a domestic or putting-out stage such that the workers come to the factory as *non*-craft workers.

Thus the essential characteristic of manufacture is the development of the division of labour which increases the rate of surplus value and capitalist control of the labour process (Marx, 1976, p. 482).

The progressive introduction of machinery into the production process defines the transition from manufacture to modern industry. In the modern industry phase machinery acts like the detailed division of labour to reduce the labour time necessary to produce commodities and thus to increase the rate of exploitation by the production of relative surplus value.

We can see from Table 3.1 that before modern industry the means of production are separated from the workers largely in form only, by virtue of the ownership of capital. In day-to-day workshop relations the workers continue to exercise a measure of control because of their skills and technical knowledge despite the increasing division of labour. This means that formal subordination allows a material basis for continued worker resistance to the capitalist objective of accumulation. However, the introduction of machine-based production fractures this basis for worker resistance and ushers in the period of the real subordination of labour to capital. Modern industry is the period where 'The production process has ceased to be a labour process in the sense of a process dominated by labour as its governing unity.' (Marx, 1973, p. 693). The entire production process can be 'designed and organized without reference to traditional skills and crafts'. To put it another way, the man/product relation gives way to the machine/product relation and jobs and tasks are treated as the *residuum* of the machine/product link (Brighton Labour Process Group, 1977, p. 2; Davis and Taylor, 1972, pp. 12 and 300–1).

The transition to machinofacture has three effects. Firstly there is the increasing *scientific* organization of work. Science and technology are harnessed as productive forces. Secondly, there is an increasing *transfer of skill*:

Along with the tool, the skill of the worker in handling it, passes over to the machine . . . This destroys the technical foundation on which the division of labour in manufacture was based. Hence, in place of the hierarchy of specialised workers that characterises manufacture there appears in the automatic factory

Table 3.1   *The development of the capitalist labour process*

	Simple cooperation	*Manufacture*	*Modern industry or machinofacture*
Technology	Not machine-based work. Traditional handicraft production	Not machine-based, but the erosion and fracturing of traditional handicrafts	Machine-based
Division of labour	No systematic division of labour within the workshop	Detailed division of labour	Detailed division of labour related to a machine process
Mode of control		Formal subordination	Formal plus real subordination
Dominant mode of extracting surplus value		Absolute surplus value	Relative surplus value
Working-class divisions		Skill hierarchies plus barriers between crafts	Mechanization breaks down skill divisions and produces a mass of unskilled labour

the tendency to equalise and reduce to an identical level every kind of work that has to be done by the minders of machine.

(Marx, 1976, p. 545)

Thirdly, the harnessing of science and the transfers of skill undermines the material basis of worker resistance to capital and creates the potential for a new structure of capitalist control.

Apart from defining the technical and social characteristics of each phase of capitalism, Marx attempted to explain the transformation in the labour process by reference to the structural dynamics of the capitalist mode of production. The basic dynamic of capitalism is that of capital accumulation and changes in the labour process are linked to a shift in the dominant form of extraction of surplus value: a shift from 'absolute' to 'relative'. As Marx puts it, 'The production of absolute surplus value turns exclusively on the length of the working day, whereas the production of relative surplus value completely revolutionises the technical process of labour and the groupings into which society is divided.' (Marx, 1976, p. 645). In general, absolute surplus value relates to the duration of labour and intensity of labour whereas relative surplus value refers to the productivity of labour.[2]

But why should capitalism be characterized by this logic of accumulation? Marx argues that capitalists are driven by competition between units of capital and by antagonistic class relations continually to revolutionize the production process to increase productivity and to gain a temporary advantage over competitors. The forces of competition compel capitalists continuously to extend their capital. This results in the introduction of labour-saving technologies in order to lower the wage bill, the displacement of labour, especially skilled labour, and the weakening of the power of working-class opposition. It is within these processes that Braverman attempts theoretically to locate a dynamic of deskilling.

The Marxist theory of the labour process is by no means adequately developed (Gintis, 1976, p. 37; Burawoy, 1979, p. 27; Cressey and MacInnes, 1980, p. 5). In constructing a theory of advanced capitalism various writers have elaborated ideas and suggestions that were largely underdeveloped in Marx's own writings, but at the same time they have 'accepted Marx's view of the labour process and have therefore missed the significance of its transformation . . .' (Burawoy, 1979, p. 202). In general, Marx's work on the labour process leaves us with four basic questions. Firstly, is the notion of a shift from FSL (formal subordination of labour) to RSL (real subordination of labour) an adequate theorization of the control relation at the point of production? For Marx mechanization solved the problem of labour control, such that the workers disappeared as an active force in shaping the relations of production.

Secondly, given Marx's definition of modern industry in terms of continuous flow production and automatic machinery is there a fourth phase of the labour process after modern industry? If so, how is it to be characterized and understood? Is Marx's periodization of the path of development correct? At times Marx suggests that the crucial transition to real subordination occurred during the Industrial Revolution, whereas writers like Braverman argue that there was a protracted transition from 'formal' to 'real' capitalist control of the labour process. More broadly, is it possible to characterize the labour process of an *entire epoch*?

Finally, it should be noted that Marx's work is ambiguous in relation to a simple deskilling thesis. Though he repeatedly pointed to a capitalist fragmentation process, he appeared to recognize a contradiction between deskilling and employers' needs for a multi-skilled flexible labour force (see Marx, 1976, p. 618; Elger, 1978, p. 14). We can attempt to answer some of these questions and move towards a theory of capitalist labour processes by examining the recent Braverman-inspired debate.

Braverman's contribution to the study of the labour process

Until recently Marxists have tended to ignore the development of the labour process. With their eyes on 'The Revolution', a hundred years of industrial change has been unexamined and unanalysed. Braverman's work is a powerful attempt to shift the focus and update Marx's work on production, as opposed to exchange relations.

Braverman assumes that Marx can be read as propounding a straightforward deskilling thesis and, as a result, his analysis revolves around the notion of deskilling. The concept of deskilling refers to four processes: (i) the process whereby the shopfloor loses the right to design and plan work; i.e. divorce of planning and doing; (ii) the fragmentation of work into meaningless segments; (iii) the redistribution of tasks amongst unskilled and semi-skilled labour, associated with labour cheapening; and (iv) the transformation of work organization from the craft system to modern, Taylorized forms of labour control.

Braverman's work is readily available and rather than providing yet another resume I wish briefly to underline his contribution to sociological thinking. (For a competent summary of Braverman, see Coombs, 1978.) Traditionally the academic study of work and work relations has been distributed among managerial studies and organization theory, industrial relations, the sociology of occupations, and something called industrial sociology. However, industrial sociology never amounted to an integrated subject, as Baldamus curtly noted: 'There is as yet no specifically sociological theory of industrial organization. What is usually called industrial sociology consists basically of

empirical investigations, loosely organized around a few general concepts.' (Baldamus, 1961, p. 5). Braverman's major contribution was to
smash through the academic barriers and offer the potential for the
birth of a new, *integrated* approach to the study and history of work.

In relation to Marxist studies Braverman's major theoretical contribution has been to shift the object of study from formal ownership
relations to control of the labour process. In connection with this
objective Braverman assumes that there is a fourth phase of capitalism –
monopoly capitalism – and he seeks to characterize this phase in
relation to the labour process. In brief, Table 3.2 shows how he adds a
fourth column to Table 3.1.

*Table 3 .2   The phase of monopoly capitalism in terms of the labour process
according to Braverman*

Technology	Automation
Division of labour	Detailed division of labour based on Taylorism and related to automatic machinery
Mode of control	Formal plus real subordination only occurs now. It did not occur under machinofacture
Dominant mode of extracting surplus value	Relative surplus value (but Braverman does not seriously discuss this aspect)
Working-class divisions	Mass of unskilled labour, including large groups of unskilled clerical and service labour, but decollectivization of workers has occurred

Implicitly (because he nowhere makes his disagreements with Marx
plain) Braverman suggests that Marx compressed history and depicted
an historically complete transformation to capitalist society when, in
fact, the full working out of the logic of capitalism was delayed until the
twentieth century. Thus Braverman suggests a different periodization
of the transformation of the labour process to that of Marx. For Marx,
the real subordination of labour to capital occurred during machinofacture, whereas Braverman suggests that at the turn of the century
there were still significant areas of production within which workers,
especially craftsmen, maintained real control over aspects of the labour
process (Stark, 1980, p. 90). According to Braverman, it was Taylorism
and associated changes in the industrial application of scientific knowledge that completed the transition to real subordination. There is
much else in *Labor and Monopoly Capital*, but I now wish to turn to a
critique of Braverman.

Beyond Braverman

Despite the value of Braverman's work as an extension and re-writing of Marx and as a stimulus to bringing the labour process into the arena of radical debate, nevertheless the weaknesses of the book are becoming increasingly visible. Of the criticisms of Braverman's work four areas have proved serious blockages to further theorization.

(a) Historical inadequacy

Whilst Braverman appears to offer an historical argument starting with the development of management in the late nineteenth century, in fact the work is largely devoid of historical or empirical content. This has a number of consequences, of which the most important is that the work is permeated by an idealized conception of the traditional craft worker. Despite assertions to the contrary, it is clear that handicraft labour under petty commodity production is made the measure of all production processes. This criterion confuses deskilling *within* capitalism with changes *across* modes of production (Cutler, 1978, pp. 79 and 84). In so far as 'craft control' is *not* identified with petty commodity handicraft production, it remains an unexamined concept. I will attempt to develop more adequate conceptions of the modes of control in nineteenth century British industry in Chapter 6.

The further consequence of Braverman's lack of historical specificity is that it is difficult to locate the specific context and targets of Taylorism (Elger, 1978, p. 36). It is easy to paint a picture of 'a unilinear decline from the homogenously skilled working class of the nineteenth century to the homogenously unskilled working class of the twentieth' if one ignores the historical realities of a stratified labour force and the pre-Taylorite forms of control (Stark, 1980, p. 94). This argument is also developed further in Chapter 6.

(b) Class conflict as an object of theorizing

Braverman seeks to set out universal characteristics of 'labour' as a general category in the production process. Because of his benchmark of independent handicraft production it is assumed that the severance of conception and execution under capitalism is inimical to the essential character of human work, such that 'labour' continuously attempts to subvert capitalist work arrangements. Therefore workers come to the factory gates as the carriers of a universal recalcitrance to capitalist authority.

This ontology of the universal characteristics of 'labour' has two significant consequences. First, it ignores the fact that the arenas of influence and control may be the school, the family and other non-work social institutions, such that workers come to the factory gates prepared to contribute effort in terms of customary standards and even *beyond* the bounds of organizational rules and work specifications (Baldamus, 1961; Bendix, 1974; Hyman and Brough, 1975).

Second, by assuming a universal recalcitrance on the part of 'labour', Braverman, paradoxically, is able to avoid consideration of *specific* trade union or shopfloor resistance to the process he describes. He tends to ignore or minimize the role of class struggle in the shaping of the labour process such that the employer is 'portrayed as having uncontested, unilateral control over the labour process' (Zimbalist, 1979, p. XII; Friedman, 1977).

Moreover, if one assumes a universal worker resistance to capitalist control, it obscures the essential variability of worker resistance: some changes are resisted more than others, some groups resist more than others, some groups achieve a 'negotiated order', whilst some groups become a privileged elite. These points are obvious enough but such distinctions are lost within Braverman.

In sum, the continued capitalist search for control over labour makes no sense outside of labour's assumed centrality and its assumed universal recalcitrance, but both centrality and recalcitrance may vary (Cutler, 1978, p. 77).

(c) Marxist functionalism and structural dynamics

Within Braverman, Zimbalist and other labour process writers there is a strong strain of Marxist functionalism. Reorganizations of the labour process are presented 'as the outcome of a conscious design rather than as the product of the struggle of contending groups' (Stark, 1980). This perspective leads to an almost conspiratorial concept of capitalism in which every event is planned by the capitalist class and is in the interests of each and every unit of capital.

In this vein Braverman substitutes for the broad processes of capital accumulation a single, overall trend – an imperative of control of the labour process. What is the nature of this imperative of control? It is linked to Braverman's philosophical view of 'natural' human labour which entails the unity of conception and execution. What this means is that the imperative to control is referred back to a philosophical anthropology of work, and is not adequately located in patterns of economic development, particularly phases of capital accumulation (Elger, 1978, p. 8; Cutler, 1978, p. 86).

Without Braverman's philosophical anthropology and his idealized conception of the traditional craft worker, is it possible to derive specific labour process imperatives from that of capital accumulation? The assumption that increasing capital accumulation entails intensifying control of the labour process in an unmediated way is based on the idea of the continued centrality of labour and the labour process, but this may vary through different stages of capitalist development. It is important to realize that appropriation of surplus value may occur not only in the labour process, but through other mechanisms, namely in the sphere of circulation through pricing policy and via state taxation. It could be argued that under monopoly capitalism the centrality of control over labour diminishes and the extraction of surplus value now occurs via monopoly pricing and taxation (e.g. see Wright, 1975). Braverman fails to consider this point because, though the central aim of the book is to link the nature of the labour process and monopoly capital, the nature of this link remains obscure. Given a single overall dynamic of deskilling and intensifying capitalist control, the transition to monopoly capitalism does not in his account alter the logic of the labour process (Edwards, 1978, p. 109). In essence what Braverman does is to take the structural solutions of one stage of capitalist development (machinofacture) and then assume that they are the structural solutions to the contradictions of monopoly capitalism.

Even if we ignore the above arguments and grant that an imperative to control is a central feature of capitalism, then there are still serious problems with this type of theorizing. For example, it is important to realize that employers have no omniscience about the possible effects of different control strategies. Thus many employers and managers in Britain showed considerable doubt and scepticism about the advantages and effects of Taylorism (see Chapter 7). Related to this point: are all employers' strategies equally dominating? For Braverman, Geoff Brown and other theorists it appears that *all* managerial arrangements confer total control, and there has been little theoretical effort to construct a range of variation along this dimension (see Friedman, 1977 and Stark, 1978).

In accordance with his implicit functionalism, Braverman tends to sever the Marxian link between the productive forces and the relations of production. He concludes that there is no longer any contradiction between the forces and relations of production, only a correspondence. Therefore class conflict is left on one side as an object of theorizing and, presumably, it can only now be expressed outside, and in spite of, the capitalist labour process or in the labour market (Wersky, 1979, p. 115). In general Braverman completely abandons any attempt to locate contradictory tendencies within the capitalist mode of production or contradictions within specific strategies of control. It is at precisely this point, in exploring the contradictions of each level of capitalist development and of specific managerial strategies that the work of Wright, Friedman and Edwards moves beyond the limitations and premature theoretical closure of Braverman. In so doing, they return to more useful Marxian methods of analysis.

(d) The unproblematic implementation of Taylorism
Braverman takes the logic of Taylorism to be the logic of capitalism and
treats as unproblematic, both historically and theoretically, the institutionalization of Taylorism. This position has been challenged by
Edwards who writes that Braverman

> accepts or seems to accept writings on management theory as evidence for actual
> developments on the shop or office floor. The most important example is
> Braverman's reading of Frederick Taylor's writings as though they described
> real processes rather than simply Taylor's thinking and theories. The book has
> therefore taken what are clearly ideological sources of information and treated
> them as though the processes they describe were real.
>
> (Edwards, 1978, p. 109; see also Edwards, 1979, pp. 97–104)

I will consider the Taylorism debate at length in Chapter 5, and the
historical development of Taylorism in Britain in Part II.

Towards a theory of capitalist labour processes
In the rest of this Chapter I will outline the elements of a theory of
capitalist labour processes, a theory which will be further developed in
Chapters 4 and 5. In particular, the question of structures of control
over the labour process will be more fully discussed in Chapter 4 in
connection with the Weberian tradition.

(a) The relative autonomy of the labour process
Do we need a theory of the labour process at all? It could be argued that
ideas about the production process in capitalist economies can be
entirely subsumed under a general theory of capitalism as a mode of
production.

Though the labour process takes place within an economic and
historical context, the context nevertheless rarely provides a precise
determination of work organization. There is a continuing indeterminacy to the labour process: the question always remains 'how shall
work be organized?' (Edwards, 1978, p. 112; Burawoy, 1979. One
implication of this is that in talking about modes of control at the
workplace we are talking about *employer strategies*. Employers are
faced with a choice of strategies to control and exploit labour.

Moreover, the range of capitalist choice can be extended by limited
competitive conditions. Competition is a varying and variable factor.
Andrew Friedman emphasizes that one distinguishing characteristic of
monopoly capitalism is that it provides a wider area of discretion for
large companies with monopoly power. Monopoly capitalism does not
result in changed organizational goals, but it *does* result in top management acquiring a wider choice of social instruments in order to achieve
the goals of capital accumulation (Friedman, 1977, pp. 25–6). Simi-
arly, where industry develops in close relationship with the state, as in

Japan, this often means that organizations are insulated from demand oscillations and can, like private monopolies, exercise more choice over labour strategies.

Thus, though the subordination of labour, real or otherwise, cannot be understood entirely at the level of the labour process, nevertheless the dynamics of class struggle and class compromise cannot be relegated to the political sphere because there is a relative autonomy to the production process.

(b) Labour and labour power

We discussed in Chapter 2 the centrality of the labour market to any analysis of work within capitalism. In neoclassical economics labour has the status of a commodity: it can be bought and sold, used and dispensed with. The 'labour as a commodity' perspective implies a model of employer/employee relations consisting of opposed objectives – the employer is motivated to resist worker aspirations which are liable to increase costs. In addition it is in the employer's interest to continue a worker's employment only so long as it remains profitable. Theoretically, the labour force can be 'turned over' in each production period subject only to the replacement costs of recruitment and training.

Marxist theory recognizes 'the labour as a commodity' perspective, but argues further that labour has unique characteristics which means that labour cannot be treated as a simple commodity. In Marxist theory, unlike neoclassical economics, the social relations of capitalism are not reduced to exchange relations. The key concept delineating the essential non-exchange nature of the capitalist economy is the labour/labour-power distinction. The commodity which the worker sells is not a fixed amount of labour embodied in a completed product but 'labour-power', i.e. the capacity to work. Thus the commodity which is exchanged in the marketplace (labour-power) is not the same entity which enters into the production process (labour). The consumption of labour-power is completed outside of the market or the sphere of circulation. It is consumed within 'the hidden abode of production' – the black box of neoclassical theory (Marx, 1976, Chapter 6; Gintis, 1976).

Thus there is a central indeterminacy of labour potential, an indefiniteness which must be resolved in other ways. Edwards stresses this point: 'Labour power can be bought, but between the purchase of labour power and the real appropriation of useful labour comes a wedge: the will, motivation and consciousness of the worker drastically affects the work force's productivity.' (Edwards, 1978, p. 111). To translate legal ownership into real possession the employer must erect structures of control over labour. This implies that the interior of the firm cannot be reduced to a bundle of exchange relations. Market models or notions of contract are inadequate conceptually to grasp the relations of subordination and domination governing the labour process (Stark, 1978, p. 16; Gintis, 1976, p. 42).

The labour/labour-power distinction implies that capitalism is in a perpetual tension between treating labour as a commodity and treating it as a non-commodity, that is as a continuing social relation between employer and workers. This last point can be clarified by a concrete example. During the 1960s the Cowley plant of British Leyland acquired a reputation for bad industrial relations. The man who was industrial relations manager at Cowley for much of this period (T.I. Richardson) argued that this was a direct result of treating the labour force as a commodity:

> The effects on local management, trade unions, the workforce and community generally of, for example, hiring an additional 761 men in the spring and declaring 565 redundant in the autumn cannot be calculated except by the length of time it takes to rebuild the hostile attitudes created by such matters.
>
> (*The Guardian*, 3 June 1975)

The conclusions which this example points to are also reached by Cressey and MacInnes. Criticizing both Marx and Braverman, they argue that there is a dual nature to the relationship of capital and labour. Capitalists are faced with the problems of continually transforming the forces of production. This, in turn, entails stimulating motivation and harnessing labour's creative and productive powers. Thus capitalists must to some degree seek a cooperative relationship with labour. It cannot just exploit those capacities that can be brought into play by bribery and coercion. Similarly, side-by-side with labour's resistance to subordination lies the fact that workers have an interest in the maintenance of the capital/labour relation and the viability of the units of capital which employ them. In summary: 'The twofold nature of the relationship of capital to labour in the workplace implies *directly contradictory* strategies for both labour and capital which in turn represent the working out of the contradictions between the forces and relations of production at the level of the workplace itself.' (Cressey and MacInnes, 1980, p. 14).

Thus capitalists cannot in terms of profit-maximization ignore the consciousness of workers. As Gintis notes, employers must attempt to reproduce from production period to production period forms of worker consciousness compatible with future profits (Gintis, 1976, p. 42). However, employer strategies are constrained by the capitalist realities of market and commodity relations, and it is the forms of capitalism which can square this circle which are most likely to survive.

(c) The structural dynamics of capitalism

In criticizing Braverman I have pointed out the lack of a determinative link between the logic of capital accumulation and the labour process. This implies that at the level of the firm the centrality of control over the labour process will vary. The firm is primarily a capital fund with a legal corporate personality, linked to a production process(es). But this does not mean that 'capitalist industrial enterprises are more or less solely concerned with producing commodities and selling them and that their calculation is entirely governed by these concerns' (Cutler, 1978, p. 92). Whilst the production process results in a flow of income to the firm, this does not preclude alternative sources playing a major role or even a predominant one, e.g. currency speculation, cumulative acquisition and asset stripping, commodity speculation, and credit manipulations of various kinds.

F.W. Taylor was one theorist who, along with Braverman, assumed that the production process was in fact the predominant concern of senior management. He soon realized his mistake. Having worked at Bethlehem Steel from 1898–1901 installing his managerial control system, Taylor discovered that Bethlehem's owners were not at all pleased with the effects of his system, and he was abruptly fired. The reason, according to Taylor, was that 'They did not wish me, as they said, to depopulate South Bethlehem. They owned all the houses in South Bethlehem and the company stores, and when they saw we were cutting the labour force down to about one-fourth, they did not want it.' (F.W. Taylor in Stark, 1980, p. 91).

Nor is it just a question of currency speculations and rent income, as in the above example. Surplus value has to be produced but also *realized* in the market. What this implies is that the realization of surplus value (i.e. finding markets, selling in those markets and making a profit) may be more crucial than the production of surplus value for certain firms, certain industries or during certain periods. On the shopfloor a negotiated order may have been reached, a phase of accommodation, as in the British engineering industry between 1850–1890, such that there is no thrust towards deskilling or the separation of conception and execution. Thus Soffer in considering the causes of worker autonomy in US industries over time makes the point that in firms whose profits come primarily from sales efforts (newspapers), hedging in raw materials (textiles), and speculating in style (women's clothes), production management and labour control were of secondary significance (1960, p. 145).

If then, we break the universal framework of Braverman, it is necessary to realize that there can be no theory of *the* capitalist labour process. Given the considerable diversity under capitalism the first requirement is an adequate sociological classification of industries, which we still lack (see Chapter 6).[3] In general we can conclude that the linkage between the logic of capital accumulation and transformations of the labour process is an indirect and varying one. For Braverman, Zimbalist, Edwards, Clawson and others there is an inadequately located impulsion to control which is attributed to capital. In the event, capitalist reality is more complex.

Summary and conclusions

In this chapter I have outlined the basic ideas of Marx on the labour process, especially the three phases within the capitalist mode of production. It was concluded that the Marxian theory of the labour process is by no means adequately developed and left several unresolved questions, particularly the problem of relating the schema to advanced capitalism.

Braverman's major contribution has been to update Marx and attempt to link the phase of monopoly capitalism and the transformations of the labour process. Despite the weaknesses in Braverman's theorizing, he has provided the potential for a new integrated approach to the study and history of work.

Labor and Monopoly Capital has stimulated debate and revived the sociology of work, but it also has created a number of impediments to further analysis. The main problems have proved to be Braverman's botched history with its romanticization of the traditional craft worker; the assumption of universal worker recalcitrance combined with the failure to discuss actual patterns of worker resistance; a Marxist functionalism which ignores the inevitable contradictions within all strategies of control, and, finally, the tendency to treat the implementation of Taylorism as unproblematic.

The reactions to, and critiques of Braverman suggest the need for a less rhetorical and a better-grounded theory of labour processes. Some elements of such a theory were set out in the final section of Chapter 3. Firstly, I argued that there is a relative autonomy of the labour process, such that it is necessary to introduce a concept of employer strategies. The other side of this coin is that there is no determinative link between the logic of capital accumulation and the development of the labour process. There is considerable diversity within capitalism and various threads of change.

Whilst the centrality of control over labour may vary, any system of control must take account of the consciousness of workers. Within capitalism there is a perpetual tension between treating workers as a commodity to be hired and fired and harnessing their ingenuity and cooperativeness. Thus there is a twofold nature to the capital/labour relationship. If the contradictory nature of the capital/labour relationship is accepted, then this changes the character of the control relation. Control should be seen in relation to conflict and sources of conflict *and* in relation to the potential terrain of compromise, bargaining and consensus. These arguments are developed further in Chapter 4.

4 Bureaucracy and Bureaucratization

In Chapter 3 we were concerned to examine the Marxian perspective on the labour process. This chapter draws out some useful ideas from the Weberian tradition in order to work towards a more adequate theory of capitalist labour processes.

The Weberian concept of bureaucracy

Edwards (1979) and Clawson (1980) have argued that a major capitalist strategy in relation to modern large-scale work organizations has been the development and application of bureaucratic techniques. If this is so, then it is not possible to understand modern industrial organization without understanding industrial bureaucracy. Therefore, this section is devoted to clarifying the concept of bureaucracy.

It is fruitless to struggle to achieve a single definition of bureaucracy that covers all usages and intended meanings. The concept is one which many writers have shoved their fingers into and stirred around a bit. As a result the usages of the term overlap, but there is no central core.[1] One standard sociological strategy is to accept as authoritative the concept of bureaucracy which Max Weber formulated, but this hardly solves all problems, given the multi-faceted nature of the Weberian concept. Three general points help place the Weberian notion of bureaucracy into context. Firstly Weber was largely concerned with broad historical comparisons between societies. In relation to bureaucracy he was trying to capture the essence of modern organization or administration in contrast to traditional administration.

Secondly, Weber's concepts are centred about state administration. This was the area which had developed first and fastest away from traditional organization, and a body of literature had built up around these changes, and Weber was still largely writing and thinking from within this corpus (e.g. see Albrow's discussion of German administrative theory in the nineteenth century, 1970, pp. 26–30).

Thirdly, the notion of bureaucracy was embedded within a general theory of power relations or 'domination'. Weber considered the idea of power too vague for sociological use, and that the focus ought to be on a special instance of power – namely, legitimate power. Just as appropriation converts advantages into rights, so 'legitimation' converts power into authority, but how, according to Weber, is the trick done?. The answer was in terms of specific *beliefs* about the legitimacy of power, beliefs shared by the ruler and the ruled. This implies that, in opposition to Marx, Weber's theory of domination does not depend upon economic mechanisms of control. Instead, the compliance of subordinates rests upon their attitudes towards, and perception of, the nature of the control relationship.

According to Weights (1978, p. 66):

> Weber fails to explain how 'values' or 'meanings' come to be shared by a plurality of social actors. Furthermore, he does not explain how the 'organized activity' which 'enforces' an order is supposed to function. In fact, given Weber's individualistic approach to social collectivities, he *cannot* provide a coherent account of either, the conditions of existence of a system of 'domination' or the conditions of compliance to authority.

This conclusion is too negative, because Weber's theory of domination is constructed on the basis of sets of beliefs about legitimacy *and* the associated administrative forms. The dual nature of the theory can be seen in relation to bureaucracy.

According to Albrow, Weber distinguished between a general concept of 'bureaucracy' (never spelt out but entailing an administrative body of appointed officials) and his ideal type (Albrow, 1970, pp. 41–2). The ideal type of bureaucracy was a specific form of 'bureaucracy', and also of legal authority systems. It represents bureaucracy in its most 'rational' form. There are ten defining characteristics, or 'empirical elements' as Mouzelis calls them. However, no writer on bureaucracy simply lists these ten elements. Weber listed five beliefs constituting the basis of 'legal authority', eight 'fundamental categories' of rational-legal authority systems, and the ten elements of the ideal type, but the typical tactic is to meld together some elements from each list, and call that 'bureaucracy', leaving the remaining characteristics to slip over the edge of relevance.[2]

We can, perhaps, summarize the five overarching beliefs about legal authority as a belief in a set of abstract, impersonal rules, applicable to everyone (see Weber, 1947, pp. 329–30). The remaining elements can be divided into two categories: those that describe the official's relationship to the organization and those that are largely concerned with the structure of control. The former largely consists of those structural conditions which surround the appointment, promotion and dismissal of individuals, and thus can be generalized in terms of the notion of an employment relationship. The sets of elements are summarized in Table 4.1.

It is clear from Table 4.1 that bureaucracy as an ideal type represents the intersection of rational-legal authority (one of the three forms of domination) with bureaucracy as a general administrative form based on officials.[3]

Legitimacy and consent

As has been pointed out, Weber conceptualized the forms of domination in non-economic terms and stressed instead the relationship of legitimation. There is a major problem relating to the nature of legitimacy which has led to a debate concerning the relative weight to be

*Table 4.1   Weberian ideal-type bureaucracy**

Structure of control	Employment relationship
(1) Continuous organization and bound by rules (WA1) (2) Hierarchy (WA3) (3) Systematic division of labour, with the necessary and delimited powers (WA2) (4) Work performance is governed by rules, which may be either technical or legal (Plus specialized training) (WA4) (5) Written records and communications (WA7)	(1) Separation from means of production and administration (WA5) (2) Non-appropriation of office (WA6)
(6) Unified control system i.e. monocratic (WB10)	(3) Formally free labour (WB1) (4) Appointment on basis of contract (WB4) (5) Selection based on technical or professional qualification (WB5) (6) Career system based on either (a) seniority or (b) merit (WB8) (7) Fixed, money salaries and pension rights (WB6) (8) Full-time commitment, i.e. sole or primary occupation (WB7)

* The bracketed codes refer to Weber, list A (i.e. Weber, 1947, pp. 330–2) or list B (on pp. 353–4) plus the specific number given it by Weber. List A refers to the characteristics of legal authority systems, of course, while list B refers to those of the ideal type. This leaves four characteristics unaccounted for. WA8 is *not* a characteristic of bureaucracy, but simply a statement that, 'Legal authority can be exercised in a wide variety of different forms . . .' (Weber, 1964, p. 332). WB2, WB3 and WB9 are repeats of WA3, WA2 and WA5 and WA6 respectively. Weber provides no explanation of this repetition.

attached to subjective conceptions of legitimacy (Stinchcombe, 1968; Cohen *et al.*, 1975; Weights, 1978). Without considering the philosophical details of this debate, two basic points emerge. To begin with, the concept of legitimation should not be theoretically stretched beyond its explanatory power. In industrial organization, for example, managers face a recurrent task of re-establishing their legitimacy. As Hyman neatly puts it, 'It is a fluent and shifting frontier: the limits of management authority and employee obedience are imprecise and always open to renegotiation.' (Hyman, 1976, p. 97). Legitimacy is never total and never granted once and for all.

In relation to this point, we still lack a vocabulary of concepts for discussing ideological relationships. As a result it is necessary to theorize a pattern of legitimacy concepts. Firstly, there are general cultural norms which create overarching patterns of legitimacy orientations. For example, the *formal* subordination of labour (i.e. the right of the employer to market the product) is not generally challenged in the West. Four hundred years of moral inculcation surround property rights such that British capitalists are not faced with the open 'pilfering' at every stage of the production process which occurs elsewhere. In India, for example, it is reported that up to 15 million tonnes of coal 'disappear' every year (*Financial Times*, 7 January 1981).

Secondly, there are organization-based legitimacies exemplified by ideologies of technocracy. Managers may spend considerable time and effort sustaining such ideologies. For example, in 1976 Meriden Worker's Cooperative was in need of technical advice and help, and three GKN managers were made available, at no cost to the co-operative, to help sort out production and technical problems. But why should GKN, a large engineering company which is one of the staunchest supporters of the Conservative Party, act as a fairy godmother to a workers' cooperative? The answer was clearly provided by an article in the *Financial Times*:

It was probably attractive for a company like GKN to be able to demonstrate *the essential role of management* in any industrial structure – even if the demonstration was not always welcome.

(*Financial Times*, 15 February 1977, emphasis added)

Acceptance of property rights and management expertise clearly play an important part in the constant negotiations within each enterprise of the frontier of control. But this shifting pattern of accommodation cannot simply be derived from, or explained in terms of, levels of acceptance of general notions of technocracy and other management ideologies. The achievement of consent, of a *modus vivendi* between management and shopfloor, also crucially depends upon the construction of definite trade-offs and interactions, which may have little to do with generating or reflecting, large-scale legitimations. Thus we need to conceptualize particular acceptances of hierarchical authority. This problematic of 'particular acceptance', of day-to-day compliance, cannot be subsumed under the concept of legitimacy, nor treated simply as a level of legitimation. If this argument is accepted, then it is useful to distinguish between the notion of 'legitimacy' and 'consent' (Burawoy, 1979). Such a distinction is supported by the frequent observation that non-acceptance of a foreman's instruction can occur within an overall framework of legitimation and by the opposite argument that 'legitimacy' is too strong a concept to apply to most workers' attitudes towards management; instead there is bargained consent or resigned acquiescence (Gouldner, 1954; Fox, 1971).

Consent is frequently achieved outside of formal organizational procedures in what has, traditionally, been described as the 'informal' structure of the organization. It is a major failing of labour process theorists to focus only on the formal structure of organizations and ignore the insights of traditional industrial sociology.

In considering the limits of formal rationality it is important to remember that all rule-based authority structures depend upon the interpretation of rules and procedures by middle management and foremen. Further, the orientation of foremen and departmental managers to the formal structure may be very different from that of senior management. Most crucially foremen have no career stake in the operation of formal control systems, and often such systems are regarded as an externally-imposed nuisance. Thus, in considering the system of rules it is necessary not only to consider the locus of authorship but also to ask, who polices the rules? If we look at collective bargaining and union/management relations, then a simple set of dichotomies leads to the following picture presented in Figure 4.1.

Figure 4.1 reminds us that consent can be achieved by the active participation of informal groups such that 'the informal or worker-organized structure of the workplace may be more productive of surplus value than the formal structure set by the capitalist' (O'Connor, 1975, p. 318). In a paradoxical way this occurred at the Longbridge plant of British Leyland in the 1950s and 1960s. According to a senior trade union official:

Under piecework the shop stewards controlled the track. It was their job to see their group made its money. They made sure all the components were in the right place at the right time, and one worker did not slack and impede the next man down the production line.

(Quoted in the *Financial Times*, 31 January 1981)

In general Figure 4.1 suggests that simple models of an organizational structure which assume unilateral rule-determination and unilateral rule-enforcement are extremely simplistic. Above all it is

Figure 4.1   The authorship and guardianship of rules

Locus of guardianship of rules	*Locus of authorship of rules*	
	Unilateral – management determined	Multilateral
Unilateral	Ideal-type bureaucracy	Frequent situation with industry-wide agreements, where managers left to impose the rules
Multilateral	Paternalistic control	Shop-steward agreement or worker participation

necessary to consider the orientation of the participants to organization rules. One example will illustrate the variability of such orientations.

In an interesting study of a United States plant, Bensman and Gerver examined the rule about the use of a 'tap' in aircraft assembly. The tap was a tool which cut new threads over the original threads of a nut and thus facilitated the alignment of nuts and aircraft plate openings. In addition, this re-threading weakened the aircraft structure and made it more likely to shake apart with severe vibration! Thus 'the use of the tap was the most serious crime of workmanship conceivable in the plant' and a worker could be summarily fired for merely possessing a tap.

The rules, then, were clear enough. They were also systematically violated by most experienced workers and all foremen. Indeed, 'the foreman instructs the worker in [the use of the tap], indicates when he wants it used, assists the worker in evading the plant rules, and when the worker is caught, goes through the ritual of punishment' – a ritual which is almost entirely ceremonial. This collaborative violation of factory rules occurred because of the pressure of work-flow on all participants, workers and foremen alike, and because the formal rules were set by an external agency; namely the US Air Force. Thus the evasion of rules becomes an acceptable behaviour, and is stabilized as a permanent aspect of the work organization (Bensman and Gerver, 1963, esp. pp. 590, 593–4 and 597).

Managerial authority then is only one form of control: to understand the processes of decision-making and behaviour in an organization it is necessary to go far beyond the on-the-spot orders that are given by

a superior to a subordinate, to go beyond the immediate command/
obedience relationship. Perrow also echoes this view:

> the vast proportion of the activity in organizations goes on without personal
> directives and supervision – and even without written rules – and sometimes in
> permitted violation of the rules. We tend to pass over this 'residue' which
> constitutes perhaps 80 per cent of the behaviour, by invoking general concepts
> such as habit, training, socialization, or routine.
>
> (1972, p. 156)

Actual shopfloor behaviour and relationships must be seen then not as
consequences of the unilateral imposition by management on a passive
workforce of specifications and prescriptions, but a two-way exchange
in which an accommodation concerning the meaning and relevance of
such prescriptions is achieved in exchange for some level of commitment to the existing distribution of authority, and to working
objectives.

In Chapter 3 I argued that the labour process theories were incomplete. Deskilling is not enough, as craft skills are not the only obstacle
to capital: new forms of work organization create other opportunities
for bargaining leverage. Job re-design does not necessarily solve the
problem of control. Therefore *all* control strategies require some
degree of integration or even incorporation of the labour force. In this
chapter we have discovered that the Weberian theory of domination
also is incomplete, in that it is excessively dependent upon an un-
differentiated notion of legitimation. Theoretically, there are *levels* of
legitimation, and there is a level of day-to-day compliance which has
little to do with legitimation, but is best termed 'consent'.

Job design, structures of control and the employment relationship

In Chapter 1, it was argued that more complex typologies were necessary in order to discuss employer strategies because such strategies were
frequently composite, mixed and even contradictory. Having outlined
neo-Marxian and Weberian perspectives on the labour process, it is
now apposite to set out the basis of such a typology.

In general we can distinguish three levels of structuration of work
organization: first, there is the level of the division of labour and
technology, in other words the area of work design. Though the design
of the production process itself has an element of control in-built, it is
nevertheless at the second level that control features are more overt.
The second level of work organization includes the formal authority
structure of the factory, plus the monitoring system. Thirdly, there is
the wider framework of the capital/labour relationship arising from the
relation of job positions to the labour market. This, in turn, links to the
division of labour via the concept of labour substitutability, but does
not reduce to the first level of structuration because of wider labour

market processes, general employer strategies and trade union/employer bargaining processes.

In sum, there are three general categories which can be used to analyse all forms of work organization: the division of labour and job design, structure of control over task performance, and the employment relationship. I will attempt to demonstrate in Chapter 5 the value of those categories in an analysis of Taylorism.

The notion of three levels of structuration of the labour process raises the question of whether there are relatively independent dynamics? Can Taylorization for example, affect one level, whilst other levels of work organization remain unaffected? The answer, I believe, is that whilst there is a tendency for changes in job design, control structures and employment relations to go together this is only a tendency and not a necessity. Deskilling can occur without increasing bureaucratization. Indeed, paradoxically deskilling can occur with continued craft control. In order to understand this paradox it is necessary to analyse craft control (or the social relations of craft production) in more detail than has been done. This is attempted in Chapter 6, and the main point to underline here is that craft control can be eliminated at one level (e.g. job design) and can still be maintained at another level, such as a continued pattern of shopfloor control and the continued influence of craft unions over recruitment (Montgomery, 1979; Stark, 1980).

Similarly, whatever happens at the level of the structure of control does not *determine*, though it may influence, work design. Though as I shall argue in Part II mass production, mass markets and the introduction of new technology formed the base for the erection of bureaucratic structures of control, nevertheless the bureaucratization of the administration of production does not *entail* deskilling.

The notion of separate dynamics, of independent sources of variation, leads us to an important distinction in relation to the nature of bureaucratization. Table 4.1 is a visual reminder that the changes of Weberian ideal-type bureaucracy can be grouped into two general sets: the structure of control and the employment relationship. Given the separate dynamics argument, it is then possible to conceive of bureaucratization of the structure of control and bureaucratization of the employment relation as two different processes. Crozier indicates the importance of such a distinction:

There is an important distinction to be made between rules prescribing the way in which the task must be performed and rules prescribing the way people should be chosen, trained and promoted for various jobs. Subordinates fight rationalization in the first area and want it in the second, and supervisory personnel do just the reverse.

(Crozier, 1964, p. 161, footnote 33)

The point here is that bureaucratization is an attempt to impose a mesh of regulations, of predictabilities on others, whilst manoeuvring to retain as much freedom and choice for oneself as possible. For employers and managers the preferred position is to situate workers within a tight set of rules and constraints, whilst retaining the freedom to add and subtract tasks to existing jobs, to promote 'blue-eyed' boys etc. For workers the preferred situation is strictly-controlled task allocation and promotion by seniority, combined with the freedom over work-pace and work-methods.

One point to be stressed is that bureaucracy creates not only a distinctive form of institutionalized control, but a distinct form of employment relationship based on worker commitment to the organization. It is necessary to emphasize some notion of the employment relationship because the point of production perspective pursued by Braverman and other labour process theorists is a limited one. The most crucial dimension of the employment relationship is that of dependency. Dependency is determined by two broad factors: alternative sources of need satisfaction and the capacity of subordinates to organize. I will deal with each of these points in turn.

In connection with dependency the most important aspect is the availability of alternative employment. This in turn depends on the size of the industrial reserve army through time plus the organized attempts of employers to carve up the labour market. For example it is not often realized that Japanese paternalistic employment practices in large firms are reinforced by the structure of the labour market. Most Japanese newspaper adverts call for workers *under* 30. This means that employees leaving a large firm get 'pushed down to the bottom of the dual economic structure, a bottom made up of small firms which paid lower wages, had poorer working conditions and were unable to guarantee employment security' (R.E. Cole, 1971, p. 129, and R.E. Cole 1979, p. 244). The best British parallel to these structured dependency relations is the Big Four British banks, who typically recruit from school, do their own training and expect their staff to stay for life, with the exception of young females who are expected to 'topple-out' of the organization into marriage. This type of employment relation is enforced by an unofficial agreement among the Big Four banks not to employ any staff who have left another bank. As a result there is virtually no labour market in British banking as evidenced by the fact that managerial vacancies are neither externally nor *internally* advertised (Littler, 1976; *Financial Times*, 25 October 1976). What these two examples illustrate is that once a worker accepts that he can no longer move, he is more likely to accept company policies. Resistance in any form is extremely difficult where no alternative employment opportunities exist. Japanese organizations and British banks are simply extreme examples of a bureaucratic employment relationship, involving stable employment with considerable job security and established patterns of career progression.

Weber saw the career system as a significant element in the employment relation side of his bureaucratic model, and this element has been emphasized by some recent writers including Edwards (1979) and Stinchcombe (1974). Stinchcombe defines 'bureaucracies' as both cognitive and motivational systems, and attempts to construct a theory of bureaucratic motivation. This asserts that the rewards which bureaucracy offers are promotions to higher offices. Second, these rewards must be tied to performance. Moreover such a system is only effective if men subjectively see their lives as a succession of promotions, i.e. if they have a career consciousness. Clearly the extent to which workers are locked into an organizational career system such that future status becomes entirely dependent on the organization is crucial.

Though it is of primary importance, workers do not just need jobs. There are also pervasive needs for health and welfare facilities. The relevant distinction here is between enterprise-related welfare versus state welfare. If we take Japan as an extreme example again, then the non-transferable welfare schemes of Japanese companies could only have their full effect of increasing dependency if the availability of welfare outside the firm was minimal. Thus Japanese employers' associations have consistently opposed state welfare schemes (Crawcour, 1978, pp. 235 and 244).

In general the vulnerability of workers is at a maximum when anyone to whom the worker might turn for recourse has close ties with management and when the employer controls health facilities and living conditions. This was often the case in US company towns and we can see that the ideology of paternalism or welfarism reflects a structured dependency (see Norris, 1978).

A second source of worker dependency relates to the capacity to organize in opposition to employers. Two factors seem to be of general significance here: the capital/state relationship and divisions amongst the working class. It is important to remember that classes do not exist separately from their relations to the state. The political struggle between classes intersects and cross-cuts relations at the point of production. The forms of state intervention and control provide a crucial context for the development of the labour process. In particular state-backed industrial development often means that organizations are insulated from demand oscillations and can, like private monopolies, exercise more choice over labour strategies (see Chapter 10).

If we turn to examine working-class divisions, then it is clear that there is a dynamic of fragmentation counterposed to that of collectivization. Divisions within the working class have a deeper basis than that of skill. As Blackburn and Mann point out, the conflicts between skilled and unskilled are echoed by differences

between male to female, between native-born and immigrants, between ethnic groups, between young, middle-aged and old, and between those privileged by an internal labour market and those not so privileged . . . The essence of the division is the same: it is between established and new workers, that is between those already established in the process of production and those recently brought into it by the expansion of capitalism.

(1979, p. 300)

Blackburn and Mann are here pointing to the importance of a basic dynamic of capitalist expansion, which creates continually re-occurring division within the working class based on job-rights and job-security within the labour process.

Having clarified the concept of an employment relationship, especially in relation to bureaucracy, it is pertinent to make a primary distinction between different forms of employment relation, which is crucial to later analysis. I have already indicated the distinction between a structure of organizational commitment versus a structure of limited employment contracts with employees returning to the labour market every few years. But underlying such distinctions are conventional organization theory ideas about the employment relationship which ignore the patterns of history. Much early industrialization was based on the *avoidance* of direct employer/employee relationships and the reliance on existing patterns of subordination. Thus a primary distinction is that between those organizations based on *direct* employment and control, and those based on *indirect* employment and control, such as the domestic system, tut-work and internal contract. In many ways the difference between direct and indirect employment and control is more fundamental than the bureaucratic/non-bureaucratic division in organizational sociology. This argument is elaborated and historically supported in Chapter 6.

Summary and conclusions

In this chapter, I have attempted to clarify the concept of bureaucracy. The notion of bureaucracy was located within Weber's theory of domination, and some confusions and ambiguities were analysed. We concluded that bureaucracy as an ideal-type represents the intersection of rational–legal authority with 'bureaucracy' as a general administrative form based on officials. One major problem in connection with labour process theory is the nature of legitimacy. It was concluded that it is necessary to theorize levels of legitimation and a concept of everyday compliance which may or may not exist within an overall framework of legitimation but is certainly not theoretically identical. 'Loyal' employees may go on strike whilst apathetic employees may not.

In the third section of this chapter I argued that there are three general categories which can be used to analyse all forms of work organization including Taylorism: the division of labour and job-design, the structure of control and the employment relation. Like many sociological concepts the 'division of labour' is dual-faced and can refer to a static description of job-roles within organizations or to the basic dynamics (deskilling versus upgrading) of the job structure. The structure of control suggests a typology of modes of control or employer strategies. There is no clear agreement on such a typology, because such strategies are frequently composite, mixed and even contradictory. The value of a threefold distinction is that it permits analysis of mixed strategies. Thus it is a superficial level of analysis simply to look at the interior of the workshop. There is a wider framework of control arising from the dictates of capitalist markets. The employment relation refers, in part, to the relation of job positions to the labour market. In addition, it was pointed out that a crucial dimension of the employment relationship is that of dependency, which allows us to distinguish between different forms of employment relation. An additional dimension, which is historically very important, is that between direct and indirect employment and control.

Finally, we noted that the three analytic categories have an empirical significance in that there may be independent sources of variation. In particular there is a distinction to be drawn between the bureaucratization of the structure of control and the bureaucratization of the employment relationship. This distinction is important in understanding the phenomenon of Taylorism (or scientific management) which is analysed in Chapter 5.

5 The Taylorism Debate

In Chapters 2–4 we have considered Marxian and Weberian perspectives on the labour process and suggested some theoretical concepts which are useful for the analysis of managerial strategies. In this chapter I will use these concepts to analyse Taylorism, but first it is pertinent to outline the Taylorism debate which is a key issue in recent labour process theorizing.

Paradoxical perspectives
Industrial and organizational sociology has frequently misconstrued the significance and meaning of Taylorism such that it has been treated as an *ideas system* only. A good example of this perspective is provided by Miller and Form (1964) in their textbook on industrial sociology.

From 1900 to 1920 Taylorism provided the dominant ideas about the 'worker' and worker-motivation, but money was not enough and a new great idea was taking root. The view of the worker as an individual personality emerged strongly about 1920 to command the stage. From 1920 to 1940 the worker was seen as a psychological complex, but then 'Psychological Man' faltered, and sociology entered industry. Man had neighbours! (Miller and Form, 1964, pp. 645–84).

This storyline continues to permeate and influence even recent works on industrial and organizational sociology. For example, Rose (1975) spends three chapters considering Taylorism largely as a managerial ideology, as a mode of understanding industrial behaviour, and concludes that Taylorism was 'refuted by the opposition it generated'. Similarly, Fox (1974) largely concentrates on Taylorism as a managerial ideology, as a mode of legitimation, which failed. In general, this perspective on Taylorism sees it as a failed ideology, a vision by technocrats which appeared around 1900, only to sink into the mists of the past about 1920.

However, there is another line of thought which treats Taylorism rather differently. Instead of regarding it as a discredited ideology, it is taken as a form of work organization, or a set of principles underlying work organization. The most recent champion of this view is Braverman who argues for the central importance of Taylorism:

The popular notion that Taylorism has been 'superseded' by later schools of industrial psychology, or 'human relations', that it 'failed' – because of Taylor's amateurish and naive views of human motivation or because it brought about a storm of labour opposition or because Taylor and various successors antagonized workers and sometimes management as well – or that it is 'outmoded' because certain Taylorian specifics like functional foremanship or his incentive-pay schemes have been discarded for more sophisticated methods: all these represent a woeful misreading of the actual dynamics of the development of management.

(Braverman, 1974, pp. 86–7)

This view of Taylorism as a significant set of design criteria structuring work organization down to the present-day is echoed by many writers who have studied the design and organization of work. For example the only available survey of job-design practices in US companies concluded that: 'Current job-design practices are consistent with the principles of rationalization or scientific management.' (Davis *et al.*, 1955, p. 80; see also Friedmann, 1955; Trist, 1973, pp. 95–9; *Work in America*, 1973, pp. 17–19; Klein, 1976, pp. 14–17).

These two views of Taylorism create a strange paradox: on the one hand it is a failed ideology, and, on the other, it represents the basic principles of the structuring of work down to the present.

There are a number of inter-linked reasons for this paradox. Most crucially there has been a failure to relate structure and ideology. Too many writers have considered it adequate to locate Taylorism within a flow of ideas, and ignore, often for lack of evidence, any other level of social reality (e.g. Haber, 1964; Child, 1969; Bendix, 1974). Associated with this type of conceptualization has been a failure to realize that 'managerial ideologies' cannot be treated as equivalent; they cannot be arranged along *one* dimension. Thus there is little meaning in conceptualizing Taylorism, welfarism, human relations and so on as equivalents, as types of 'managerial philosophies', which succeed each other with the ebb and flow of history. The reason for the lack of equivalence is simple. All ideologies have structural implications, but some have more than others.

In considering the influence of managerial ideologies, we need to remember the three levels of structuration distinguished in Chapter 4: namely work design, the structure of control and the employment relationship. Taylorism was a management package which affected all three levels, whereas the structural implications of human relations and welfarism do not reach down to the level of work design.

It is only when we turn from an abstracted ideological flow to consider the processes of institutionalization, that historical confusions begin to sort themselves out. There are two major points here. Firstly, all processes of institutionalization and diffusion take time. There will always be an historical lag between the ideas of intellectuals and those of active practitioners. Priests and warriors never think alike. Thus human relations did not 'happen' in the 1930s. It only became institutionally significant in the USA in the 1940s and the 1950s in Britain. It is possible to ignore this cultural lag only at the cost of not locating ideas and idea-systems within *any* social space.

The second point we can label the 'Ambrit Fallacy'. This refers to the continual tendency to fuse the history and culture of the two very different societies, namely America and Britain, and the attempts to draw sociological conclusions on the basis of this unrecognized conflation. The reason that Taylorism hangs suspended in an historical vacuum in relation to British industrial history is the direct result of the Ambrit Fallacy.[1] Thus, the historical heyday of Taylorism in Britain was not pre-1914 but in the inter-war years (see Chapters 8 and 9).

Apart from the implicit debate between traditional industrial sociology and more recent analyses, there has been an explicit debate between labour process theorists about the influence and implementation of Taylorism within capitalism. Broadly there are four different views:

(1) As Braverman argues, Taylorism was central to the structuring of the capitalist labour process.
(2) Taylorism was an extreme expression of processes that were occurring anyway.
(3) Taylorism had a widespread *ideological* impact, but practically was not significant.
(4) Taylorism was not of major significance. It proved to be a contradictory and impractical method of labour control.

(See Braverman, 1974, pp. 85–138; Palmer, 1975, p. 32; deKadt, 1976, pp. 65–7; Palmer, 1976, pp. 68–70; Edwards, 1979, pp. 97–104; Clawson, 1980, pp. 31–2; Stark, 1980, pp. 91–2).

In order to assess these debates we need a clear and operative understanding of the concept of Taylorism. This I attempt to provide in the next three sections of this chapter.

The principles of Taylorism

Taylorism grew out of the systematic management movement in the USA in the 1880/90s (see Chapter 11). Like some of the other early management reformers, only with a greater intensity, Taylor believed in the original sin and the original stupidity of the worker. According to

Taylor 'the natural instinct and tendency of men is to take it easy, which may be called "natural soldering" ' (Taylor, 1903, p. 30). Moreover, any man phlegmatic enough to do manual work was too stupid to develop the best way, the 'scientific way' of doing a job. Thus the role of the workman was a passive one. They should 'do what they are told to do promptly and without asking questions or making suggestions' (Taylor, 1909). This managerialist view of labour can be contrasted to the populist view. According to Bryan Palmer (1975), under nineteenth century modes of work control in the USA many workers saw themselves as the sole creative factor in production. Taylorism and the rationalization movement generally undermined the populist view and substituted a concept of labour as a passive factor of production, a mere appendage of the machine. Secondly, it is interesting to contrast this view of original sin and stupidity to the Japanese Confucian view of original virtue (Dore, 1973, pp. 277 and 401–2; see Chapter 10).

As I have emphasized, Taylorism was both a system of ideological assertions and a set of management practices. If we turn to look at scientific management as a set of practices then we can proceed to analyse it in terms of three general categories: job design, the structure of control over task performance, and the implicit employment relationship.

It is clear that Taylorism involves systematic analysis of the labour process and the division of labour, followed by their decomposition in accordance with several principles.[2] The systematic analysis of work (Taylor's First Principle) was in order to develop a 'science of work'; and this systematic job analysis forms the basis for the calculation of production costs, the establishment of standard times for every task and the associated incentive payment system.

The decomposition is based on the following principles:

(1) *A general principle of maximum fragmentation* This prescribes that after analysis of work into its simplest constituent elements, management should seek to limit an individual 'job' to a single task as far as possible.

(2) *The divorce of planning and doing (Taylor's Fourth Principle)* This principle in particular is based on the idea that the worker is too stupid to understand his own job.

(3) *The divorce of 'direct' and 'indirect' labour* 'progressively suppressing that part of the worker's activity which consists of preparing and organizing the work in his own way' (Palloix, 1976, p. 52). This principle is given little theoretical attention but is very significant on the shopfloor. It is an essential component of more intensified work. Indeed it is the Taylorian equivalent of Babbage's principle. All preparation and servicing tasks are stripped

away to be performed by unskilled, and cheaper, workers, as far as possible.

(4)   *Minimization of skill requirements and job-learning time*
(5)   *Reduction of material handling to a minimum*

These five principles constitute a dynamic of deskilling. Taylor had generated a system for taking labour (i.e. job-roles) apart. In general, then, Taylorism embodies a dynamic of deskilling, though it should not be thought that it was the only cause of an increasing division of labour. Taylorism was *both* a consequence and a cause of deskilling and the corresponding coordination problems.

Earlier theorists such as Babbage had no clear idea of the problems of, and the means of, re-integration of the fragmented job roles. Systematic management grew out of the intensified problems of the integration of the new division of labour. These had been created by larger factories, more specialized machines and job-roles pre-Taylor, and the failure of traditional modes of management under changed conditions. The second major aspect of Taylorism then is the new structure of control, of integration, which it offered. This had a number of aspects.

(a) The principle of task control (Taylor's Third Principle)
This element has been obscured by the circumlocutory way in which Taylor described it. He talked about 'bringing the science and workmen together'. What it means in practice is a 'planning department' which plans and coordinates the entire manufacturing process:

The work of every workman is fully planned out by the management at least one day in advance, and each man received in most cases complete written instructions, describing in detail the task which he is to accomplish, as well as the means to be used in doing the work . . . This task specifies not only what is to be done but how it is to be done and the exact time allowed for doing it.

(Taylor, 1911, p. 39)

This is how 'science' and the workman are brought together. It should be emphasized that a crucial aspect of this 'bringing together' is the prescribing of uniform practices and operating procedures – standardization in other words. This represents a historical shift towards a more total control, a new level of control, over the labour process. In practice, the idea of a planning department with its conglomeration of functions envisaged by Taylor at the apex of the organization was rarely realized.

Complete task control could not be achieved simply by a planning department and standardization. Other mechanisms were necessary.

(b) Functional organization

This principle is usually lost sight of because it was rarely put directly into practice. Even the early acolytes had reservations about functional foremanship (Nelson, 1975, p. 72). Nevertheless, functional organization should be noted for several reasons. Functional organization is important as a prescription because it represents the idea of a *division of management*: a movement away from a single hierarchy.

For Taylor, the role of the foreman and the gang-boss was too wide, too powerful, and not clearly circumscribed. It needed to be subdivided and deskilled as much as the roles of the workmen:

Functional management consists in so dividing the work of management that each man from the assistant superintendent down shall have as few functions as possible to perform. If practicable the work of each man in the management should be confined to the performance of a single leading function.

(Taylor, 1903, p. 99)

Thus Taylor advocated dividing the shopfloor foremen into four (setting-up boss, speed boss, quality inspector and repair boss), and placing them under the control of the planning department. Like workers foremen became subject to the rule of clerks.

Braverman, and many other writers, use the following quote to illustrate the Taylorian attack on craft autonomy: 'All possible brain work should be removed from the shop and centred in the planning or laying-out department . . .' But nobody completes this quotation. Let us do so: '. . . leaving for the *foremen* and *gang-bosses* work strictly executive in nature.' (Taylor, 1903, pp. 98–9, emphasis added; cf. Braverman, 1974, p. 113). Furthermore, this statement occurs in the midst of a long section in 'Shop management' analysing the need to subdivide *managerial* roles. The implication I want to draw is that Taylorism and functional organization had an historical significance in relation to 'over-powerful' foremen and internal contractors as much as to craft deskilling.

Secondly, functional organization is significant because it was taken seriously by non-Western societies: Russia, and China to a lesser extent.[3] Indeed Brugger seeks to characterize Taylorism in terms of this principle. This is a novel way of looking at Taylorism and deserves consideration, if only because discussion of Taylorism tends to be resolutely ethnocentric. The argument is simple: within large complex organizations there are two basic ways of achieving organizational goals and solidarity – technologically or ideologically. If we relate this distinction to the structure of authority, then we get the possibilities illustrated in Figure 5.1.

The value of this perspective is that it locates these particular Taylorite ideas within a frame of possibilities, and suggests what

Figure 5.1   Types of authority structure and solidarity

Authority structure	Type of solidarity	
	Technological	Ideological
Staff-line	Modern, Western industrial organizations	Large Japanese organizations 1947–mid-1950s
Functional	Taylor model	Some Chinese experiments in the 1960s

happened to the Taylorian model in practice – namely a shift to staff-line organization. Taylor's prized 'planning department' became a series of departments clipped onto the side of the existing authority structure.

(c) Time study and the creation of a monitoring system
The institutionalization of time study represents the creation of a *separated* monitoring system over subordinate activities. The time study and scheduling system depends upon the workers filling in job-cards and/or time-sheets which constitute a flow-back of information to the planning departments, and enables them to determine effort-levels and compare performance. The point to be emphasized is that this flow of information largely bypasses the foremen, bypasses, that is, the existing authority structure.

The reduced 'observability' in large, complex organizations because of the increased physical separation and reduced congruence of superior/subordinate skills led to upper levels of management becoming progressively more isolated from knowledge of task performance in its details.[4] Thus as we move from specialization to fragmentation of labour it creates different types of problems which must be solved at the level of the structure of control, especially if the dynamic of deskilling is to continue. However, the fragmentation of tasks provides a measurement and quantification potential which, in turn, provides an information-flow potential so that senior managers can overview a production system and 'manage by exception'.

(d) Incentive payment system
The significance of this element of Taylorism has been much overrated

and misunderstood. I will attempt to understand the real significance of incentive payment systems below.

(e) Work group strategy

It is important to question the conventional version of Taylorism, which maintains that Taylor knew nothing of, nor about, work-groups, and their significance for the organization. According to the accepted version Taylor adopted an economistic view of working-class motivations, such that the only point of contact between managers and men is the pay envelope (cf. Thompson, 1913, p. 631). This is a superficial level of analysis. Taylor knew all about work-groups. He knew about solidary work-groups. He knew about their significance in regulating output; he called it 'systematic soldering' because he did not like it (Taylor, 1903, p. 32). Thus 'human relations' represents the 'discovery' of that which Taylorism had been concerned to destroy – work-group solidarity.

Given this perspective, 'human relations' represents a different managerial tactic in relation to work-groups. The Taylorite tactic is to try and break the power of the work-teams and work-groups by pressure, and, by appeal to individual ambition, to atomize the workforce.[5] Human relations represents an alternative approach; it represents a pale suggestion of 'ideological integration', of ideological control (see Figure 5.1). The latter as a dynamic process is best expressed by Brugger in relation to Chinese experience. The Chinese approach

seeks to focus loyalty not only upon the formal organization, but upon levels both higher and lower than the organization. At the lower level . . . *to infuse existing levels of group solidarity with commitment to the same values as the formal organization*. At the higher levels, it seeks *not* to extend the focus of loyalty through a hierarchy of formal organization, but to focus it upon a particular symbol cluster which is the source of legitimacy not only of different levels of formal organization but also of informal groupings.

(Brugger, 1976, p. 268, emphasis added)

This pattern of ideological control is important in understanding Japanese work organization, as we shall discover in Chapter 10.

Thus discussion of Taylorism in terms of whether it represents too individualistic an understanding of the social realities of work organization is doubly to misunderstand Taylorism, and the historical path which it represents.

The third aspect of Taylorism relates to the employment relation. It is this which enables us to clearly relate Taylorite work organization to bureaucracy. The employment relations embodied in Taylorism have been brought out most clearly by L.E. Davis:

there is a minimal connection between the individual and the organization in terms of skill, training, involvement and the complexity of his contribution, in return for maximum flexibility and independence on the part of the organization in using its manpower. In other words, the organization strives for maximum inter-changeability of personnel (with minimum training) to reduce its dependence on the availability, ability or motivation of individuals.

(1966, p. 302)

Davis calls this relation the 'minimum interaction model'.

What Davis is pointing to is the crucial concept of labour substitutability. Routinization of jobs maximizes substitutability, such that individuals, work-groups and even entire departments can be replaced more easily. In practical terms this means that any modern personnel department will have a known replacement time for each grade of labour, composed of two elements: recruitment-time and training-time. Recruitment-time varies with the pool of unemployment and training-time with the extent of deskilling. Thus Taylorite routinization of jobs is a push towards minimum interaction employment relations and a real 'commodification' of labour.

In practice there are limits to minimum interaction and hire and fire policies. Theoretically, these have been emphasized by Cressey and MacInnes (1980). As was pointed out in Chapter 3, capitalism is in a perpetual tension between the commodification of labour versus recognizing and utilizing the social relationships of employers, foremen and workers. In practice these limits were discovered by Ford.

By the time that Henry Ford came into business Taylorism had begun to affect the US engineering industries. Consequently, Ford

Figure 5.2   Types of paternalism

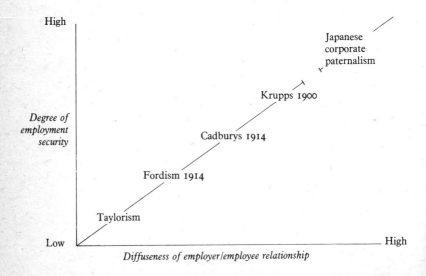

took over some of the essential aspects of Taylorism (the divorce of planning and doing, the fragmentation of jobs, each task allotted a specific time, etc.), but he also went further by introducing two further principles. These were the flow-line principle and a new method of labour control.

The new method of labour control used by Ford revolved around the 'Five Dollar Day'. One effect of the implementation of Taylorism and flow-line principles was that workers deserted his automobile plants in droves. For example in 1913 Ford required about 13,000 workers 'to run his plants at any one time, and in that year over 50,000 workers quit' (Beynon, 1973, p. 19). (For the links between Taylorism and Fordism see Sward, 1972, pp. 34–5). The minimum interaction principle of Taylorism was proving *too* expensive, and the answer that Ford came up with was the Five Dollar Day. This was a wage package which guaranteed high rates of pay. However, not everyone qualified for the Five Dollar Day. The conditions were six months' continuous employment, aged over 21, satisfactorily personal habits at home and work (cleanliness and prudence) and no consumption of alcohol or tobacco. All these criteria were checked by Ford's newly established 'Sociological Department'! This aspect of Fordism enables us to see the relation between Taylorism and paternalism.

The relation between Taylorism and paternalism is not always clear, an obscurity which is exacerbated by the vagueness surrounding the concept of paternalism. It is useful to link the two concepts explicitly in terms of the employment relation. In addition, such a clarification enables us to locate Japanese corporate paternalism which is discussed in later chapters. In order to construct a chart of paternalism it is necessary to note that paternalism essentially involves a diffuse employer/employee relationship, with an employer's concern for the non-work life of an employee (Abercrombie and Hill, 1976). This diffuseness of the employment relationship is associated with the degree of employment security. If we relate these two dimensions then we get the picture in Figure 5.2

Taylorism as we have seen is associated with casualized employment and a minimum interaction relationship. One of Taylor's close associates asserted that he did not 'care a hoot what became of the workman after he left the factory at night, so long as he was able to show up the next morning in a fit condition for a hard day's toil' (Copley, 1915, p. 42). For Taylor, welfare schemes and paternalistic modes of management were objects of ridicule (Palmer, 1975, p. 40). Fordism, with its paternal repressiveness and the attempt to stabilize high rates of turnover by the 'Five Dollar Day' is, so to speak, two steps up from Taylorism (for Cadburys, see Child, 1964; for Krupps, see Pounds, 1952; for Japan, see Chapter 10). Despite Fordism and the threads of paternal capitalism, minimum interaction continues to be the economic reality for many workers in the secondary labour market.

The relationship of Taylorism to bureaucracy

It is common to see Taylorism as part of a wider 'rationalization movement' or as one type of a formal or classical theory of administration.[6] However, little attempt is made systematically to relate Taylorism to the Weberian concept of bureaucracy. This failure to do so has led to serious consequences. The major effect has been to leave Taylorism isolated from the main body of sociological theory such that it is something to throw bricks at but never to use as a tool of analysis.

In order to relate Taylorism to the concept of bureaucracy it is necessary to remember the fundamental distinction within the Weberian model which was made in Chapter 4. In that chapter it was pointed out that apart from the five over-arching beliefs about rational legal authority, the remaining elements of the ideal type can be divided into two categories: those that describe the official's relationship to the organization (or the 'employment relationship') and those that are largely concerned with the structure of control (see Table 4.1).

If we examine Taylorism in the above context, then it is clear that Taylorism represents the bureaucratization of the structure of control, but not the employment relationship. Taylorism does not involve, nor imply, a career system (WB8), nor fixed salaries (WB6). Instead it involves what we have called the minimum inter-action relation between individual and organization.

In relation to the structure of control aspects of the bureaucratic model, Taylorism takes continuity and hierarchy for granted. In addition the Taylorites sought to introduce a systematic division of labour (WA2); work-performance governed by rules based on 'science' (WA4); and a system of written instruction and communication (WA7). The Taylor idea of a planning office was an attempt to achieve a unified system of control (WB10), but with a functional system of organization. Therefore it was not strictly monocratic.

In relation to the employment relationship aspects of the bureaucratic model, Taylorism tends to take non-appropriation, free contractual labour, and full-time commitment (WA5, WA6, WB1, WB4, and WB7) for granted. The notion of 'scientific' selection (WB5) was a major, explicit principle in Taylor's writings. In practice the idea was little developed.

The central significance of a career structure within an organization has been suggested by many writers (see Chapter 4). Career structures and career motivation are a major, definitive characteristic of 'bureaucratic' organization, and this element can be used to distinguish between different types of rational legal work organization. Thus the major characteristic of Taylorite work organization is the lack of any notion of a career system. It is this which distinguishes it from other available models of organization at the turn of the century; for example those based on the public service organizations such as the police, the railways and the post office.[7]

Wage/effort exchange

The purpose of this section is to look at Taylorism from a rather different perspective – that of wage/effort exchanges. This perspective, elaborated by Baldamus, has been recently championed by Ackroyd (1974). Both writers argue that it should be the central thread of industrial sociology. However, such an approach seems to me to be complementary to more general ideas on the structure of control and the processes of the division of labour.

An entire literature has built up around payment systems since the 1890s. It has frequently dominated managerial discussions of work organization, and Taylorism itself has become ensnared in this form of interpretation. Taylor's 'wage-conscious' audience at the American Society of Mechanical Engineers were largely impervious to his ideas of a system of management, as he bitterly complained.[8] This perspective has continued, such that the notion of incentive wages is still seen as the predominant element in Taylorism. This is a mistake. Rather than allow the literature and concepts of payment systems to swamp socio-logical analysis, it is necessary to do the reverse: to penetrate payment systems with precise analytic tools.

Let us start by attempting to deflate the fundamental distinction within payment system literature: that between time-wages and piece-wages. It is necessary to recognize the common basis of all types of wages: 'But in the practice of industry, whether a man be employed on a time-wage or on piece-wage, both the time occupied and the work done are, as a rule, taken into account . . . time-wage very often has a piece-basis, and piece-wage has in practically all cases a time-basis.' (Schloss, 1898, p. 13).

In other words, time-wages are usually based on mutual expectation about the quantum of work. For example, many foremen and sub-contractors in the latter part of the nineteenth century would set production quotas. Similarly, piece-work involves implicit assump-tions of earning so much per day, or per week. Thus, as Behrend argues, every employment contract involves both a wage-rate bargain and an effort-bargain (Behrend, 1957).

Thus the sociological significance of Taylorism in relation to wage/effort exchange does *not* lie in a simple shift to piece-work. Indeed, Taylor himself argued that his system of management could be applied *under any payment system*, and concludes that a variety of payment systems can be used in the same factory depending on circumstances (Taylor, 1903, p. 80). Given this, the important question in relation to payment systems relates to effort determination: how do workers decide what effort to put into their work? There are three broad answers: (i) custom and practice; or (ii) based on formal standards; or (iii) a conflictual tension between the two. It is this distinction, rather than the usual classification, which is sociologically and historically important in relation to payment-systems.

Using the above distinction it is possible to construct the classification of wage/effort exchange systems depicted in Figure 5.3. This classification brings out the crucial aspect of Taylorism in this regard, and indeed Taylor saw his system in this way: 'this whole system rests upon an accurate and scientific study of unit times, which is by far the most important element in scientific management' (Taylor, 1903, p. 58).

In addition, the above classification overlaps with a second distinction. It is possible to distinguish between wage/effort exchange systems in terms of their 'transparency'. Some payment systems, such as simple piece-work, make the relation of effort to earnings transparent; (both supervisors and workers are fully aware of the effort bargain involved for each task) whilst other systems completely obscure the effort/wage relationship. The relevance of the notion of 'transparency' to the Taylorite payment schemes is that they attempted to make the wage/effort relationship *more* opaque than simple piece-work in order to provide a built-in rate-cutting factor. The way that this was done is as follows: instead of just mapping the output rate onto a wage-scale, a third intermediary scale is introduced, namely an 'effort-scale'. This is usually derived from some output target or 'standard job-time', and this effort-scale provides an apparent arithmetic rationale for the wage-scale, and obscures the relationship between the output rate and the

Figure 5.3   Wage/effort exchange systems

	Informal Standards of effort	Formal Standards of effort
Piece-work or time-wage	Unilaterally determined	Bilaterally determined
	e.g. the Taylorite system	e.g. standard price lists

wage scale. For Taylor and his acolytes, such as Gantt, there was no explicit effort-scale, but under the Bedaux system, introduced later, and important in Britain, there was a comparative scale – based on 'B' units, such that a workman was judged to be working at 60B or 70B and so on (see Chapter 8).

Hobsbawm argues that during the nineteenth century there was a slow withering of the customary, traditional ideas concerning labour effort. This occurred through a collective learning process; a collective reorientation to the market system (Hobsbawm, 1964, pp. 350–1). However, it is not just a question of the slow assimilation of the 'rules of the game'. A traditional, normative basis to levels of work effort must be socially constituted. In this case standard effort-levels are built into the occupation or skill. Therefore, if job-roles are fractured during an accelerating division of labour, an increasing number of workers are thrust into positions for which there are no customary standards. It is this which constituted a major part of the 'labour problem' at the end of the nineteenth century.

Thus Taylorism represents the historical switchover from traditional effort-norms to the creation of new social mechanisms for constituting effort standards. However, at this point in the argument we encounter another paradox.

Baldamus and other writers have emphasized that time-study rests on pre-existing notions of wage/effort relationships and of the level of effort in a particular work situation:

Whether one is successful or not in finding the 'required' standard times depends decisively upon the discovery of the preconceived, habitually maintained standards of normal exertion in any type of operation. The true purpose of scientific objectivity in the practice of work-measurement is precisely the opposite of what it claims to be in theory: . . . The true purpose . . . is to guess as consistently as possible the purely subjective element of effort standards, and subsequently to adjust rates of pay in accordance with them.
(Baldamus, 1961, p. 47; also see Behrend, 1957, pp. 503–15; Behrend, 1961, pp. 102–18; Hyman and Brough, 1975, pp. 13–14)

How can a time-study practitioner discover pre-existing notions of effort-levels where there are none? If work-study was a managerial solution to the widespread *lack* of traditional effort-norms, how can it be based on 'prevailing notions of the right level of effort'? The answer, I think, is that most research on the operation of work-study is based on ongoing systems, where the work-study practitioner is concerned with minor method or product changes. However, in a situation of more radical job-changes, a situation of fragmentation and associated technological change, the work-study engineer is a more active participant in establishing the standard effort-levels than some writers would have us believe. For example, in the 1920s and 1930s in Britain, many factories established assembly and sub-assembly lines for the first time, fragmenting many jobs in the process, and the deskilled workers, often women, brought to the bench ignorance and often credulousness about 'the right level of effort'.

One distinction introduced by Baldamus enables the argument concerning the relationship of bureaucracy to Taylorism to be completed. This is the distinction between effort stability and effort intensity controls. Effort stability mechanisms shift 'effort' about, so that it is stabilized between people and overtime. Effort now comes in neat packets, and all the 'packets' dance to the same rhythm. It is not only necessary to iron out effort, but also to boost it up. This is the aim of effort-intensity controls. They are not necessarily *separate* from effort-stability controls in practice. Some means of control (e.g. training, incentive schemes) can have a dual function. However, this distinction enables us to understand the different significance of two aspects of the Taylorian work-study process. Rate-setting, that is establishing a rate for a job, is primarily a matter of effort-intensity control. It is at this point that any 'speed-up' effect is inserted into the task situation; whilst once established, incentive schemes are primarily a matter of *stabilizing* effort, or effort routinization.

It is important to note that stabilizing effort ensures calculability and predictability within the organization. For Weber, bureaucratic organization ensured a high degree of calculability, but when we look at the bureaucratization of the structure of control in industrial organizations, then what Taylorism adds to the Weberian elements (work-study, monitoring system, incentive payment system) is concerned with the processes of determining and fixing effort-levels. Once production tasks are observed, analysed, timed and recorded, then knowledge of them can be rendered independent of any individual or work-group, such that given outcomes can be replicated, taught and built into the formal organizational structure.

Summary and conclusions

If sociology is to understand the changes in the forms of work organization from the late nineteenth century to the present, then it is necessary to penetrate beyond the cliches about Taylorism. In particular, it is necessary to avoid construing Taylorism as an abstracted ideas-system, and to avoid the 'Ambrit Fallacy'. Thus we have analysed Taylorism in terms of the division of labour, the structure of control over task-performance, and the implicit minimum inter-action employment relationship.

Further, Taylorism represents a form of organization devoid of any notion of a career structure or job security for the majority, unlike other forms of organizational model available at the turn of the century, such as the railways, and the post office. Therefore Taylorism can be defined as the bureaucratization of the structure of control, but not the employment relationship. This aspect of the Taylorite model permits a clearer conceptual comparison with both the Weberian notion of bureaucracy and managerial strategies such as Fordism and paternalism.

In industrial organizations calculability essentially involves processes of determining and fixing effort-levels. Thus Taylorism also represents the historical shift to the creation of new social mechanisms for constituting effort-standards within an accelerated dynamic of deskilling. It is this rather than incentive wages which is the crucial element in Taylorism in relation to wage/effort exchange.

In this chapter we have been concerned to analyse Taylorism largely based on Taylor's own writings. This leaves out of account the contradictions of a Taylorite strategy and the context of implementation, both of which are crucial aspects of Taylorism *in practice*. These aspects will be considered in later chapters. Moreover in assessing the influence of Taylorism in Britain it is important not to identify Taylorism with all processes of labour rationalization. Writers such as Braverman blur any distinction between Taylorism and the wider trends of mechanization, job fragmentation and systematic management. In opposition to this, it is theoretically necessary to bear in mind a clear distinction between Taylorite rationalization and non-Taylorite rationalization.

In the next four chapters we will look at the historical development of the labour process in Britain between about 1870 and the beginning of the Second World War. This period in many ways was the crucial period for the crystallization of the British pattern of capital/labour relationships.

Part Two   The Bureaucratization of Work Organization in Britain, 1870–1939

6   Nineteenth Century Modes of Labour Control

Nineteenth century workshop relations

There are two contradictory models of nineteenth century workshop relations which are widespread. Firstly there is the 'Old Wilfred Workmaster' view. This assumes direct, personal relationships between an owner-manager and all the workers, associated with an authoritarian, centralized form of control (e.g. Kynaston-Reeves and Woodward, 1970, pp. 53–4; Litterer, 1961, pp. 469–70; Edwards, 1979, pp. 25–7). This model of simple, direct control, with its overtones of the heroic entrepreneur, is historically misleading, because it was only applicable to a minority of firms. This type of control we will term 'entrepreneurial control'.

Secondly, in total or partial contradiction to the 'Old Wilfred Workmaster' conception is the assumption of widespread craft control. It is this second model of relationships which permeates Braverman's work. It is the transfer of job-knowledge from the crafts and its monopolization by management which Braverman sees as the essence of Taylorism and modern capitalism. The assumption of craft-control ignores considerable differences between industries and indeed between the workshop situation of craft and non-craft workers. In this and the next section I will suggest a more adequate means of conceptualizing nineteenth century structures of control over task performance which highlights some of these differences.

There was no general theory of organization during the Industrial Revolution. There was a surprising lack of management theory and conscious planning especially in relation to labour and labour control (Pollard, 1968, pp. 296–301; see also Hobsbawm, 1964, p. 352; Payne, 1974, pp. 32–3; Bendix, 1974, pp. 202–3). This was partly because of the widespread avoidance of direct employer/employee relationships.

As Hobsbawm points out, 'Capitalism in its early stages expands, and to some extent operates, not so much by directly subordinating large bodies of workers to employers, but by sub-contracting exploitation and management.' (Hobsbawm, 1964, p. 297). Thus the immediate employer of many workers was not the large capitalist, but an inter-mediate, internal contractor who had a contractual relationship with the over-arching employer, and in turn was an employer of labour himself. The employer provided the fixed capital, supplied the raw material and much of the working capital and controlled the sale of the finished product. The contractor hired and fired, supervised the work process and received a lump sum from the employer for completed work. The contractor's income consisted of the difference between the wages he paid to his employees or gang (plus the cost of any working capital he might provide) and the payments from the employer (Schloss, 1898, pp. 180–1; Gospel, 1978, p. 2; cf. Buttrick, 1952, pp. 205–6).

In addition, the contractor was sometimes responsible for his own financial control and much of his own purchasing. This enabled the capitalist to shift part of the risk of operating onto the contractors: the capital risks were spread as well as the managerial problems. In practice, the extent of the autonomy of the internal contractor varied among industries and over time such that no single concept can capture adequately all the traditional and hybrid situations.

Considerable confusion surrounds the notion of sub-contract be-cause of the failure to distinguish between *external* sub-contract and *internal* contract. The continuance of internal contract through the nineteenth century reflected inside the factory the continuance of petty workshop production outside the factory. Nevertheless, external sub-contract, or outwork, which merges into ordinary commercial relation-ships, does not represent a cohesive structure, and is not relevant to the gist of this chapter.[1]

Apart from variations in autonomy, the institution of internal con-tract varied along a skill dimension. The basis of the contracted work-group could vary from a skill or craft to unskilled gang-work, such as dockwork and navvying. Related to this skill basis is the size of the work-group. As Pollard points out, most industries varied between 'having a small number of sub-contractors as in mining, or large numbers of skilled workers as sub-contractors each employing only a few child or unskilled assistants' (Pollard, 1968, p. 59; also Hobs-bawm, 1964, pp. 299–300). Thus the internal contract system was not only a mode of authority on the shopfloor, but the social form within which the perpetuation of skills took place, if there *were* any skills to be passed on.

Given the absence of systematic management theory, what were the existing social relations which were carried over into the early large work organizations? In general, there were three main types of internal contract which can be distinguished in terms of traditional patterns of relationship:

(a) Familial relations and familial control
For example in cotton-spinning the skilled spinners were put in charge of machines on the understanding that they paid and recruited their own child assistants, and the employer did not deal with the assistants at all. Initially, the children employed were the spinner's own family, and this reproduced the domestic working situation (Lazonick, 1979). It is important to note that the children and helpers were not necessarily learning the trade.

(b) The master craftsman role and craft control
A good example of craft control is provided by the nineteenth century ironworks. The ironmaster paid and recruited his own men, determined hours of work and discipline, and even the organization of production. Moreover, whenever an ironmaster moved to another iron-works, he took all his workers with him (Pollard, 1968, p. 201). The primary commitment was to the master and not to any wider organization, or any wider social group. Similarly, in shipbuilding the shipwrights employed their own gangs, and apprentices were bound to the craftsmen not the yard owners (Pollard and Robertson, 1979, p. 164).

(c) Team work on a gang basis with a gang boss
This form of work organization is exemplified by the docks and the well-known butty-system in the coal mines.[2] (For the docks see Smith and Nash, 1889; for the butty system see A.J.P. Taylor, 1960 and Goffee, 1977). The gang bosses tended to assimilate their position to that of craftsmen, but it is a mistake to see these work-group relationships in terms of craft control: the reality was different. The position of the 'ganger' was more vulnerable, and was often based on extraneous factors, such as the personal relationship to the employer, as much as intrinsic, skill-based factors.[3]

Thus the bases of authority were different in the three cases, but all three relationships were relations of legitimated dependence and subordination. And these sets of relationships were institutionalized into British nineteenth century industry within the mechanism of internal contract.

Stone (1973) and other labour process theorists tend to confuse craft control with internal contract and to see the blurred amalgam as an embryonic form of workers' control which, correspondingly, limited capitalist control over the production process. This argument needs to be turned on its head: we need to understand the reinforcing advantages of internal contract for capitalists. These were fivefold: firstly it was a flexible mechanism that enabled the work system to meet 'sharp fluctuations in demand without having to carry a permanent burden of overhead expenditure' entailed by a large office staff (Hobsbawn, 1964, p. 298). Secondly, not only did it spread capital risks, it enabled capital risks to be determined in the first place: the employer was saved from numerous complex cost calculations. Thus systems of internal contract acted as a substitute for accounting. Thirdly, internal contract provided financial incentives, and a path of upward mobility, for key groups of workers. Fourthly, it bypassed the awkward fact that many employers lacked technical skills and technical knowledge. Finally, it was the agency of effort stabilization and task allocation. In general, internal contract systems and delegated modes of control provided a historical solution to the contradictions between the increasing size of firms and simple entrepreneurial control, especially in the context of scarce managerial resources.

A great deal has been written on the recalcitrance of the working class to factory life; of the need to create a new work discipline and abolish 'Saint Monday'; of the need to break the back of the workers across the new machinery, but what is often lost sight of is that the capitalist use of existing forms of subordination and dependency within a contract framework meant that the management of labour became a subsidiary problem to the 'external' problems of building roads, docks, and so on. As Bendix puts it:

For the subcontractors . . . could manage the workforce of the early enterprises more or less on the basis of existing and cumulative tradition of the master-apprentice relationship. As it is probable that English industrialization would have been greatly retarded if these traditions had not remained intact long after entrepreneurs and their spokesmen had begun to attack this and all other aspects of traditionalism in economic life.

(1974, p. 55)

None of this is to say that internal contracting did not act as a means of job control, a structural support of craft and non-craft skill, but this needs to be seen within the overall capitalist context. In terms of the labour market the contractor controlled hiring and firing and he could use this power to maintain an exclusiveness and control access to jobs (Hobsbawm, 1964, p. 299). Similarly, their control over task allocation and the power to make decisions affecting production increased their strategic position on the shopfloor.

Moreover, many sub-contracted work-groups maintained either a skill-hierarchy or a hierarchy based on length of attachment to the ganger. For example, in the flint-glass industry, the basic work-team was called a 'chair'. It consisted of a 'gaffer', a 'servitor', a 'footworker' and a boy or 'taker-in'. Early in the nineteenth century the 'chair' was a sub-contracted work-group, and the gaffer enjoyed virtually unlimited power over the underhands. Control of hierarchies such as these enabled contractors to restrict the work-activity and status of under-hands, learners and apprentices. It must always be remembered that underhands could be as technically-skilled as the 'gaffer', and this constituted a running threat to skill status and the contractor's position. Many of the early British trade unions were primarily associations of internal contractors and they often used the union to develop a set of rules regulating the work done by helpers and underhands (War-burton, 1939, p. 35; Fox, 1955, pp. 62–9; Clegg, Fox and Thompson, 1964, p. 15; Goffee, 1977, p. 46; cf. Ashworth, 1915, p. 36). However we will note in later sections that internal contracting is a flexible mechanism which could be used during periods of economic crisis for deskilling.

So far I have emphasized that industrial and organizational sociology has neglected the historical significance of internal contract. Having argued this in an ideal-typical way, it is important to introduce some necessary qualifications. In general, nineteenth century British industry presents a varied and complex picture. In particular the scope of internal contract was limited by two factors. Firstly, it was unusual for a nineteenth century British firm to place all its operations under forms of internal contract. Typically, a proportion of the labour force would be directly employed. Indeed some of the early nineteenth century factory labour was coerced, most notably the pauper-apprentices, though these would rarely amount to as much as a third of the labour force (Pollard, 1968, pp. 194 and 203). Secondly, the contract system did not extend to all industries. As we shall see below, some new industries and some service organizations represented alternative models of direct employment and control.

Moreover, other mechanisms of control were important. For example in the pottery industry the employers made extensive use of the magistrates' courts to enforce breaches of contract under the Master and Servant legislation. At periods during the nineteenth century there were four or five such cases per week in the potteries, and it must be remembered that until changes in the legislation in 1867, any breach of contract by a worker was generally a criminal offence (Burchill and Ross, 1977).

Nevertheless, various forms of internal contracting were wide-spread. Pollard, for example, concludes that internal contract was prevalent throughout the entire range of industries, and Hobsbawm echoes this. The system was particularly well entrenched in textiles, mining, ironworks, and shipbuilding, which were the basic industries of the early period of industrialization. Even within areas of direct employment the foreman would normally be granted absolute and arbitrary powers to hire and fire and set pay rates. Thus traditional foreman/worker relations were still modelled on the capitalist/worker power relationship (cf. Nelson, 1975, pp. 34–48; Edwards, 1979, p. 33).

To summarize this section: nineteenth century British industry presented a spectrum of modes of control consisting of

(1) Entrepreneurial control; i.e. simple, direct control.
(2) Internal contract systems; these included familial control, craft control and the gang-boss system. All three forms of internal contracting involved delegated control and co-domination.
(3) Traditional foremanship; this was often modelled on entrepreneurial control such that it too entailed delegated control.

The advantages of the above typology are that it enables us to move away from simple and limited ideas of craft control, or from confused ideas of the labour aristocracy and it provides the beginnings of an analysis of various patterns of shopfloor control within non-bureaucratic work organizations.[4]

Classification of British industries in relation to modes of control

As I pointed out in Chapter 1, many of the current controversies over craft control and deskilling would be clarified if we had an adequate sociological classification of industries. Whilst it is not comprehensive, I attempt such a classification below.

The starting point must be the capital/labour relationship. The important aspects of this relation are

(1) The extent of pre-planning or pre-conceptualization of the production process;
(2) The extent of employer dependence on 'skill' and worker abilities generally;
(3) The extent of employer dependence on pre-existing forms of group or cultural solidarity and subordination.

The third aspect is usually neglected, but is a crucial factor in labour control. If we bear these three dimensions of the capital/labour relation in mind, then this leads to the ninefold classification of industries set out below. In Table 6.1 a primary distinction is that between those organizations based on direct employment and control and those based on indirect employment and control. Some new industries which involved considerable pre-planning, and the large monopolistic service organizations, constituted systems of *direct* employment and control throughout the nineteenth century. It is a mistake, however, to see these organizations, including the service organizations, emerging from the cultural chrysalis as full-blown bureaucracies in the early part of the nineteenth century. On the contrary bureaucratization was a slow, stumbling process. For example, the *Report of the Commissioners on the Post Office 1854* complains of the continuing lack of unified career structure, areas of patronage, and the extent of collegiality (GPO Archives, Post 59/179, 1854, *passim*, esp. pp. 2–4, 6–7 and 30). Given that complete bureaucratization of these types of organization took fifty years or more, then it is an historical perversion simply to characterize these organizations in terms of bureaucratic control.

Within the category of indirect control there are three main threads. The principle of classification here relates to three types of traditional relationships described in the previous section. Finally, it is worth noting the 'outwork' trades as a separate group, largely distinct from the internal contract industries.[5] Thus the structurally-based classification of nineteenth century work organizations, plus some indications of structural trends through the century are as outlined in Table 6.1.

The classification in Table 6.1 should make it clear that systems of internal contract did not cover the entire spectrum of industries and organizations in the nineteenth century. Specifically, the subject of internal contract excludes categories A.1, A.2, A.3 and C.1. Moreover, the extent of craft forms of internal contract was even more limited. Secondly, the classification of industries should sensitize us to the fact that the trends and timing of change have been different in different industries. The transformation of the labour process in, say, textiles has been different from that in gang-work industries and different again from process, pre-planned industries. Broadly, forms of internal contract survived longest in categories B.2.a and B.3, and still survive today in the building industry with its articulation of internal and external sub-contracting.

Newly established industries and firms tended to assimilate to one of these patterns of labour control. For example, new, mass market food drink and tobacco firms and some electrical engineering assimilated to A.2, whilst non-traditional assembly industries such as vehicles assimilated to B.2.a and B.2.b (see Zeitlin, 1980).

Bearing in mind the problems of historical generalization, what was the extent of internal contracting and traditional modes of control in British industry by the 1870s and 1880s? Unfortunately, the available sources tend to be vague or inconsistent. Pollard, in his discussion of management during the Industrial Revolution, notes 'how much of the older system was left in the interstices of the new factory organization, making adjustment easier and postponing . . . the development of modern management techniques' (Pollard, 1968, p. 18). Nevertheless, Pollard exaggerates and misinterprets the modernity of work relation-

Table 6.1   Classification of British Industries circa 1870

(A) *Direct employment and control*

    (A.1) *Process, pre-planned industries*

        Some new industries, usually of chemical or quasi-chemical nature, began on a relatively large-scale and involved considerable pre-planning of the production process (e.g. brewing, distilling, sugar refining and soap-boiling). All these industries involved heavy work, employed a low proportion of boys and women *and* few skilled men. And they all tended to be more centralized, with direct employment, and little internal contract.

    (A.2) *Semi-planned industries*

        Some industries, primarily food, drink and tobacco, involved light work and employed a *high* proportion of boys or women, plus, again, few skilled men.

    (A.3) *Monopolistic service organizations*

        The post office, railways, and the police, for example. Usually these were in a monopoly or quasi-monopoly position.

    (For A.1 and A.3 the direction of change through the nineteenth century was towards bureaucratization of the structure of control, followed by bureaucratization of the employment relationship. (For the basis of this distinction, see Chapter 4.))

(B) *Indirect employment and control or direct employment and indirect control*

    (B.1) *Industries founded with a domestic background*

        Textiles and some final-goods industries, for example.

    Though the kinship content of the contracted work-group was drained away in industries such as cotton, the minder-piecer system survived the introduction of new technology through to the 1870s (Lazonick, 1979). In hosiery there was a faster shift to direct modes of control.

    (B.2) *Industries founded on a craft basis*

        (B.2.a)   Traditional assembly industries, such as shipbuilding, coach building and building itself.

        (B.2.b)   Metal industries, e.g. iron, brass.

        (B.2.c)   Others, such as the glass industry and the potteries.

        All these groups (B.2.a,b and c) employed a high proportion of skilled men, and were founded on an internal contracted craft basis.

    (B.3) *Gang-work industries*

        Such as the extractive industries, docks, etc. In these industries systems of internal contract proved the most resilient.

(C) *External sub-contract*

    (C.1) *The 'sweated trades'*

        These were largely the consumer goods industries, such as clothing, boots and shoes, toys, etc.

---

ships in the early nineteenth century, and correspondingly neglects the continuities of traditional relationships, especially the survival of internal contract, as he himself admits (p. 53). This makes him an unreliable interpreter of events in some respects.

Bendix makes no attempt to specify the timing of the demise of contract systems, but generally seems to regard them as surviving throughout the nineteenth century (1974, p. 57). Samuel, who is only considering mineral work, where internal contract was the characteristic form of employment, largely agrees with Bendix (Samuel, 1977, pp. 33–4, 73–5). Dobb, following G.C. Allen, suggests that as late as the 1870s, sub-contract was still widespread (Dobb, 1963, pp. 266–7). Hobsbawm suggests that 'straight sub-contract was certainly declining fast *from the* 1870s', and that 'in the building and engineering industries, it was certainly fighting a rear-guard action by the 1850–73 period . . .' (Hobsbawm, 1964, pp. 299–300). On the other hand, Schloss, writing in the 1890s, observes that 'sub-contract is a system so widely adopted throughout the length and breadth of British industry that any attempt to make here an exhaustive enumeration of the trades, in which it is met with, would be altogether impracticable'. Later he asserts that 'sub-contract, in fact, is practically ubiquitous' (Schloss, 1898, pp. 197–8 and 202).

Some of this difference is accounted for by the fact that different writers are using the term 'sub-contract' to refer to different practices. For example, Schloss tends to combine internal and external contract. Nevertheless, apart from examples of external sub-contract in various industries, Schloss provides numerous examples of *internal* contract in a wide variety of industries. These included a large Midlands ironworks where almost every operation was performed under sub-contract, brickworks, the shipbuilding and engineering industries, London mantle factories, etc. (Chapters XIV and XV).

In sum, the available historical evidence is not sufficient to be definite about different industries and precise practices, but it is fairly clear that by the 1870s and 1880s, internal contract in some form was still widespread in a large number of British industries in categories B.1, B.2 and B.3. Only in the direct employment and control industries (A.1, A.2 and A.3) were there clear signs of non-traditional forms of labour management. For example, systematic appointment and promotion procedures including an internal labour market and a systematic division of labour, the lineaments of bureaucracy, were achieved in the Post Office by the 1870s (GPO Archives, Post 60/81, 1877). However, there is no evidence of organizational diffusion from these industries and firms to other sectors.

The decline of traditional modes of control
So far in this chapter we have been concerned to establish and underline the extent and significance of contract systems up to the 1870s and 1880s. Now we turn to the core of the argument – the demise, and the circumstances of that demise, of internal contracting.

We have made clear in previous sections that the pace of evolution may vary among different industries such that stage theories of industrial development can be misleading. The industries that were most affected by the pressures of the last quarter of the nineteenth century were iron and steel, metals generally, and engineering. Shipbuilding was affected to a much lesser extent. These were the industries which were at the forefront of industrial change and influenced other sectors later in the twentieth century. In what follows, then, the discussion is limited to these specific industries.

In metals and engineering the last quarter of the nineteenth century saw the demise of traditional modes of control and the beginnings of a dramatic transformation into new forms of work organization. As Stearns points out, the evolution of industrial work was not a steady process, and this period marks a sharp change in the division of labour and the structure of control (1975, p.2). This transformation of the labour process raises the questions of why the process occurred when it did, and what were the mechanisms of transition?

In the last quarter of the nineteenth century a number of pressures were generated which gnawed away at the existing structures of control within metal-working firms. The period 1873–96 was the period of the 'Great Depression', though there is some debate amongst economic historians as to the economic unity of this period (see Saul, 1969). Nevertheless, some economic facts are clear enough. For fourteen years from 1873 on, with one minor respite, prices fell without cease. There is nothing comparable to this price-slide in all the previous nineteenth century: 'It was the most drastic deflation in the memory of man.' (Landes, 1969, p. 231). Thereafter, prices rose slightly up to 1891, and then fell back sharply to a nineteenth century low in 1896. This continuing, year-on-year price plummet squeezed profit margins hard. At a macro level this can be seen in the following figures:

Profits as a percentage of industrial income

1870–74	47.7
1875–79	43.3
1880–84	42.6
1885–89	42.2
1890–94	37.8

(*Source*: Feinstein, quoted in Saul, 1969, p. 42, footnote 1)

Moreover, the profits-squeeze was further exacerbated by the competitive economic environment. From the 1870s onwards, British industry was faced with growing competition in world trade: the USA and Germany were now in the industrial race. For the latter countries it was no longer a question of closing the industrial gap, but of a struggle for markets. As the Great Depression altered the setting of the wage/effort bargain, it combined with labour pressures to change the logic of the employer's position.

Three factors served to maintain labour costs during the price-slide. A more organized labour force than in the 1840s meant that money wages held-up relatively well during the 1870s and 1880s. From 1876 to 1888, money wages were very stable, never changing more than plus or minus 2% per annum (Saul, 1969; Landes, 1969). Secondly, the period of the early 1870s witnessed a widespread shift in the 'normal' hours of work. It is easy to assume that the now standard 40-hour week was achieved slowly and steadily through the decades of history. On the contrary, the pattern of change was extremely discontinuous and, as Bienefeld points out, 'the years from 1871 to 1874 brought changes that were so widespread and extensive that they can be said to have radically altered the country's conception of what constituted a day's work' (1972, p. 142).

The pattern of change for some industries is indicated in Table 6.2.

What Table 6.2 shows is that the decade 1850–60 saw very little change in the normal hours of work, and that though there were the beginnings of a general pressure to reduce hours in the decade 1860–70, the major changes, especially in engineering and the metal trades, were

Table 6.2   Average normal hours of work, 1850–80

Industries	1850	1860	% change from 1850	1870	% change from 1860	1880	% change from 1870
Engineering	59.5	59.4	−0.2	57.9	−2.5	53.9	−6.9
Shipbuilding	59.9	59.4	−0.1	57.8	−2.7	54.1	−6.4
Coachbuilding	60.4	59.9	−0.8	57.7	−3.7	54.8	−5.0
Iron and steel	59.5	59.5	0	59.0	−0.8	58.1	−1.5
Ironfoundry	60.1	59.5	−0.1	57.8	−2.9	54.5	−5.7
Building (general contractors)	60.1	58.1	−3.3	55.8	−4.0	54.1	−3.0
Pottery	60.3	60.3	0	58.4	−3.2	56.8	−2.7
Glass	56.5	56.9	+0.7	55.2	−3.0	54.0	−2.2
Chemicals	59.9	60.2	+0.5	59.2	−1.7	58.4	−1.4
Printing	59.8	58.9	−1.5	56.6	−3.9	53.9	−4.8

Source: Adapted from Bienefeld, 1972, Tables 2, 3 and 4, pp. 93, 98 and 111. The 1850 column is not strictly comparable with the 1880 column, as the data-base for the latter is wider.

concentrated in the 1870s. The early 1870s then was the period of a widespread shift to the 54-hour normal week for most organized trades, and the unorganized workers were also dragged along by events.

The changes in the normal hours of work became rooted in patterns of behaviour, such that when the decline in prices and profits stimulated an employer's offensive to regain the 'lost hours' in 1876, it met a strong opposition from trade unions and work-groups. The staunch resistance of many unions to increased hours is not surprising when it is remembered that the demand for the nine-hour day was often a rallying-point around which many unions were established or enlarged beyond local associations. To lose the nine-hour day would be to lose the original basis of unity.

A third factor working through the labour force at this time has been suggested by Hobsbawm – namely a weakening of traditional ideas about labour effort. The hypothesis is that workers began to learn the rules of the economic game, and learnt to bargain with their effort-levels (Hobsbawm, 1964, p. 351; see Chapter 5 of this volume), and certainly there was a marked fall in the rate of growth of labour productivity at this time (Saul, 1969, p. 31). However, as I argued in Chapter 5, it is not just a question of cultural or of generational change. The change in effort-norms is associated with the break-up of many older occupations, such as the fitters and turners. The point here is that an 'occupation' is not just a set of inter-linked activities, but was a job-role, incorporating a set of norms about effort-levels. Therefore, if traditional job-roles are massively destroyed, there are no customary benchmarks or standards by which to judge one's pace.

All the above factors – the prices and profit slide, the increased competition, the shorter hours, and the more powerful labour movement underpinning the shorter hours and existing wage levels – created a constellation of pressures on employers to reduce labour and capital costs during the Great Depression. The ratio of wages to profits began to climb alarmingly. Theoretically there were several possible avenues, the obvious one being the imposition of wage cuts. Despite labour opposition, some wage cuts still occurred, for example, in the building and engineering industries (Bienefeld, 1972, pp. 117–18; Jefferys, 1945, pp. 95–7). Nevertheless, the existing levels of wages were only pushed back a little. Wages held up surprisingly well, and recovered again in 1882.

A second strategy for employers to adopt is a more extensive use of labour, either by systematic overtime, or possibly shift-work. This had been the strategy widely used by employers during the 1840s deflation. For example, in one Manchester engineering firm in 1840, the working-day was extended so that it ran from 5 a.m. to 9 p.m. Despite the struggle of workers to protect the nine-hour day in the 1870s and 1880s, systematic overtime became widespread in several industries, including engineering (Burgess, 1975, pp. 13, 45 and 54–5). Indeed it was the willingness of workers to do overtime, and the removal of restrictions on overtime work, which reduced the resistance of many employers to a nine-hour day in the first place. Thus the nine-hour day held up *in name* during the Great Depression, but the formal position disguises considerable forced overtime working.[6]

Beyond wage-cuts and the more extensive use of labour lies a different path – the more *intensive* use of labour. Opposition to systematic overtime, and indeed militant demands for an eight-hour day, encouraged a shift towards a different pattern of labour utilization. But there was no overnight managerial revolution. The initial processes of effort-intensification were attempted within the existing structures of control, such as internal contract, piecemastership and traditional foremanship.

In the 1860s the system of internal contract had been widely praised by academics and industrialists, such as Lord Brassey and William Denny. Thus, Brassey asserts that sub-contract is 'beneficial alike to the master and the men. The men earn higher wages, while the master has the satisfaction of obtaining an equivalent for the wages he has paid, and completing the contract . . . with far greater rapidity.' (1872, p. 265). Sub-contract was seen as efficient, an effective method of supervision and selection, and especially as providing a channel for gradually rising in 'the scale of society' (McCulloch, *Treatise on Wages*, quoted by Schloss, 1898, p. 181). By the 1890s, the consensus had completely changed. There was widespread condemnation of contracting and it had become vilified as the 'sweating system'. The association with 'sweating' confused internal contract and 'outwork'; nevertheless this reversal of attitude is remarkable.

The reversal of attitude to contract systems can be explained by the fact that contracting and piecemastership was increasingly used to speed-up workers during the Great Depression years. Moreover, the greater predominance of piecemastership in engineering encouraged widespread 'driving'. Under piecemastership the basic time-rate of subordinates is controlled by the employer in most cases. Thus, the possibility of directly cutting wages is closed to the piecemaster, unlike other forms of contract, and the easiest avenue open is the speed-up of workers.

Effort intensification was frequently allied with the substitution of cheaper labour. Contractors and piecemasters were encouraged to hire cheap, semi-skilled labour in place of skilled labour. It needs to be emphasized that internal contract could function as both a mechanism of skill maintenance and craft autonomy or it could be used as a mechanism of deskilling. For example, Fox in discussing the metal trades in Birmingham in the 1870s has this to say:

Each subcontractor/workshop owner was paid by the employer on straight piece-prices, and made his own arrangements with his employees . . . concerning their wages. The vital difference was that while he was paid on piece-prices, he paid his team on fixed day-wages. The more economically and efficiently he organized production, the larger his profit. He usually sought this through elaborate subdivision of labour, each member of the team being kept for the most part on one or two simple skills which could be fairly easily acquired. Being under the maximum incentive to get his labour cheap, he often employed boys and youths . . . At the age of 16 or thereabouts their rising cost in wages would prompt the sub-contractor to discharge them and seek younger and cheaper labour.

(1955, pp. 59–60)

Thus the internal contract system, like Taylorism later, could function as an agency of de-skilling and dilution (Schloss, 1898, p. 221; Burgess, 1975, pp. 20–1; for American examples see Chapter 11 of this volume).

In sum, the economic storms of the Great Depression, combined with the newly emerged power of organized labour, led to contract systems as a structure of control becoming squeezed by employers, so that they reached the limits of their efficiency and potential, and during this process the social relations of contractors and men deteriorated into cries of 'nigger-driving' on the one hand and 'ca'canny' on the other, such that the question of the nature and size of the work-load supplanted wages as the major issue in labour disputes. This, in turn, led to trade union attacks on contracting given the association with sweating and pace-making.

However, pressure within unions was stifled by the fact that many of the early nineteenth century unions were primarily associations of inside contractors. For example the contractors strategic position within the Ironworkers Union resulted in a defence of inside contracting and a concern to limit the collective power of the unskilled and semi-skilled. Thus contracting in iron and steel was not finally eliminated until the underhands became organized into separate trade unions. Technical changes in the steel industry facilitated the formation of the Steel Smelters' Association in 1886 which became the union of the underhands and the divisions on the shopfloor were reflected in a conflict between the two unions – Ironworkers and Steel Smelters. There were a number of bitter disputes in the late 1880s, though the most famous case was in 1909/10 at Hawarden Bridge Steelworks, where the Steel Smelters went out on strike against the contract system and were opposed by the Ironworkers' Union. In this case, the unskilled workers were temporarily defeated. The issue went to the TUC who ruled in favour of the Ironworkers and as a result, the Steel Smelters left the TUC for six years in disgust (Pugh, 1951, p. 159). Despite this particular case, the Steel Smelters grew rapidly and wherever they secured recognition they soon succeeded in negotiating an end to internal contracting (Elbaum and Wilkinson, 1979, p. 292).

In general, many groups of unskilled and semi-skilled workers during this period (1870s–1900s) succeeded in breaking out of the internal contract frame and its associated exploitations into various forms of collective piecework (see S. and B. Webb, 1898, pp. 290–1). It was the collective pressure of the unskilled which was the vehicle of the decline of internal contract in numerous firms.

But the increasing opposition of work-groups and trade unions to contract systems was not the only factor in their demise. From the employers' side there was increasing hostility towards this intermediate stratum. Some employers became apprehensive at their ignorance and lack of control over the contractors' activities. Furthermore, there was the glint of the profits skimmed-off by the contractors in a period of declining profit-margins. Internal contract was also tied-in with traditional methods, and new technology and associated skill changes reduced the value of contracting as a method of organizing and controlling the labour process. For example in iron and steel, 'Integration of processes required centralized control and the value of the contractor as a co-ordinator of production at the level of the individual process declined, whilst mechanization at least partially shifted the control of the pace of work from the contractor to the operator of the new machines.' (Elbaum and Wilkinson, 1979, p. 284). Contracting and delegated forms of control then became squeezed for more power and control, and by increasingly organized workers resentful of sweating and resentful of favouritism.

Summary and conclusions

There is a general lack of studies focusing on the historical development of forms of work organization and changes in the labour process. As a consequence, available concepts are few and limited. I noted the limitations of the concepts of 'craft control' and the 'labour aristocracy', and sought to emphasize and develop the notion of internal contract systems and suggest its utility in understanding the nature of British pre-bureaucratic work organization. In general, classical Marxism, with its exaggerated notions of workshop subordination, overlooks the fact that Victorian industry, at least until the Great Depression, was permeated with forms of co-domination. This implies that the simple pairing of management/worker, control/subordination and capital/labour is open to question: many labouring occupations entailed supervisory functions and petty capitalist motivations.

Historical generalizations about the survival and transformations of traditional forms of control are rendered difficult by conceptual confusions, empirical ambiguities, and differences among industries. A classification of industries was suggested in order to clarify many of the current arguments over the processes and timing of changes in work organization.

If we recognize the widespread importance of delegated forms of control in British industry, then it leads us on to ask questions about their demise. As far as we can tell, systems of internal contract in some form survived until the 1870s–80s. The critical period for the decline of such systems in Britain was the last quarter of the nineteenth century, particularly in the metal and metal-working industries.

Finally, we looked at the process and the mechanisms of the demise of traditional modes of control. Simplifying and generalizing the pattern of events was as follows: the Great Depression in the last quarter of the nineteenth century shifted the economic setting of the wage/effort bargain beyond the normal trade downturn. This altered economic context combined with a stronger labour movement to change the logic of the employer's position. As a result, employers sought to reduce labour costs through a more intensive use of labour, but the initial processes of effort intensification were attempted within the *existing* structures of control. The effects of this, in turn, were twofold: first it created extensive opposition against 'sweating', amongst work-groups, trade unions and the public. Second, it led to the deterioration of social relationships between contractors and workers. Sweater and sub-contractor became interchangeable terms, and both were terms of opprobrium.

Few hands were raised to protect 'the slave-driving sub-contractor', because new ideas, new methods, and new technology influenced many employers to reach down for more control over the shopfloor. Thus contractors became squeezed from both ends. It is important to note that there are strict limits to the increase in surplus value through labour intensification, limits set by the margins of human capacities. In the long term the technical re-division of labour and the mechanization of tasks are more important. But in the short term, within the confines of an economic depression when capital is scarce and expensive, labour intensification proved to have crucial effects on the structures of control. However, the demise of internal contract and traditional forms of control only constitutes the beginning of the restructuring of work organization. It leaves open the question of what the new forms of work organization are to look like.

7 The Emergence of New Structures of Control, 1880–1914

As we saw in Chapter 6, the 1870s and 1880s witnessed the start of an accelerated decline in the extent of internal contract and co-domination in many industries; a process which seems to have been completed during the First World War. Thus in 1918, G.D.H. Cole tells us that

> In most of the coalfields the butty system has disappeared; the worst forms of the contract system have been driven out from the iron and steel industry; the power of the sub-contractor at the docks is largely gone. In fact, the pure 'contract' system, under which the engagement and dismissal of the vast majority of the workers employed, and the rate and amount of their remuneration, were in the hands of a few intermediaries between the firm and the worker employed in its works, has almost ceased to exist in any organized trade.
>
> (1918, p. 33)

And this view of the final decline of contract systems was endorsed by Goodrich in his careful survey of the industrial scene after the First World War (1921, p. 20).[1]

In this chapter I will discuss the nature and extent of changes in the labour process in the run up to the First World War, and the early British responses to Taylorism as an ideology and a management system.

Experiments and hesitancies

From the perspective of the 1880s, it was not at all clear what form the new structures of control would take: the future was open. This was a period when many industrial experiments were tried or advocated. For example there were persistent advocates of profit-sharing, co-partnership, and similar plans for worker participation. Thus a classic work by Schloss (1898) is basically a detailed plea for co-partnership, and if we turn from theory to practice, the years 1889–92 were a peak period for the introduction of profit-sharing schemes. Eighty-eight such schemes were started during this brief period (Ramsay, 1977, p. 484). In contrast, Shadwell advocated what he called the 'commercialization of labour': this meant the amalgam of sub-contract and the spreading trade unionism. In other words, trade unions should formally become labour-only subcontractors, recruiting workers, supplying labour to firms, and controlling the labour force (Shadwell, 1906, p. 140).

The best historical example of the 'commercialization of labour' is the Carpenters' Union in the USA. At the end of the nineteenth century, the leaders of the Carpenters' Union were concerned to halt sub-contracting by individual carpenters, and so they established 'business agents', who acted as union middlemen, supplying labour to companies and allocating jobs to workers. No British unions went as far as this. Indeed, the widespread reaction against contractors made the commercialization of labour increasingly unlikely. Many of the early trade unions had been associations of internal contractors, and the demise of contract in work organizations was reflected in shifts of power within unions (e.g. the National Society of Amalgamated Brass-workers: Fox, 1955, pp. 66–70) or *between* unions (e.g. the Association of Iron and Steel Workers versus the Steel Smelters Association: Pugh, 1951, p. 159). In general, the overall pattern and policy of unionism changed, and all systems of internal contract passed beyond the trade union pale.

Nor did the transition process to directly-employed labour occur without employer fears and questioning. One indication of this is provided by Schloss. In 1891 he considered the problems of a shift from contractors to directly-employed foremen, and concluded that the difficulties were 'undoubtedly of a grave nature'. What were the difficulties in the eyes of the late Victorians? Firstly, there was the problem of ineffective and inefficient supervision unconstrained by the profit-motive. Secondly, Schloss assumed that hiring and firing would remain the prerogative of the directly-employed foreman. Thus recruitment would be inextricably intertwined with favouritism and bribery and there were plenty of examples to support this view (e.g. Williams, 1915, pp. 276–7).

The crucial point then is that the late Victorians could not clearly understand how an industrial organization which was not permeated by the profit motive could function. They could not clearly see beyond petty capitalism to a Weberian model of bureaucracy and bureaucratic control. The extension of the bureaucratic idea to the shopfloor was not a foregone conclusion in 1880. It is important to emphasize this point because many labour process theorists see Taylorism and the bureau-cratization of the shopfloor as *inevitable* developments of capitalism. They were not. The structural outcomes in Britain in 1880 depended on worker resistance and supervisory resistance.

The spread of piece-work, 1880–1914

Up to the 1880s, and indeed well beyond it, time-wages were the most common form of wage payment (Schloss, 1898, p. 43; Webb and Webb 1898, p. 287, footnote 1)[2], but having said that, we need to go further and remember that these 'time-wages' occurred within the context of internal contract or piecemastership. Time-wages in the nineteenth century were not, typically, a straight day wage. This implies, amongst other things, that the wage was not guaranteed. The worker was frequently at the mercy of the contractor or piecemaster, who would often pay his men in the local pub less than they expected or were due. Indeed sub-contract served to maintain time-wages as the common pattern of payment. As the Webbs point out: 'The members of the great race of sub-contractors in all industries are always trying to employ time-workers, in order to obtain for themselves the fullest possible advantage of their own driving power.' (Webb and Webb 1898, p. 303; see also Hobsbawm, 1964, p. 353; Stearns, 1975, pp. 214–15). Thus the decay of contract systems is associated with the spread of both collective and individual piece-work. There was a widespread attempt to extend petty capitalist motives to all workers by means of piece-work.

The extent of the spread of piece-work is most easily traced in the engineering industry. The proportions of men on piece-work in engineering is as follows: 1886, 5%; 1906, 27.5%; 1927, 49.6% (Rowe, 1928, pp. 258–9). After 1906 the statistics are no longer solely referring to straight piece-work but incorporate to an increasing extent premium bonus schemes. Nevertheless, the rapid extension of piece-work is clear enough. But what is the historical significance of the spread of piece-work in terms of the capital/labour relation and modes of control?

The first point to be clear about is that piece-work in itself is not part of systematic management and bureaucratic forms of organization. We can see more clearly the relation between piece-work and the bureaucratization of the structure of control if we remember the classification of wage/effort exchange systems in Chapter 5. The basic axis of this classification is the distinction between traditional, informal standards of effort and formal standards of effort. If we now relate this distinction to time-wages versus piecework, then we get the picture shown in Figure 7.1

Historically in many industries the shift in payment systems has been in the sequence indicated by the arrows. The transition we are describing here is from box A to box B, whereas it is the transition from boxes B to C which is historically more significant, and which represents the crucial shift to formal standards of effort and bureaucratized structures of control.

If the above historical schematization is accepted, then it is important to understand the dynamics of the shift from A to B to C. Given the

Figure 7.1   Wage systems and standards of effort

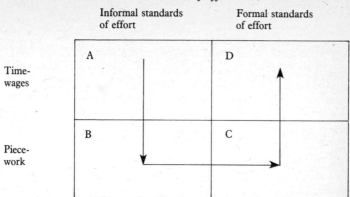

failures of internal contract as a means of effort intensification (see Chapter 6) piece-work was used as a speed-up device: once piece wages were introduced there was steady pressure to lower rates in order to force higher production, which produced widespread strikes and disputes during the period 1880–1924 (Stearns, 1975, pp. 203, 210 and 212).

The struggles over rate-cutting illustrate that the basic issue was not that of time-wages *versus* piece-work. Indeed some groups, such as the Sheffield steel workers, welcomed individual piece-work as a release from the exploitations of sub-contract. The underlying question was that of the wage/effort ratio, and the demise of contracting and the spread of piece-work lifted this underlying question out of personal disputes between a driving contractor and his men, into a more generalized struggle between employer and workers. The contractor as both employer and employee complicated the confrontation between capital and labour, however, as Fox points out: 'What had once been a graded hierarchy of economic classes, leading through from underhand to small master and thence to employer and factor, with no unbridgeable gulf anywhere in its length, was now tending to become polarized out into wage earners and employers.' (1955, p. 67).

Piece-work generated a specific constellation of problems from the employer's point of view, and this constellation of problems constituted an internal dynamic within piece-work systems which became a pressure towards shopfloor systematization. We can best see the set of problems generated by piece-work, by looking at the failures of straight piece-work in the Cardboard Box Department of a specific factory (Cadbury's) in 1909. According to Edward Cadbury:

We had always managed this department on the flat piece-rate system . . . but for some time we were convinced of the failure of this system. Our rates were based on the output of the average worker, not on the fastest; but the girls had an idea that they knew what we expected them to earn, and the fast girls deliberately avoided earning much above this wage. The introduction of new methods or new machines necessitated the fixing of fresh rates, *and it was difficult to know when the girls were working at a proper speed or deliberately working slowly*. Adjustment of rates were sometimes necessary, and this made the girls fear that increased output would merely mean a cutting of the piece-rate and possibly harder work for the same wages.

(Cadbury, 1914a, pp. 114–15, emphasis added)

This description of the situation in one department of one factory is typical of the cluster of problems generated by piece-work. First, even amongst young, largely non-unionized girls there is systematic output restriction, based on fears of rate-cutting. Second, these fears were fed by the *experience* of rate-cutting, which on the receiving end seemed *ad hoc* and arbitrary. Third, in this arena of mistrust the employer is faced with acute problems of lack of observability; lack of 'access' to the workers' performance. Sweeping away delegated forms of control leaves the employer facing the solidity of his own ignorance about shopfloor performance which in turn leads to the setting of wild or inaccurate piece-rates, corrective rate-cutting, and a vicious circle of mistrust.

The increasing failures of straight piece-work as an effort intensification device, the vicious circles of mistrust which were often created by rate-cutting, and the pressure of trade unions and work-groups to consistency and mutually agreed rates: all these factors constituted a push towards systematic management, towards a new shuffle of the capitalist cards.

Workshop re-organizations, 1890–1924

From the 1890s through to the First World War workshop re-organizations occurred in several industries, especially engineering. These changes in the structure of control, the first stirrings of systematic management, were often associated with the spread of premium bonus systems (PBS). Therefore we need to understand the nature of PBSs and how they relate to other shopfloor changes, especially the creation of a new supervisory role structure.

All PBSs have common elements. Essentially they substitute a time allowance for a piece-work price. This entails fixing time limits for each and every job. What were these time limits or allowances based on? At this period, especially in Britain, they were based on past records plus hope! They were guess-estimates, with a lot of guessing. A minimum rate was guaranteed, and if a job was accomplished in less than the time limit, a worker was paid over and above his standard wage for any time saved, but the bonus was always proportionate. Thus the 'time saved' was divided between workers and management in varying proportions.

However, as many workers quickly realized, PBSs such as the Rowan system (the most widely used system in Britain) were based on a formula such that the workers' share of the time saved was a constantly diminishing proportion. Indeed, beyond a certain mid-point bonus earned actually declines. Put another way, the labour cost of the job to the employer falls with every increase of output; it was 'an automatic price-breaker'. Clearly, this was one of its advantages to the employer, because it institutionalized rate-cutting. An associated advantage was that the system was not open-ended, the workers' earnings could not soar way above double time. This was a useful safety-net for incompetent and ignorant rate-setting, which was all too frequent (Cole, 1918, p. 51).

The defeat of the Amalgamated Society of Engineers in the 1897/98 dispute resulted in the formal acceptance of piece-work by the engineering union, despite its long history of opposition to piece-work, and in August 1902, under the Carlisle Agreement, the ASE accepted the PBS on a national basis.

The ASE's acceptance of premium bonus systems was strongly resented by other trade unions, as it weakened their own opposition and opened the factory gates to the new payment systems, but despite continued opposition by other trade unions, despite internal opposition within the ASE culminating in a 5:1 vote against the continuance of PBS in 1911, and despite the hostile 1910 TUC Report, it proved impossible to secure a united action to abolish PBSs and they slowly spread right up to 1914.

PBSs and workshop re-organizations chiefly affected the large firms in newer sectors where major capital investments were possible because of large, expanding markets, such as the cycle, motor, locomotive and electrical industries. In addition a significant area in which PB schemes were concentrated were government establishments – ordnance factories and dockyards – and in these establishments the procedures for rate-fixing were much more elaborate and formalized (TUC, 1910, p. 64). But in the bulk of the engineering industry consisting of small, unspecialized firms the instabilities of the market discouraged major innovations in the structure of control. The slow spread of PB schemes can be seen from the fact that the ASE, the union *most affected*, had less than 10% of its employed members working on the bonus system in 1909. The percentage of boilermakers, brassfounders, and sheet metal workers, etc. affected must have been well below this figure.[3]

Thus in discussing the first stirrings of systematic management in Britain pre-1914, we need to bear in mind that PB schemes had not yet affected more than a small proportion of shopfloors, and that there was a significant difference between the private sector and government establishments. In addition, not all changes in the structure of control involved a switch to some form of PBS: some firms restricted the autonomy of foremen, changed recruitment procedures, and introduced feed and speed supervisors *without* changing the payment system in a fundamental way.

In general, the workshop reorganizations entailed four essential elements from a sociological point of view. I will deal with each of these in turn.

(a) New supervisory role systems

The first aspect of the workshop re-organizations was the slow stumbling creation of a new supervisory role system. By the 1890s and the early 1900s the internal contractor and piecemaster had given away to the directly-employed foreman in many industries but this process was no simple, single change. I have tried to make clear in Chapter 6 that it is necessary to think in terms of different forms of internal contract, and what these structural differences imply is that there were patterns of change from systems of contract to traditional foremanship. These patterns are complex and confusing, but in short either the contractor became more integrated into the wider organizational frame as a directly-employed foreman, or he relapsed into the workgroup itself as a semi-supervisor (a chargehand, chargeman, leading-hand or ganger, etc.) answerable to a directly-employed foreman, or he became a 'submerged' work-group leader. Alfred Williams in his classic study of a Swindon locomotive works describes an example of the second process, where the piecemaster becomes a despised chargeman, his previous exploitations now restricted to a few privileges – primarily the right to a 10% bonus from the surplus earnt by his gang (1915, pp. 282–3).

Despite the widespread emergence of the directly-employed foreman in the 1890s and 1900s, there did not emerge a drastically altered set of role conceptions, because of the absence of a systematic management ideology. In many respects the traditional foreman performed the same functions as the larger contractors. Thus in the closing period of the First World War one employer assessed the role of the foreman in this way:

In most works . . . the whole industrial life of a workman is in the hands of his foreman. The foreman chooses him from among the applicants at the works gate; often he settles what wages he shall get; no advance of wage or promotion is possible except on his initiative; he often sets the piece-price and has the power to cut it when he wishes; and . . . he almost always has unrestricted power of discharge.
(*Athenaeum*, 1917; see also Schloss, 1898, pp. 2–3 and Stearns, 1975, p. 177)

Thus the traditional foreman was the undisputed master of his own shop, and like the internal contractor before him, he hired and fired, set wages, planned and allocated work. However, there were fundamental differences between the contractor and the traditional foreman: the foreman did not employ his own labour, his wage or salary was his main source of income, and he did not have the same petty capitalist interest in costs and profits.

The traditional foreman's power started to be modified almost as soon as it had emerged from the decay of internal contract. The period 1890–1914 was a period when the foreman's area of discretion was being whittled down by the employers and indeed was changing rapidly on some shopfloors. There were a number of aspects to these changes. Firstly there was the subdivision of the foreman's role. Feed and speed inspectors, quality-control inspectors, rate-fixers – all started to appear on the shopfloor in the early 1900s and all represented some incursion into the foreman's autonomous empire. For example, the speed and feed system under which appropriate speeds, feeds and cutting angles were worked out by a new type of specialist technician and then enforced on the machine tool operative resulted in work methods being no longer the sole prerogative of the foreman. Despite considerable shopfloor and trade union resistance to feed and speed systems, they continued to spread up to 1914 (Watson, 1934, pp. 92–3; Levine, 1967, p. 98).

Not only the 'feed and speedies', but the new payment systems had the effect of breaking up the traditional foreman's role. During the early years of PB systems the foreman himself would take on the functions of rate-fixing. However, there was an increasing tendency to develop separate rate-fixing departments, especially in the larger munitions factories. The new payment systems became *centrally* determined and administered, and this undercut the foreman's power position (TUC, 1910, pp. 25, 29, 47 and 56).

This shift to the central determination of wages entailed changes in the pattern of bargaining. No longer did individual workers and groups make their own bargains with the foreman. Indeed the division of the foreman's role reduced the bargaining capacity of that role. The value of a single-role supervisory system from the worker's viewpoint is that the locus of decision-making is visible and known – one can hope to persuade and influence 'Old Fred'. A multi-role supervisory system introduces a qualitative difference – the decision-making becomes stretched between the feed and speed inspectors, the rate-fixing department, and the foreman, and in so doing it becomes socially intangible. This withering of personal bargaining and influence relationships was a powerful stimulus to the development of shop stewards and workshop committees in the 1900s (Cole, 1923, pp. 14–15; Phelps Brown, 1959, pp. 290–2).

Perhaps the most crucial erosion of the foreman's autonomy was in relation to hiring and firing. Whereas recruitment had been at the personal choice and whim of the foreman, it was gradually replaced by a more formal system of examination and selection via a central office or 'Employment Department.[4] In general the new structures of control, which were the first steps towards systematic management, meant the insertion of a stratum of white-collar workers and technicians between the employer and the shopfloor, diminishing the role and status of the old sub-contractor and the traditional foreman (Cole, 1918, pp. 72–3; Hobsbawm, 1964, p. 297).

(b) The development of new payment systems

The second essential aspect of the workshop reorganizations was the development of new payment systems – especially the premium bonus system as we have seen above. But PB systems were not just a sphere unto themselves. It is necessary to look at what the payment systems entailed on the shopfloor and in the factory.

The development of complex payment systems meant that most large works had to create large wages departments, and all workers received 'payment through the office'. This is more significant than it sounds to modern ears, because it represented the work organization accepting responsibility for wage payments to *all* the workers. This was new. Previously the company would pay bulk sums to the contractor or piecemaster who would often pay his men in the local pub what he pleased. Many men were robbed blind – or blind drunk.[5]

Apart from the creation of a central wages office, the new payment systems entailed the continual shopfloor recording of job-times. This introduced rate-fixers onto the shopfloor, often attached to a central rate-fixing department. Not only did rate-fixing bypass the traditional foreman and harass the skilled worker, but it had a more fundamental significance. Previously the contractor or traditional foreman would have been the only superior to have known the measure of his men. Usually a skilled man himself, he had been through the trade, and knew what constituted a day's work. He could be as much the upholder of customary effort-norms as the craftsman himself (e.g. see Williams, 1915, p. 99). In general there was a congruence of superior and subordinate skills. But PB schemes brought the measuring and recording of job-times. This meant that knowledge of effort-levels and of work-performance was lifted out of the work-group or shop and made accessible to a wider range of superiors. In sum, the beginnings of task measurement increased the 'observability' of work behaviour. The establishment of time standards for jobs whilst providing the details necessary for premium bonus schemes, also acted as the basis of a new structure of control.

Some of the more far-sighted workers in the 1900s were aware of what was happening:

A riveter: '. . . the employers could now gauge the capacity of their workmen with absolute accuracy, and if a workman took the full estimated time to do his work the firm soon wanted to know the reason why'.

A brass finisher: 'One feature of the system was that each man's individual ability could be ascertained and those who were not quite up to the maximum standard of efficiency were weeded out.'

A fitter at Chatham Dockyard: 'As a general rule, the men liked the extra money but abhorred the system, which was a lever in the hands of the Government by which they could whip one man with another, and by creating rivalry between one man and another squeeze the utmost out of their employees. He would be only too glad if the Government would revert to time-rates and conditions; although now they had an accurate knowledge of a man's capacity, he was afraid that if this did occur the authorities would expect the men to do a days work on a premium bonus standard' . . .

(TUC, 1910, pp. 31, 34 and 62 respectively)

However, though the pre-1914 bonus system saw the start of job-measurement, the move in this direction should not be exaggerated. There was no systematic time study nor method study in Britain before the First World War as far as I can discover. All the observers at that time agree that the fixing of basic job-times in Britain under the PBS was *ad hoc* and haphazard in much the same way as piece-prices had always been fixed.[6]

Moreover PBSs were not based on Taylorite element time-studies and job analysis. In many ways the PB system was still based on the foreman's judgement and the skilled worker's knowledge. Essentially PB schemes accepted *past performance* as the basis for effort norms. Thus PBS represents the beginnings of a shift to formal standards of effort, but *only* the beginnings.

The haphazard nature of rate-setting meant that errors frequently occurred and equally frequently had to be corrected, with all that this entailed in mutual distrust.[7] Moreover the in-built price-cutting nature of the PBSs was not adequate for many employers – the pattern of rate-cutting, especially in the private sector, continued. Many workers saw no difference between piece-work and PBS in this respect, both were subject to the cutting-down process (TUC, 1910, p. 27). Often the rate-cutting was open and undisguised, springing from a class-based employer belief that bonus should not amount to more than time plus a quarter, or time plus a third (see Cadbury, 1914, p. 104). Equally, many work-groups worked to a time plus a quarter norm as well, and adjusted their effort accordingly. The adjustment process as the two sides attempted to reach an equilibrium is vividly described by Watson:

The original piece-price allowed for the job was 5 hours, this being based on the time taken when working day-work . . . the workers completed the job in 4 hours . . . the time was cut to 4 hours, and the work was done in $3\frac{1}{2}$ . . . It was then cut to $3\frac{1}{2}$, and the workers completed the job in 3 hours. Again the time was cut, but the patience of the workers had reached its limit and the time taken was 7 hours. The time was immediately increased to 4 hours, but with no effect. On increasing the time to the original 5 hours, the workers completed the job in $3\frac{1}{2}$ hours. Once again the time was cut . . . and the time promptly jumped to 7 hours. The workers had learnt their lesson. In this case the labour cost, which had begun at 8s.10d. gradually sank to 6s.5d. but jumped to 14s. when the workers had learnt their lesson.

(1934, pp. 40–1)

It was the widespread, persistent rate-cutting that did more than anything else to generate and reinforce opposition to PB schemes before 1914, but beyond the changing structure of control, beyond the whole army of new supervisors and inspectors were two other factors that are crucial to an understanding of the workshop reorganizations in Edwardian Britain.

(c) Changes in the employment relationship: paternalism and casualism

In the last two sections we have looked at the beginnings of the bureaucratization of the structure of control, but the employment relation also changed with the demise of internal contract and piece-mastership and the development of 'payment through the office'. Generally, there was a fundamental shift to a directly-employed and directly-controlled labour force, but there are other aspects of the employment relation that we need to consider.

If the employers gained control of hiring and firing from contractors and traditional foremen, then what were they going to do with that control? Given the growth and extension of product markets and the greater potential for influencing that market, it was theoretically possible at the turn of the century to institute a system of job security in large industrial organizations taking the model of the public service organizations, such as the railways, police and post office. Or it would have been possible to create security for a central core of workers, and leave the rest as 'floaters'. Or it was possible to casualize labour almost completely.

There were some signs of a turning towards paternalistic forms of organization between 1880 and 1914. There was a tradition of patern-alism in Britain which had been formed and practised by such figures as Robert Owen and Titus Salt, but the tradition was thin and spasmodic. Nevertheless, the Quaker employers, such as Rowntree, Cadbury and C & J Clark, provided a new impetus to paternalistic practices in the 1890s and 1900s. New model factory villages, such as Earswick in York and Bournville in Birmingham, were built. Moreover, there was a new emphasis: a shift from housing and community work to a concern for factory amenities and working conditions (Gospel, 1978, p. 21). Apart from the ideas of garden factories, of better design and light, air and cleanliness, there were serious efforts to develop medical and educational facilities, and even pension plans. The various welfare programmes were sometimes brought together under the control of a new kind of manager, called the welfare secretary (Meakin, 1905). This was the precursor of the modern personnel manager and the personnel department.

This apparent recrudescence of paternalism has been historically highlighted and labelled 'welfarism' or 'industrial betterment' but the extent and significance of welfarism pre-1914 has been grossly overestimated. Welfarism only ever affected a small minority of firms, primarily Quaker ones and the vast majority of employers did not interest themselves in the conditions of the workers (Phelps Brown, 1959, p. 75; Child, 1969, p. 35). Moreover welfarism was largely confined to factories employing large numbers of women and girls. In general, there was a lack of employer enthusiasm for welfarism and no evidence that employers' organizations encouraged welfare work (Gospel, 1978, p. 23).[8]

The restricted coverage of welfarism partly arose from lack of resources because industries such as engineering were characterized by a small firm structure. A mass of small non-specialist firms were unable to provide the capital which extensive welfare schemes required. Moreover, labour was frequently hostile to paternalistic proposals, suspicious of anything that smacked of company unionism and which threatened to supplant or rival the services provided by unions or autonomous organizations. This was particularly true of skilled workers with their Samuel Smiles traditions of thrift and independence. Thus the very group which employers might wish to influence were saturated in values of self-help and staunchly resistant to dependent employment relationships (Melling, 1980; Crossick, 1978). Even foremen proved suspicious of welfarism. In general there was little sustained impetus to company-based welfare in Britain compared to state welfare.

As we discussed in Chapter 5, the concept of paternalism requires at least two dimensions: the degree of employment stability, and the extent of employer concern with the non-work life of the employee. Typically a paternalistic organization entails increased employment security and considerable employer concern for the diffuse aspects of the employer/employee relationship, but clearly one is possible without the other. Welfarism, as practised in Britain, offered very little in the way of increased job security. Not only did British employers turn their backs on any notion of a more secure job system, but the introduction of PB schemes and the associated workshop changes actually increased the casualization of labour. For example, at the Vickers armaments factory at Erith, the introduction of premium bonus in 1909 meant that if no work was readily available then men were sent home with the consequent loss of pay. This casualization arises from the fact that under the contract system the contractor does any work planning and programming that needs to be done, but the workshop reorganization of the 1890s and early 1900s meant that this function shifted away from the contractor or traditional foreman to middle management. As the early management systems began to generate detailed information concerning labour costs, the upshot was that men, skilled and unskilled, were sent home by the foreman if labour did not match work flow (TUC, 1910, pp. 52–4). More generally in engineering there was an increase in the practice of 'standing off'; i.e. forcing men to accept periods of temporary unemployment for days or weeks with the oscillations in production or market demand (Cole, 1918, pp. 75–6). As the Webbs have pointed out, there was a long and extensive tradition of casualism in British industry and the dockers were only a particularly dramatic and publicized example of casualism (Webb and Webb, 1909, pp. 186–9).[9]

Forcing the workers to accept the burdens of fluctuating demand and production was particularly common in Britain because of the continued dominance of small firms, non-specialized firms, and the relative absence of production planning. Systems of internal contract are very flexible organizational forms which are not only substitutes for labour management, but also for shop planning (see Chapter 6). The pre-1914 changes in the employment relation and the emergence of direct employment and direct control were out of step with the evolution of shop planning. As late as 1916, one commentator was asserting that planning:

is rarely done in a systematic way by British manufacturers. The number of works in which it is even attempted can be counted on one hand. Very often there is no planning at all; it is left to the operative and rule of thumb. Generally, there is some planning of a rough and ready kind, but some of the most famous works in the country are in such a state of chaos that the stuff seems to be turned out by accident.

(Shadwell, 1916, pp. 375–6)

Thus the widespread lack of internal shop planning intensified the casualizing employment effects of the seasonal and trade cycles.

(d) Changing work-group relationships

Apart from the employment relation, the workshop reorganizations of 1890–1914 influenced the social integration of industrial organizations at a different level. As I have pointed out in Chapter 6, contract systems involved a modal pattern of work with a dependence on semi-autonomous work-groups. In general, any system of indirect employment will result in strong work-groups because the 'formal' and 'informal' structures tend to coincide. Therefore, we need to ask: what happened under the new systems of control to these work-groups and work-teams?

Though in some factories the work-groups were fractured, with the consequent competitive individuation, in many industries and factories the work-groups survived, but now they were unanchored into the production system. There was an increasing divorce between the formal and informal systems of control. The work group endured, not as a mechanism of explicit control, as it had been under internal contract, but 'as a submerged, impenetrable obstacle to management's sovereignty' and influence (TUC, 1910, pp. 35–6, 39–41; Montgomery, 1974, p. 518). Of course the 'uncoupling' of the small work-group was not a universal process in all industries. It partly depended on the changing supervisory pattern. Where there were attempts to create semi-supervisors such as chargehands and under-foremen, then these men were more likely to be seen as members of the work-team and to exert some influence over it (e.g. see Williams, 1915, p. 53).

However, a strategy of incorporation in which employers were careful not to uproot the links between a supervisor and his men faced contradictions itself. Top management worried about the continuation, or formation, of supervisor/work-group solidarity *vis-à-vis* themselves, especially with the spread of unionist and socialist ideas and the mounting labour unrest between 1890 and 1914. As one shipyard manager warned his directors in 1903:

a question which is causing us grave concern is that of our Ironworker, Carpenter and Joiner Underforemen. Owing to the great fluctuations in the amount of our work in the last ten or twelve years, the larger number of these men seem reluctant to throw themselves heartily on the side of their employers on account of not knowing . . . when they may be disrated and have to work as mates with the men at present under them and with whom they live in adjacent flats . . . These men are our non-commissioned officers and our economical production is largely dependent, especially in the shipyard, on them.
(John Brown and Co. Ltd., UCS 23/3 Minutes, 1903. Quoted in Melling, 1980, pp. 209–10)

Generally in engineering and metal-working there were repeated warning voices ranging from Colonel Dyer in the 1897/8 dispute to an editorial in *Engineering* in 1916 which emphasized that a modern foreman 'should belong to a social caste as distinct as possible from the workers, in order to counteract any tendency that might otherwise manifest itself for foreman and workers to make common cause' ('The foreman of the future', *Engineering*, 5 May 1916). Consequently, there was a spasmodic employer policy or practice to emphasize the differences between workers and their immediate superiors, and their supervisory function was stressed at the expense of their traditional role as participants in production. In addition there were attempts to wean foremen away from the workers' trade unions and organize them in the Foremen's Mutual Benefit Society established by the Engineering Employers' Federation in 1896–9.

Thus the employers' strategy of re-defining the role of the foreman and attempting to integrate him into management often led to the same consequences as a less sophisticated strategy: it resulted in the dis-association of work groups, and created the potential for the emergence of a rival work-group leadership, such as the newly-emergent shop stewards.

We can see in these historical developments some of the contra-dictions of the capitalist labour process itself. Continued employer dependence on existing forms of solidarity and subordination in an attempt to maximize the creativity and reliability of labour power renders control of the labour process incomplete. Alternatively, attempts at direct control result in reduced flexibility and cooperative-ness.

Management ideology and responses to Taylorism

Hobsbawm has argued that employers' beliefs in the first part of the nineteenth century (up to 1840s) concerning labour led to a total neglect of productivity and efficient labour utilization. Productivity was simple – it was a matter of long hours and the speed of the machines. Thus, the 1816 Royal Commission was incredulous at Robert Owen's suggestion 'that his output had dropped less than in proportion to the reduction in hours. . . . They repeated the same question about six times and clearly thought Owen mad or dishonest.' (Bienefeld, 1972, footnote 59 p. 267). But in the latter part of the nineteenth century, especially during the Great Depression, the idea of 'labour efficiency' began to be diffused as a general notion. Labour utilization became an object of study, and there are the beginnings of a management literature. However, before 1914 the development of new ideas and practices in Britain did not congeal into an integrated theory of organization, as they did in the USA. Indeed this is one of the major differences between the bureau-cratization process in the two societies (see Chapter 11), and is reflected in the response to Taylorite ideas crossing the Atlantic.

The early British responses to Taylorism have been carefully docu-mented by Urwick and Brech, and Levine. They show that Taylorism had a relatively small influence on British industry before the First World War, apart from a brief spurt of interest just before the outbreak of the War (Urwick and Brech, Vol. II, 1948, p. 88).[10]

When the wall of indifferences and lack of understanding of Taylor-ism in Britain was finally breached in the run-up to the War, the reactions were largely hostile. For example, *The Engineer* ran a series of hostile leaders on Taylorism from 1911 through to 1914. Thus in 1911, *The Engineer* proclaimed: 'We do not hesitate to say that Taylorism is inhuman. As far as possible it dehumanizes the man, for it endeavours to remove the only distinction that makes him better than a machine – his intelligence.' (*The Engineer*, 19 May 1911, p. 520; also 12 April 1912, 25 April 1913 and 14 November 1913).

Liberal and Quaker employers such as Edward Cadbury were also highly critical of aspects of Taylorism. For Cadbury, the main dangers attached to Taylorite forms of organization were that they would lead to excessive speeding up, debase the worker, tend to produce a *low-wage* economy and cause serious conflicts between capital and labour (Cadbury, 1914a, pp. 103–6). However, Cadbury was not totally hostile to Taylorism, and recognized both its importance and that scientific management was bound to 'become general in time' (Cadbury, 1914b, p. 327). Nevertheless Cadbury as probably the leading management intellectual of his time, and one of the few British employers to have actually read Taylor, responded to the new ideas with caution and distrust.

Thus, in so far as British employers and managers were aware of Taylorism there was a conscious rejection of the American model. Partly this was because of the pattern of demand for many engineering products in Britain. There was a limited mass market, and fewer opportunities for standardization and the specialization of tasks. The extent of mass production before the First World War was patchy indeed. Levine could only discover *traces* in sewing machines, the cycle trades, some newer branches of engineering, and some electrical trades and he concludes that it was not until the First World War and the enormous demand for standardized items, such as shells, that 'standardized repetition work took the place of the varied and variable output' of much of British manufacture before the War (Levine, 1967, pp. 52–3; Hobsbawm, 1969, p. 175).

Moreover, British employers, especially in engineering, rejected a high-wage strategy which was an essential element of the American model because of class-based notions of appropriate wage-levels. Instead, the Engineering Employers' Federation in the aftermath of the 1897/8 dispute sought to *reduce* wage levels in the face of foreign competition (*The Engineer*, 14 April 1913; Levine, 1967, pp. 63–4 and Zeitlin, 1979). In addition British engineers stressed the high administrative and supervisory costs associated with Taylorism and were unconvinced of the profitability of scientific management:

The proof of factory management is to be found in the sales department. Unless scientific management enables us to produce more cheaply or more quickly than before, it is of little avail. We have yet to learn that British works managed on American lines have paid higher dividends than British works, managed on British lines.

(The Engineer, 14 November 1913)

Given this ignorance, indifference and pre-War hostility to Taylorism, then it is not possible to maintain that a widespread shift in employers' beliefs had occurred before the First World War, unless it can be shown that some other ideology had swept through the capitalist ranks, whereas the paternalism and welfarism of Quaker employers such as Cadbury were clearly confined to a small minority.[11] This lack of a dominant ideology meant that few employers were able to conceptualize clearly alternative strategies and, as a result, combined traditional labour management with gradual change.

Summary and conclusions

This chapter has surveyed the emergence and extent of the new structures of work organization in the period 1880–1914. The changes that did occur should not be exaggerated nor misinterpreted. The spread of piece-work should *not* be seen as an integral part of systematic management, as it left the determination of effort-norms on a customary basis. Instead, piece-work generated a typical constellation of problems that constituted a push towards systematic management.

Similarly, despite many assertions or assumptions to the contrary (e.g. Burgess, 1980, pp. 83–4) Taylorism was not important in Britain before 1914. There was a limited wave of rationalization in the 1890–1914 period primarily affecting the engineering and metal-working industries, but this was not Taylorite nor Taylor-inspired. The innovations had their roots in indigenous methods pioneered by the large armaments firms.

We examined the workshop reorganizations which *did* occur during this period, many of which were associated with the spread of premium bonus systems. Clearly, there was a widespread change to a directly-employed and directly-controlled labour force, but this provided no impetus for more secure job systems. On the contrary, as far as one can determine, casualism increased.

On the shopfloor itself, the employers failed to incorporate work teams within the newly developing formal structures of control. This created the potential for the development of a rival work-group leadership, and this new shop steward leadership was stimulated by the changes in wage/effort exchanges. The spread of new payment systems, such as the premium bonus schemes, meant the development of task measurement and the beginnings of formal standards of effort. All these changes affected the traditional foreman's role, and the foreman/worker relationship. In general, there was a steady erosion of the foreman's previous autonomy and power position, and its transfer to a new stratum of technical staff.

It should not be assumed that the workshop reorganizations were solely and exclusively aimed at the workers. Top management was frequently as much concerned with the attitudes, motivation and power position of the foreman. Senior management wanted to encase the foreman/worker *relation* in rules, and not simply exercise greater control over the manual operatives. As Gouldner points out,

> bureaucratic rules flourish, other things being equal, when the senior officers of a group are impressed with the recalcitrance of those to whom they have delegated a measure of command . . . bureaucratic patterns are particularly useful to the degree that distrust and suspicion concerning role performance has become diffuse and directed to members of the 'in-group', as well as those on the outside.
>
> (Gouldner, 1954, p. 168)

This problem 'the enemy within', was not new of course. The widespread distrust of agents or managers at the end of the eighteenth century led many contemporaries to argue that industrial capitalism was sociologically impossible! (Pollard, 1968, pp. 23–5). What was new was the solution to the miasma of distrust. In the early nineteenth century the typical solution was an organizational form based on the principle of coordinated self-interest, namely systems of sub-contract, the whole framework permeated by the profit motive. In the early twentieth century the solution, or the beginnings of a solution, was the elaboration of bureaucratic rules – the development of a water-right code of internal laws, with successive levels of monitoring of subordinate activity.

But by 1914, this development had not advanced to the point that the traditional pivotal role of the foreman had disintegrated. The foreman remained a powerful hire-'n'-fire figure. Even when there was standardization of procedures and the creation of centralized departments, these could always be informally bypassed.

It is important to re-emphasize that the workshop reorganization during 1890–1914 only affected a small percentage of firms, primarily metal-working ones who were in the vanguard of industrial change. The majority of firms remained unaffected, and even in the firms that *were* affected, the current of change only represented the first stirrings of systematic management. Certainly the workshop changes did not amount to the complete bureaucratization of the structure of control by any means. In general, change was slow and hesitant. Top management failed to move quickly to re-structure completely shopfloor control because new ideas and new managerial practices had not congealed into an integrated theory of management in Britain. Because of this, British employers did not have the social resources to create effective alternatives to traditional foremanship even if they had wanted to.

If we accept that 1880–1914 was a period of the decay of internal contracting and other traditional forms of control, that it was a period of organizational experimentation and of employer hesitancy, often in the face of supervisory resistance, then the question arises of when Taylorism was institutionalized in British industry. When were bureaucratic forms of control imposed on the shopfloors of British factories? This question takes us on to an analysis of the inter-war period.

8 The Inter-war Years: Rationalization and the Bedaux System

Rationalization and the development of the firm

The primary focus of this book is the labour process. However, in understanding changes in the labour process and management it is necessary to consider wider structural factors, particularly economic relations between firms and ideological currents within society. In many ways the First World War was a watershed for all levels of structuration.

Britain emerged from the First World War into a new economic, industrial and social landscape. Economically the War had been a period of full employment and labour shortages, of rising prices, and of state planning and control. Not only had the Government taken control of the railways and coal-mines, but by 1918 the Ministry of Munitions had become the largest employer in the country. State intervention had developed slowly during the First World War, and had been carried out in an *ad hoc*, pragmatic way. Nevertheless, the changes were real and by the end of the war, there was the potential to develop a different version of capitalism (Harris, 1972, pp. 36–9).

There were changes too in the internal practices of firms. The enormous and continuing demand for munitions, for the tools of war, had created stable markets for many factories and led to the increasing development and use of mass production methods and some standardization. Moreover, industrialists were impelled to staff their factories with unskilled labour, especially women, and this labour shake-up had let to the erosion of skill differentials.

On the industrial relations front the employers faced a transformed labour movement. Trade unions had gained a new status and power, and there had been a shift to national, centralized wage bargaining. At the plant level the 'Shop Stewards Movement' had frightened conservative industrialists and forced many works managers into formal consultation with workplace representatives for the first time.

The war-time developments left the ruling class in an uneasy tension between old strategies and new, between going backwards or forwards. On the one side there were the 'reconstructionists' for whom the years of war had inculcated several lessons and these were promulgated as the precepts of a new social era. The propaganda of the reconstructionists revolved around five basic points:

(1) The belief that the Victorian competitive market system was beyond redemption: 'seven-tenths of the old competition was wasteful', and a new era of cooperation was beginning to take shape (Industrial Reconstuction Council, 1918, p. 9). Associated with this belief was the view that 'The industries of the country are no longer regarded as the property or possession of private individuals or corporations. They are regarded as public trusts whose existence in private hands is tolerated for certain benefits they confer on the community, and they must be compelled as the price of their existence to contribute more and more to the common good.'
(Richmond, 1917, p. 24; also Industrial Reconstruction Council, 1918, pp. 10 and 13).[1]

(2) Moreover, it was now possible to think and act in terms of an industry or trade as a corporate unit, and it was suggested that this view should be given a permanent institutional identity by means of Trade Parliaments or self-governing trade associations (Industrial Reconstruction Council, 1918; Benn, 1918).

(3) Thirdly, there were new ideas of the government's role and its relation to industry. These ideas varied, but the common element was the assumption of a much greater interventionist role in the economy, possibly via the Trade Parliaments. It should no longer be 'nobody's business to enquire why typewriters should all be made in America, or [until the War] optical glass in Germany'. A new theory of government was required in which economics was central (Industrial Reconstruction Council, 1918, pp. 40–1).

(4) The new spirit of cooperation between capital and labour should not be lost, but should be institutionalized in the Trade Parliaments or Joint Industrial Councils (Benn, 1918).

(5) There should be permanent forms of inter-firm cooperation of an industry-wide basis for the purposes of scientific research and export marketing (Industrial Reconstruction Council, 1918, pp. 30–1 and 33–5).

In essence the reconstructionists were outlining a new national corporatism, the sinews of a corporate society.

The utopian ideas of the reconstructionists left more industrialists untouched. The majority of the business classes were 'restorationists', yearning for a return to pre-war conditions, to the pre-war social order. Even if the 800,000 dead could have been resurrected and stuck back into their social slots, the changes in expectations and attitudes could not be easily bundled into the attic like a chest full of war mementoes. However, this did not prevent the restorationists from trying.

The opportunity was provided by the immediate post-war boom which, with its hopes of easy prosperity, seemed ample justification for business optimism and provided an excuse and an occasion for 'restoration' and de-control. Many government controls were quickly ended. Price controls largely ceased in 1920 along with rationing of raw materials. The Ministry of Munitions was wound up and 105 of its 245 factories were sold to industrialists; and all government hesitancy about de-control aroused a crescendo of shrill cries from the press, especially the *Daily Mail* (Mowat, 1955, pp. 28–9). Thus, despite the hopes and plans of the reconstructionists, the mechanisms of state control were dismantled with nervous speed, and there was a rapid scurry to return to an isolated economic individualism (Hobsbawm 1969, p. 214; also Urwick, 1929, p. 131). The end result was, as Mowat says, 'In the bonfire of controls the plans for the re-organization of industries were also consumed.' (Mowat, 1955, p. 29; also Pollard, 1969, p. 90).

However, after the brief boom of 1918–20, and the restorationists' triumph, the central fact of the inter-war experience was economic depression – 'to the labourer it meant the dole, to the employer it meant over-capacity' (Hannah, 1976a, p. 31). As the Depression continued, as unemployment got worse, not better, it forced a re-evaluation of economic and social beliefs. It became more difficult for traditional capitalists to talk as if the slump in trade was merely a temporary set-back. As the traditionalists grew silent and retreated, the reconstructionists reset their banners under the name of 'rationalization'.

In the inter-war years rationalization was a term used in a variety of ways. For the World Economic Conference of 1927, rationalization had a broad meaning:

Rationalization, by which we understand the methods of technique and of organization designed to secure the minimum of waste of either effort or material. They include the scientific organization of labour, standardization of both materials and products, simplification of processes, and improvements in the system of transport and marketing.

(Quoted in Urwick, 1929, Appendix B, p. 154)[2]

But for most British proponents of rationalization it had a more limited meaning; they used it to refer to large-scale horizontal mergers of firms, plus, often a lesser theme, the application of scientific methods of management and control.

For others, 'rationalization' represented a recognition and desire to replace the failing market system with 'a new Industrial Science which will convert commerce and industry into units regulated according to laws more or less exact' (Barley, 1932, p. 17; also Myers, 1932, pp. 54–5). There was an increasing desire by rationalizers to gather up the innumerable actions of innumerable men into a centralized system of control over economic life. Clearly these views constitute a continuous thread with the ideas of the reconstructionists.

The foremost proponent of rationalization ideas was Lyndall Urwick who was the Director of the International Management Institute at Geneva, and when it folded in 1930 became a management consultant. Starting from Taylorite ideas he saw rationalization as a natural extension of 'scientific management' beyond its limited application to individual firms to the wider spheres of an entire industry and the distribution process (Urwick, 1929, p. 134; also Myers, 1932, pp. 54–5). Influenced by developments in the USA and Germany Urwick thought that rationalization within an industry and within the firm would enable Great Britain to attain that 're-organized national economy which is essential'. Urwick published his main advertisement for rationalization in 1929 and the book is an uneasy mixture of the zealot's tendency to see the incipient emergence of that which he advocates, plus complaints that in Britain nobody takes rationalization seriously. In relation to the former tendency, Urwick argues that increasingly scientifically-based economic understanding has led, and will lead, to greater control and smoothing out of economic fluctuations (Urwick, 1929, pp. 38–9 and 86–7) – and this statement was published in the same month – October 1929 – as the Wall Street crash and the onset of the worst global economic depression in living history! Seldom has a message been quite so savagely kicked in the head by concomitant events.

What was the material basis for the rationalization movement in the inter-war years? This question requires us to shift focus from the ideological plane and briefly look at merger activity and industrial concentration. In Britain there was a fundamental tension between industrial and financial capital. This arose from the fact that the original landed class transformed itself into a capitalist class well before the rise of industry, and put its money into trading ventures. Thus there was a pre-industrial commercial elite based on the City of London and international trade. As a result landowners and merchants were *not* interested in financing industry as the industrial revolution gained momentum (Francis, 1980, p. 3). Instead industry was left to minority groups and 'marginal men', such as the Quakers and immigrants. Such groups did not have access to large sources of capital because the controllers of resources within society will only transfer resources to embryonic organizations provided the elite structure of the organiz- ations is judged to be 'safe' and accommodates their interests. Cut off, then, from the City of London the early industrial enterprises were largely based on *self*-financing. This British pattern of development can be contrasted to the Continental and the Japanese patterns (see Chapter 10). The British pattern of self-financing had consequences for the link between family and firm.

The link between family and enterprise in Britain proved to be a tenacious one. Though the Joint Stock Companies Acts of 1856 and 1862 created the legal foundations for a corporate economy, indus- trialists were *not* active supporters of the legislation. By the 1880s limited liability companies constituted a tiny minority of industrial organizations, and the preferred organizational form was the private company. According to Payne: 'entrepreneurs operated within organ- izations which show little alteration from those of their pioneering forebears. Certainly there was little movement towards the divorce of management from ownership, towards the elongation of organizational hierarchies.' (Payne, 1974, p. 20). This pattern of control continued well into the twentieth century and, in contrast to the USA and Germany, large organizations in early twentieth century Britain were distinguished by this continued dominance of proprietorial and familial management (Chandler, 1976, p. 40; for Germany see Spencer, 1979, pp. 51–2, and Kocka, 1971, pp. 155–6).

The continued familial framework of many British industries meant that the development of new organizational forms was impeded. The problems that this set up were very evident in the organizations created by a turn of the century merger wave. Many of these mergers involved the coming-together of large numbers of small firms (e.g. the Salt Union, 1888, involved 64 firms and the Bleachers Association, 1900, involved 53 firms), and they often encountered severe managerial problems. Without a new theory of organization or management these multi-firm amalgamations resembled confederations of family firms. Thus the Calico Printers Association, formed in 1899 from 46 separate companies, had a board of 128 directors including 8 managing directors in its early years (Utton, 1972, pp. 154–5; Payne, 1974, p. 22). Many of these early combines 'were run more as debating societies than as unitary organizations', and there was often little attempt to create a centralized administration with an integrated production and market- ing policy, nor to unify operations by standard costings systems (Hannah, 1976, p. 83; Chandler, 1976, pp. 36–7). Thus by 1914 there had been little significant dilution of proprietorial control. Given that families and entrepreneurs attempted to keep ownership and control as long as possible, when can the rise of corporate capitalism be dated in Britain?

Though there are some problems with the data, the general trends and periodization of industrial concentration beyond the First World War are well summarized by Hannah:

First, after several decades of perhaps slightly increasing concentration, there was, in the decade following the First World War, a substantial and rapid rise in industrial concentration as a result of which the largest 100 firms gained control of perhaps one quarter of manufacturing output. There then followed several decades of stagnant, or possibly even declining, concentration so that the level of 1930 was probably not exceeded until the early 1950s, by which time the second substantial upward movement was clearly under way.

(Hannah, 1976, p. 105)

These trends can be seen in Figure 8.1

In general, it is clear that 1919–39 was a period of the rapid development of corporate capitalism in Britain, such that by 1939 Britain had as high a concentration of capital as any other Western society. It is important to note this periodization of the shift from entrepreneurial to corporate capitalism, because much writing, especially in sociology, tends to confuse and combine the USA and Britain, a point we noted in relation to Taylorism as well.[3]

Thus the material basis for the rationalization movement was the increasing concentration of capital plus the development of the so-called new industries. A range of new industries typically founded around the turn of the century – chemicals, motors, electrical engineering, synthetic textiles – grew steadily through the inter-war period,

Figure 8.1   Number of firm disappearances by merger each year

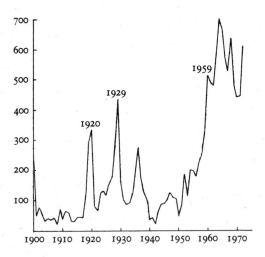

Source: Hannah, 1976a, p. 107.

and began to replace in economic importance the old, staple industries. Thus in June 1923, 21.1% of the labour force was employed in four of the traditional industries, and this percentage had declined to 10.7% in June 1938 (Ministry of Labour Report, 1938, summarized in Branson and Heinemann, 1973, Appendix, Table 4, p. 369). There were important differences between the new and old industries. Typically, the new industries required large units of production and greater concentrations of industrial capital. In addition, the technical base of the new industries was more advanced and they frequently incorporated mass production techniques. The size of these organizations and the capital concentrations meant that such firms were often more inflexible than the small firms of the Victorian economy: they did not relish the free-for-all of the traditional market place. It was above all these new aggregations of economic power that provided a base for the rationalization movement.

Having discussed the shifts in the realm of ideas and the material basis for those changes, it is now possible to turn to examine the concomitant changes at the level of the labour process.

Bedaux: a new form of Taylorism

After the death of Taylor in 1915, the American Efficiency Movement threw up several successors who offered 'new' managerial systems which in fact had their roots in Taylorism. Of these, the most important was the Bedaux System, named after its founder Charles E. Bedaux.

Bedaux is an interesting and little known character. He was born in 1886 in Paris, but, as the black sheep of the family, emigrated to the USA in 1906. In the United States he took a variety of jobs selling life insurance and promoting a toothpaste which also removed inkspots! Eventually he worked for a Grand Rapids furniture company, and developed the system which was to make his fortune. In 1918 he founded the first Bedaux consultancy firm in Cleveland, and the success of his management system was such that he became the owner of two networks of Bedaux companies, one in the United States and one international, with offices from Chicago to Berlin to Bombay.

In 1927, with a fortune in his pocket, Bedaux returned to France to live in luxury at his own chateau near Tours. During the 1930s Bedaux moved more and more towards fascist politics, and became friendly with the Nazi elite, particularly Dr Robert Ley, the Labour Front leader. The Duke of Windsor, after his abdication in 1936, was married at Bedaux's chateau, and Bedaux arranged a German tour for the ex-king. However, an attempted American tour for the Duke and Duchess of Windsor had to be cancelled, because Bedaux's support aroused a storm of protest from the American press and American trade union leaders. For example, Francis Forman, President of the United

Textile Workers, is quoted as saying: 'Mr Bedaux is a man who has made his money from the sweat and labour of the textile workers. I suggest he takes the Duke and Duchess on a tour of the southern textile districts to interview the men and women who are wandering around on relief as a result of his system.' More important than the interrupted holiday plans of the Windsors was the fact that the fiasco of the cancelled tour led to an internal company revolt against Bedaux. Bedaux, close to breakdown, had to surrender control over his American company, though he retained 55% of the stock and control of Bedaux International. This defeat must have come as a shock to Bedaux, a person full of his own grandeur. As Janet Flanner put it, 'whatever type of modern management he may have counselled to his customers, his own was feudal, simple and single. He was it.' (Flanner, 22 September 1945, p. 29). Nor was Bedaux's defeat confined to the USA. The British Bedaux office imitated the American palace revolt, and insisted on instituting a directorate, who, they thought, could run the British business with less publicity and suggestions of fascism.

Bedaux retreated to his French chateau, and after the fall of France in 1940, he became an industrial adviser to both the Nazis and the Vichy government. Bedaux had always had a strong sense of himself as engaged on a mission (e.g. see Bedaux, 1917, p. 110). Such was his profound belief in his system, that he thought that production organized by his methods could do away with poverty. Moreover, he believed that an efficient society could come only from a revolution on the right, led by engineers and technocrats. It was his humanitarian duty, as an inspired systematizer, to build society up on a new technical basis. It was these views, echoes of course of Howard Scott's technocracy (see Akin, 1977), that made Bedaux welcome the Nazis as a new European elite.

During his period in Nazi France Bedaux became positively metaphysical in his thinking. He managed to sell to the aged Marshal Petain, Vichy head of state, a new social philosophy called 'equivalism'. This involved a new Bedaux unit called a 'bex' which apparently measured production qualified by mental effort. It was intended to be a perfect payment system which would reward each man in proportion to his contribution to society. In addition, bexes were to take the place of money, and would serve as stable units of exchange and thus eliminate all speculation. Whether old Petain understood all this or not, to Bedaux's mind it was clear enough: it was 'Capitalism within the form of Communism' (Flanner, 22 September 1945, p. 30, and 6 October 1945, p. 41).

In 1942 Bedaux was captured in the Allied invasion of North Africa, where he was directing a fantastic scheme to build a 2000 mile peanut-oil pipeline across the Sahara Desert! As a naturalized American,

Bedaux was taken back to the USA and faced trial for treason. Rather than stand trial he committed suicide in February 1944.

Bedaux's bizarre biography is a side-show, but it has one important effect: it served to link Taylorism and 'scientific management' to fascism. As a result, the work-study profession has sought to avoid any overt connection to Bedaux in the post-war period (e.g. see the brief and embarrassed reference in Randall, 1969, p. 78; cf. Franks, 1970, p. 150).[4]

The widespread success of Bedaux was in part because he was an excellent and very effective salesman. Taylor had been concerned to get himself accepted *intellectually* and presented his papers to professional conferences and meetings. In contrast, Bedaux eschewed professional debate and set out to sell himself to employers and managers. Thus, Hasbrouck Haynes, another efficiency engineer and a competitor to Bedaux, who devised the Haynes 'Manit' System (see Alford, 1924, pp. 931–3), presented his scheme to the American Society of Mechanical Engineers in 1924: Bedaux never did. Bedaux also succeeded because he offered a management package which did not require total re-structuring of management. Theoretically at least,

Taylor's system was expensive and slow to install, requiring at least three years for a given plant. It involved painstaking and protracted investigation of every aspect of the productive process. It met resistance because it also involved a major re-structuring of management and restriction on the authority of traditional management.

(Layton, 1974, p. 383)

Bedaux on the other hand, offered a system which appeared to be quick and easy to install and which could be clipped onto the existing, traditional management structure. Moreover, dressed up in the language of science, the Bedaux system offered greater management power at the expense of the worker, and gave management the sense of being able to comprehend and control effort inputs.

Demonstrating the crucial importance of Taylorism during the inter-war period depends upon an acceptance of the link between Taylorism and Bedaux. There are three points to make about this. First, a close reading of Bedaux's only book shows his indebtedness to Taylor and other emulators such as Harrington Emerson. The work is clearly within the mainstream of systematic management. Moreover this work, *The Bedaux Efficiency Course for Industrial Application* (1917), was used as a training manual for Bedaux consultants in Britain between 1926 and 1932.[5] Secondly, the early British recruits to the Bedaux Company were selected on the basis of their knowledge of Taylor's works (Brownlow, p. 1.1). Thirdly, we can look at the practices and effects of Bedaux and it is clear that job analysis and job

simplification, the increasing bureaucratization of the shopfloor including work-study, and the advocacy of minimum interaction employment relations were essential Taylorian principles (see Chapter 9).
Overall, it is evident that Bedaux was one of the most important figures
in the international spread of scientific management in the inter-war
years and crucial to the diffusion of Taylorian workshop practices in
Britain. Even when the popularity of Bedaux declined, many of the
firms that discarded the Bedaux system itself, went on to use other
forms of 'rationalized' management. Thus, Bedaux, the man and techniques, did open the way for the spread of neo-Taylorite systems.
Certainly, the history of 'scientific management' in Britain in the
inter-war period is largely the history of Bedaux (Livingstone, 1969, p.
49).

Basic elements of the Bedaux system
In essence, the Bedaux system was a comprehensive structure of control over the labour process, whose installation offered employers
reduced costs through 'scientifically' established effort-norms leading
to increased labour productivity and proportionately reduced labour
costs. In general, the system is not well understood, and this section
describes the essential elements of the Bedaux system.[6]

According to Layton, 'Bedaux claimed to have solved the problem
which had eluded Taylor, namely that of discovering the precise,
scientific relationship between work and fatigue' (Layton, 1974,
p. 382). Taylor's position had been open to attack, and indeed was
attacked in Britain and the USA, because he never could effectively
ground in science his notions of a 'proper task'. Taylor wrote almost
nothing on fatigue and rest periods and when questioned about over-
work, as at the Hearings of the House of Representatives, he could only
fall back on personal experience, assertion and cliché (e.g. see Taylor,
1912, pp. 122–6, and 143). What Bedaux did was to attempt to combine
the emerging studies of fatigue and Taylorism. 'In place of the arbitrary
allowances utilised by Taylor, Bedaux claimed to be able to determine
the exact proportion of work and rest needed for any task.' (Layton,
1974, p. 382). How did he do this?

Bedaux attempted to determine the relation between elementary
work motions – lifting, pulling, pushing, pressing, etc. – and necessary
rest periods. Using a concept of 'strain', he asserted that:

For a muscular effort of a given power the ratio of strain is directly proportional
to the rapidity of motion and completion of the cycle.

Moreover:

For a muscular effort of a given power the duration of work and rest periods is
inversely proportional to the rapidity of motion

(1917, p.274, and Morrow, 1922, p. 241)

These so-called laws of work allowed Bedaux to build up a 'relaxation curve' which showed the rest times which were necessary to offset working time, the whole thing based on the length of the work cycle. In fact this relaxation curve soon had various additional 'fiddle' factors added, such as some extra allowance for the sequence of motions (varied versus non-varied) and allowances for body position. In practice, the rest allowances were *ad hoc*, composite figures mingled with guesstimates and assessments of what the local labour market would bear. Moreover, as Layton points out, 'There is no convincing evidence that Bedaux ever engaged in any scientific or experimental investigation: his results and methods were not subject to critical review by informed researchers in the field.' (Layton, 1974, pp. 382–3; see also TUC, 1933, p. 11).

Nevertheless, Bedaux's ideas had an appeal because they covered one of the embarrassing areas of nakedness manifested by Taylor. Once employers had the capacity to determine the exact nature of 'strain', and thus the exact allowance for relaxation, they were in a position to arrive at a *universal measure for all work*. Within the Bedaux system the universal measurement was the Bedaux Unit or the 'B'. This was defined as follows:

A 'B' is a fraction of a minute of work plus a fraction of a minute of rest, always aggregating unity, but varying in proportions according to the nature of strain.

(Morrow, 1922, p. 243)

It is the 'B' which is the really ingenious notion in the whole system. By incorporating the rest allowance in the unit of effort, Bedaux, at a stroke jumped over the minefield of comparability of work in a pseudo-scientific blur.[7]

The keystone then, of the entire system is a unit of labour measurement the 'B', equal to 60 seconds, composed of a certain number of seconds of working time, plus a proportion of relaxation time. This unit of labour measurement made it possible to make comparisons of the relative efficiency of workers, departments and factories, even though the types of work were substantially different (TUC, 1933, p. 6; American Federation of Labor, 1935, p. 940; Richardson, 1954, p. 79; Layton, 1974, p. 382). If it is possible to reduce all work activity – the worker at the milling machine, the lathe operator, the assembly worker, the female packer and the supervisor's supervising – within a single measuring grid, then all barriers to 'observability' have been broken. It is possible for the first time to set up a monitoring and control system which provides the work manager with a comprehensive picture of all work activity throughout the plant. This was what the Bedaux system offered.

However, a means of labour measurement does not, in itself, provide a basis for control: it is also necessary to establish effort norms. Again the 'B' had this double function. As the allowance for relaxation is built into the Bedaux unit, an operative taking the normal amount of rest should produce *on any job* 60B per hour. Thus the universal norm is 60B. Any work done in excess of this standard attracted bonus. In practice, the Bedaux consultants regarded 80B as an attainable target and attempted to push operatives and supervisors towards this effort level. This difference between practice and theory represents an important inconsistency common to most neo-Taylorite systems. If 60B is a 'scientifically established' effort-norm, combining work and compensating relaxation in the proportions appropriate for the average worker, then an 80B target implies one of two things – either 80B necessitates the worker sacrificing rest-time considered essential for health and continued efficiency, or it implies improvements in methods and facilities which should have been made before time studies were taken (Richardson, 1954, p. 81; cf. Bedaux, 1917, p. 210). We can see here an internal contradiction between creating a pseudo-scientific rationale for effort-norms and devising a speed-up system.

Given the 'B' as a tool of labour measurement and the in-built effort norms, the effect of Bedaux was to spin a structure of routine data-collection around the production processes of the factory which determines which causes of production delay have most administrative attention paid to them (Stinchcombe, 1974). The ideological aspects of this procedure reside in the nature of the causes of production delay and production loss picked out by the system and, correspondingly, the causes which are ignored. Essentially the Bedaux system picked out the individual performances of workers and supervisors. This can be seen in another basic element of the system – the Factory Posting Sheet. The idea of this was to post up weekly, or sometimes daily, the work performance of each individual operative. All workers whose output fell below 60B were recorded in coloured ink. The rather naive psychological ideas behind this system were that it would provide workers with targets to aim at, provide regular feedback on performance, and even tap the well-springs of competition. According to Bedaux himself, the objective was:

To encourage the racing spirit, which at the beginning carries the working force into exaggeration, which afterwards subsides to a more normal attitude, the production of each individual is published every day. . . . Workers, even of the most unskilled class – we have in mind a certain Polish class of labour doing unattractive work which is usually filled by illiterate men – go to these labour reports daily to compare their production with that of others. We have seen an old Polish worker go to the board to have a younger man show him his number, and after seeing that the points made the day before were written in red, indicating that the standard had been passed and a premium earned, go back to his work with a renewed energy born out of a spirit of peaceful confidence in the future.

(Bedaux, 1917, p. 294)

In reality, of course, the Posting Sheet acted as a visible warning to individual workers that if their performance did not improve, then they would be 'assisted' by the foremen, or moved to another department, and finally sacked. It was this visible and public weeding out process which helped to arouse so much resentment against Bedaux.

Bedaux, being no fool, was aware that one effect of his system was the increased casualization of labour. His response was to turn the situation on its head and argue that his system *increased* job tenure, because a group of well-managed, efficient workers earning a good bonus would themselves demand the removal or sacking of ineffective co-workers. 'It is no longer the employer who tries to dispose of a labourer because he refuses to produce. The request comes from the employees themselves, who wish to keep their premium earnings as high as possible.' (Bedaux, 1917, p. 306). In order to institutionalize these motivations, Bedaux proposed a committee on self-discipline which would be responsible for judging and recommending the dismissal of 'chronic low producers' (pp. 306–7). Whatever the merits or deceits of Bedaux's scheme, there is no record in the British Bedaux Archives of such a committee being established.

The measures of performance set-up by Bedaux also acted as the basis of the reward system. The wage-rate fixed for a 60B performance was regarded as a minimum wage whatever the actual performance, i.e. the day-wage was guaranteed. Any output above 60B attracted a 'premium' or bonus. In general the bonus was calculated such that each B point earnt 1/60th of the base rate of pay. This did not result in a proportionate rate of increase. As Philip Livingstone puts it

The mathematics of a Bedaux scheme was straightforward. In concrete terms, if a man earned £3 a week for producing 40 articles, Bedaux offered him £4 a week if he produced 80. Put in these terms, the confidence trick is too obvious, but the logic was confused by jargon and a certain amount of downright untruth. For instance, Bedaux always started from the premise that the man should have been producing 60 articles for his £3, and thus if he produced a third more – 80 – he got a third more pay – £4. What could be fairer?

(Livingstone, 1969, p. 50)

Under a straight piece-work scheme labour costs are static and total costs are relatively constant. The Bedaux scheme sharply reduced total costs, and was regressive in that bonuses became harder and harder to earn. But, at least originally, the situation did not end there. Bedaux also argued that a worker was only able to work above a 60B performance because of the assistance of the indirect workers and supervision. Therefore the production workers only received 75% of the available bonus, whilst the other 25% went into a reserve fund to provide bonuses for the indirect workers – the foreman, and even the production control managers (Bedaux, 1917, pp. 291–2).

Not surprisingly this 25% creaming-off scheme aroused unpleasant memories of profiteering contractors and gang-bosses, and led to cries that 'they steal some of our bonus and give it to the bosses'. The virulent opposition to this aspect of the Bedaux payment system resulted in it being de-emphasized, such that by 1933 the TUC Report was able to state that the division of the bonus was no longer an essential feature of the system, and that the Bedaux Company now had no objections to the entire 'premium' going to direct labour (p. 5). And through the 1930s in Britain this was increasingly in fact the case.[8]

During the early period of Bedaux the recommended practice was to introduce the system whilst ignoring the methods and equipment used. (Bedaux, 1928). As a result Bedaux was frequently criticized for not doing enough in terms of method improvements, but, on the contrary thrusting all the burden of increased output onto the workers (*Harvard Business Review*, July 1924, p. 477; American Federation of Labor, 1935, p. 938; Pearson, 1937, p. 71). This was certainly the line adopted by the Taylor Society who, fearful of the charge of 'speed up', struggled to disassociate itself from the Bedaux system.[9]

However, there are limits to the extent that methods, tools and machinery can be ignored, especially because the introduction and use of any payment-by-results system depends on the work being standardized, routinized and measurable. Thus in practice, before establishing the time standards in a particular department, it was considered necessary to re-organize the work on a more efficient basis. The external influencing conditions of a task (e.g. regularity of material supply, routing of work, machine speeds and feeds etc.) were standardized so that effort-norms would be established in terms of the improved facilities and methods of operation. Consequently Bedaux was as much a vehicle of standardization and the re-division of labour as it was of systematic sweating (see Chapter 9).

If the Bedaux system appears to be complex, then appearances are correct: it was. It was not easy for the average worker to understand how his pay-packet had been calculated and this complexity combined with the artificial 'science' meant that the Bedaux system was less open to collective bargaining than simpler payment systems (Dobb, 1928, p. 66; Laloux, 1951, pp. 146–7).

Diffusion of the Bedaux system

The pressures of the First World War and the American involvement in the war led to a flow of ideas concerning Taylorism and scientific management across the Atlantic. For example, various technical missions sent to the USA returned with practical experience of, and occasionally enthusiasm for, Taylorism (Devinat, 1927, p. 28). After the War Taylorism became embedded within broader perceptions of

America as a model of industrial productivity and economic prosperity. Such visions of progress and prosperity acted as cultural conduits by means of which ideas of Taylorism seeped into the European consciousness. However, according to Maier, there was a pattern of receptivity to these ideas, and both Germany and Italy proved more receptive than Britain (Maier, 1970, p. 37). It was not until the late 1920s and early 1930s that the problems of the British economy, and employers' desperate attempts to lower costs, created broad and continued interest in Taylorism.

Between the end of the First World War and the mid-1920s, Taylorite schemes began to filter into British shopfloors and factories with initial attention given to time-study and more systematic payment systems. At an ideological level there was some reconciliation between industrial psychologists who had opposed Taylorism and scientific management (Devinat, 1927, pp. 33–4; Lee 1921, p. 70; Sheldon, 1923, pp. 179–84; Child, 1969, p. 60). Indeed Devinat argues that this led to a new form of Taylorism in Europe marked by a coalescence of psychology, the First World War's fatigue studies and Taylorite ideas of systematic job analysis and costing. In some ways, as we have seen, Bedaux exemplified this mergence of ideas.

Table 8.1   The number of firms using the Bedaux system in 1937

USA	500
Canada	28
Britain	225
France	144
Italy	49
Belgium	22
Germany	25
Holland	39
Austria	5
Switzerland	4
Spain	2
Scandinavian countries	24
East European countries	25
Australia	17
Other countries	17
Total	1126

Source: Based on Laloux, 1951, p. 11

Note: These figures should be treated as indicative only. All data about Bedaux are subject to two problems: first Bedaux was a very secretive man who, for example, always kept his American office ignorant of what his European offices were doing. Second, and relatedly, commercial secrecy combined with public relations and salesmanship led to a number of misleading publicity pamphlets.

In 1926 Bedaux, as an American consultancy firm, established a permanent office in Britain for the first time, and was extremely successful in speeding up the process of the diffusion of neo-Taylorite ideas. Nor was the success peculiar to Britain. Bedaux's system spread first in the USA and Canada, but by the 1930s there were nineteen offices around the world and schemes had been installed in at least twenty-six different countries. Table 8.1 shows the number of firms that had installed Bedaux systems by 1937, according to Laloux.

Bedaux clearly enjoyed a remarkable international success. His system swept American and European industry and created a fortune for its founder. Despite at least two American imitators, Haynes 'Manit' and Dyer, no other managerial control system had such a widespread success (see American Federation of Labor, 1935, p. 936, and Nadworny, 1955, p. 179).

After a slow start in the late 1920s, the Bedaux system spread rapidly during the 1930s in Britain. This was partly because the firms involved were in the new and expanding industries of the 1930s – food processing, light engineering, motor components (though not motor vehicles), chemicals, etc. However, this is not the entire story. Bedaux was also applied to more traditional industries, such as iron and steel, textiles and hosiery. By 1939 approximately 250 firms had utilized Bedaux techniques including ICI, Lucas, Joseph Lyons and Wolsey. Moreover, many of these firms were industry leaders and acted as a guide to other firms in the same industry. As a result Bedaux became the most commonly used system of managerial control in British industry.

In Table 8.2 there is an analysis of the Bedaux archives which shows how the firms that used the Bedaux managerial control system were spread across industries.

This pattern of influence is important because according to labour

Table 8.2   *Distribution of the Bedaux system by industrial sector* (%)

Food, drink and tobacco	13
Chemical and allied	11
Coal and petroleum	1
Metal manufacture	10
Mechanical engineering	6
Instrument engineering	1
Electrical engineering	6
Vehicles (mainly motor components)	3
Textiles	21
Other manufacture	23
Services and distribution	6

(n = 183 firms)
(percentages are rounded)

process theory Taylorism was the rabid destroyer of the craft system. The evidence shows that the industries that were most affected (food, drink and tobacco, chemical and allied, and textiles) were the industries which had *not* been established on a craft basis, but depended on unskilled or semi-skilled labour. The Bedaux archives show that job analysis and job fragmentation did occur in these industries during the process of Bedaux systematization, but such processes cannot be subsumed under a model of 'craft deskilling'. This argument is taken up again in Chapter 9.

Summary and conclusions

It was pointed out that the main characteristics of the pattern of ownership and control in British industry have been long, continued familial control associated with self-financing, and, correspondingly, a late shift to corporate or monopoly capitalism in comparison with other societies. Additionally, there has been a relative independence from the state conditioned by a *laissez-faire* ideology. The First World War raised expectations that this pattern would be transformed into a new rational corporate society: expectations which were fuelled by the immediate consequences of the War. There was widespread awareness of the Russian revolution and an upsurge in the claims of trade unions. But the hopes of the 'reconstructionists' and the diffusion of scientific management were both blocked by the general crisis of over-production in 1920/21 and the mass of surplus labour which suddenly flooded onto the labour market.

The inter-war years did see a dramatic concentration of capital such that by 1939 British industry was as highly concentrated as the American. This capital concentration provided the material basis for a renewed rationalization movement which, however, was much weaker than in other societies and had little influence on the shopfloor. There was a general failure to spread the gospel of scientific management which was associated with a lack of business schools and management institutions in Britain.

After the First World War the US scientific management movement divided into the pure Taylorites, for whom organizational salvation could only lie in the strict application of Taylor's principles and methods, and a group of systematizers who were willing to take on board the early industrial psychology and fatigue studies as a part of 'scientific management'. The most successful and commercial of these neo-Taylorite schemes was the Bedaux system. It became the most common system of managerial control in Britain. It was particularly acceptable to employers because it limited the restructuring of management implied by classical Taylorism, and enabled the control system to be clipped onto the existing management structure.

Bedaux developed, or said he had, a universal measure of work – the 'B' – which incorporated the rest allowance into the unit of effort. With this standard of measurement, it was possible to make comparisons of the relative efficiency of workers, departments and entire factories. Thus Bedaux offered, for the first time, a monitoring and control system with which to gain a comprehensive picture of the work activity of a whole production process. Bedaux's monitoring and control system entailed spinning a structure of routine data collection over the shop-floor and the worker, which created a system of accountability for production losses. This monitoring system also acted as the basis of a premium payment system.

In Chapter 9 we will examine the patterns of opposition to the Bedaux system and the overall effect on the labour process.

9 Case Studies in Control and Resistance

Obtaining detailed historical material on shopfloor events is unquestionably difficult, and the Bedaux archives decisively extend our knowledge of the development and institutionalization of 'scientific management' in Britain. Amidst a mass of technical data, we can gain an insight into day-by-day shopfloor relations in 200 firms across the entire range of industries. Moreover, the overriding significance of Bedaux is that it was the main vehicle for expressing and institutionalizing the Taylorite message in Britain in the inter-war period (Thurley and Wirdenius, 1973, p. 7).[1]

The Bedaux material on microfilm is a mass of minutes, meetings and technical detail. The consultants worked in many firms for four years or more which resulted in several thousand pages of documentation on each company. Thus, in order to see the wood from the trees, it is necessary to be very clear about what questions we are directing at the data. In essence, we want to ask the following:

(1) What structural pressures did Bedaux, as a group of change-agents, exert on the labour process in the inter-war years? For example, did the recommendations and changes frequently result in job simplification and deskilling? Or is the Braverman thesis simply misleading?

(2) What were the major sources of resistance? Was it just a question of shopfloor worker resistance based on strategies of independence, or were other organizational strata significant factors?

(3) What were the Bedaux and employer strategies for overcoming resistance?

(4) What were the patterns of development and eventual outcome, especially from a comparative perspective?

All these questions are complex, and involve many subsidiary questions. Nevertheless, they provide a basic organization of relevance and irrelevance. The rest of this chapter consists of two detailed case studies

in contrasting industries – one labour intensive, the other capital intensive. Both case histories involved famous and long-drawn-out strikes
and the archive material allows us to see the shopfloor dimension of
these disputes for the first time. The conclusion draws on the rest of the
Bedaux archives and primary sources to place these studies of control
and resistance into context.

Wolsey Hosiery Company, 1930–4

The hosiery industry is a traditional industry which passed through
a putting-out stage. In the eighteenth and nineteenth centuries the
domestic system was the basic form of organization, especially in
the East Midlands. Generally mechanization and the concentration of
capital were slow to appear in hosiery and, as a result, the transition to a
factory system occurred relatively late in the 1870s. Consequently the
1870s Education Acts had been passed, which prevented child labour
within the factories. However, this did not preclude the use of internal
contracting. Under the domestic system the middlemen between
village stockingers and merchant hosiers were called 'bagmen'. Many
bagmen became small manufacturers and internal contractors within
larger factories, and they often employed their own family.

After the concentration of workers into factories there was a dynamic
towards the introduction of peripheral workers and the 1890s was the
crucial period for the substitution of women for men on power frames.
By the end of the nineteenth century women far outnumbered men in
the factories, and the rapid influx of women represented the advent of
unorganized unskilled and semi-skilled work. By the 1930s the ratio of
women to men was 4:1 and the process of deskilling had advanced to
such a point that hosiery manufacture had become primarily 'women's
work'.[2]

Though by the 1930s there were several large companies, including
Wolsey, in the hosiery industry, it was still the case that firms employing under 200 workers accounted for 86% of firms and about 40% of
employment. Moreover, 'the emergence of large firms did not imply
any marked tendency towards concentration of manufacture in large
plants'. Structural change took the form of a merger of firms rather
than the concentration of manufacture. Indeed, the shift from owner-
dominated firms to federations of firms within a parent company was
not really widespread in the hosiery industry until the 1960s (Wells,
1972, p. 202). Partly this was because the hosiery industry had always
been one in which the barriers to entry were low, and the change to
factory production apparently made little difference. Thus, with the
multiplicity of firms and the ease of entry the industry was highly
competitive (Wells, 1972, pp. 186–7; Friedman, 1977, p. 167). Apart
from the pattern of intense domestic competition, foreign competition

was a problem for the hosiery producers. This was particularly the case in the late nineteenth century and early 1930s.

The combination of highly competitive conditions facing the Leicester hosiery firms plus a scattered female labour force resulted in worker resistance to managerial control strategies being weak and poorly organized. Trade unions were late to develop, and often had little bargaining power. The transition to factory production in the latter part of the nineteenth century stimulated a defensive trade unionism among skilled men workers, but few women workers joined unions. Even by the 1930s only about 20% of women hosiery workers were unionized in comparison to a 40% union density for the men (Friedman, 1977, pp. 168, 171, 172 and 173; R. Gurnham, letter to writer 20 November 74; Walton, 1952, pp. 188–209; Wells, 1972, pp. 209–10).

The Wolsey Hosiery Company is not typical of the entire industry, but it is fairly representative of the twelve larger firms in hosiery manufacture. In 1930, it was a group with eight factories in and around Leicester, employing in total about 5000 people. In many ways Wolsey was the leading firm in the industry, and as such had the pick of the labour market – 'You were considered to be a little bit above the ordinary factory worker if you worked in Wolsey'.[3] Thus the firm was able to recruit lower middle-class and skilled workers' daughters. This made unionization of the female workers at Wolsey even more intractable. As the union secretary puts it: 'I had the job of trying, many, many, times, to organize these people and failed utterly, you couldn't touch 'em at all.' (Moulden interview, 1979).

Between the Wars, the hosiery industry was one textile industry, unlike the cotton and woollen industries, which was not greatly dependent on exports. It also benefited from an expanding domestic market because of changing fashions and consumer needs. As a result, despite the overall economic context, hosiery was largely a growth industry (Wells, 1972, pp. 170–1). Nevertheless, the hosiery industry was not insulated from the economic problems of the late 1920s and early 1930s, problems which were exacerbated by import penetration on one level, and, on another level, led to an employer search for lower labour costs. Ernest Walker, the managing director of Wolsey, thought the answer lay in modern, American-type labour control, and in the summer of 1930 wrote to Bedaux to invite them to systematize the main Wolsey plants in Leicester. On Thursday, 21 August 1930, the Bedaux consultants visited the Wolsey factories for the first time.

The structural pressures of Bedaux
What were the main effects of the Bedaux systematization at Wolsey during the four years 1930–4?

Firstly, Bedaux advocated and pushed through a general policy of job-fragmentation and deskilling. With non-machine-paced tasks there was a general divorce of direct and indirect labour, such that 'all preparation and servicing tasks are stripped away to be performed by unskilled, and cheaper, workers as far as possible' (see Chapter 6). For example, Bedaux decided that the maximum number of operatives required in the cutting room was 24 instead of 50. Half of the work was considered quite unskilled, and could be done by junior operatives at a lower rate of pay. It was decided with management that operatives could be withdrawn from the department a few at a time during the next few weeks 'taking advantage of the present shortage of work as an excuse for cutting down staff' (F.9, R.5).[4] In general the re-designing of manual tasks was in the direction of greater fragmentation (e.g. see F.9, R.5, 29, 61, 64, 66, 77, 80, 85, 144, 166, 175, 176, 177 and 183).

With machine-paced tasks as at the Bruin Street Knitting Factory, Bedaux consistently advocated a policy of 'stretch-out'. For example, in the Komet Half-Hose Department, Bedaux considered that the operatives had unnecessary intervals between working and recommended a stretch-out from six Komet machines to nine per operator. The knitting process was the traditional hosiery skilled task, but the new machines such as the Komets further reduced the necessary skill. Thus in order to get the operatives to operate these machines 'very liberal piece-rates have been in use', not only at Wolsey but generally in the Leicester district. As a result, the level of earnings had no technical basis, i.e. no basis in work routines, and Bedaux recommended that they be *reduced*. Thus, the general policy advocated by Bedaux was one of increased effort norms through stretch-out and direct labour cheapening through wage reductions (F.17, R.1–9).

The Wolsey management was cautious about such confrontational tactics and decided that it was necessary to consult the union. Therefore, at a board meeting on 14 February 1933, it was agreed that the correct approach to the trade union was to assert that the proposed changes were not Bedaux-inspired, but a definite decision of the directors, which had to be taken on account of the present position of trade. Secondly the Board emphasized that the company intended to use the service of men as opposed to women operatives, as much as possible, and, thirdly, that the displaced operatives would be given other work 'as far as possible' (F.17, R.5).[5] In this case the reaction of the Hosiery Workers' Union was to accede to management's proposals, partly because the additional male workers, rather than women, provided a more stable union membership (F.17, R.5 and 6).

In relation to the structure of control at Wolsey's several themes are prominent in the Bedaux reports. Instead of a pattern of foreman control Bedaux pushed through the principle of centralized task control. For example, in the fancy department cutting room (the shop where the knitted fabric is cut before being made up) the operatives were shifted from a situation of self-reliance including individual job knowledge, mixed with occasional supervisory cajoling, to a situation where all tasks are based on written, formal instructions. These 'instruction cards' included the effort norm, in terms of B's, for each job: 'This inclusion will now mean that an operator will be able to procure her pattern on which will be posted her full instructions regarding "lay-up"; weight; waste, and B-values for the job.' (F.9, R.172; see also R.8, 16, 137, 139, 143, 166, 174; cf. F.W. Taylor, 1911, p. 39).

As the systematization of the Wolsey factories proceeded, so the quality of products became an increasing problem. Bedaux had created a chain of consequences requiring a *complete* switch to a more bureaucratized control structure. Thus, at a meeting on 4 October 1932 (two years after Bedaux had started at the Abbey Park Mills Plant), it was agreed to place quality control on a centralized, bureaucratic basis. We can summarize a complex set of changes in Table 9.1.

We can see in this set of changes a further diminution of the power, autonomy and responsibility of the departmental foreman. The foreman becomes encased in a set of formalized standards, attempting to violate each of the standards as infrequently as possible (Woodward, 1970, p. 51).

Table 9.1 *Formalization of quality control at Wolsey, 1932*

Previous situation	1932 changes
1. No examination department. Examiners come under departmental supervisors	1. New, centralized examining department, under one supervisor
2. Fixed lay-out of examiners	2. Flexible system
	3. Draw up charts and percentages of faults to help new supervisor decide where to put his men
	4. Display these fault percentages in each department
	5. Set up a points system of faults and assess each department against an agreed standard. If this standard is exceeded in any one week, then disciplinary action would be taken against the worst offenders
6. Examiners were old operatives	6. Get rid of old operatives and recruit 'the right type' of worker

Source: Based on Bedaux Archives, F. 9, R. 181

One effect of task control and the creation of monitoring systems is a flow of data from the shopfloor to a higher management. This effect is shown clearly at Wolsey. By 7 July 1931 (eleven months after starting work at Abbey Park Mills), Bedaux started issuing *daily* analysis sheets for the use of senior factory management. These showed a range of data for each and every department including the 'losses' of the department relative to an ideal standard of efficiency, and the names of workers who had not reached the 60B level of performance on the previous day.

The point of these daily analysis sheets was that they acted as the basis of control. Thus Bedaux recommended that 'every operator who does not attain her required standard should be spoken to, to ascertain any difficulties which she may be experiencing'. Essentially, Bedaux regarded 60B as a minimum 'schedule of performance' such that continued failure to meet this effort norm merited dismissal (F.9, R.32, 41, 53, 55, 76 and 151). In addition, the recommended routine was that departmental 'losses' should be investigated *every day* 'with a view to their total elimination' (F.9, R.55).[6]

The final element of the structural pressures exerted by Bedaux concerns the employment relationship. The Abbey Park Mills factory employed approximately 1300 female and only 60 male workers. Many of the 1300 women were young girls who started there after school and were likely to leave soon after marriage. However it is easy to assume that the employment relationship was more transitory than it was in practice. Though there was a shifting population at Wolsey, the hosiery trade was one which employed a big percentage of married women, and the average stay of a girl at Wolsey was about twelve to fourteen years (Moulden interview, 1979).

Nevertheless whatever the length of time the women workers stayed at Wolsey they were still treated as casual labour. The hosiery trade was subject to seasonal fluctuations in demand and workers could be 'stood-off' without either notice or pay, and were frequently subject to short-time working (F.9, R.11, 20, 22, 40, 48, 50, 81, 98, 102, 104, 107, 109, 110, 111, 169, 179, 216; F.A. Wells, 1972, p. 188). During Bedaux's period at Wolsey the question of employment guarantees came up as a solution to fears of unemployment and increased short-time working, and a minimal change occurred: it was ruled that if workers are bought onto the clock in the morning or afternoon, then they must be allowed to stay the whole of that morning/afternoon period, even if there is no work. Bedaux strongly opposed any employment guarantee and even opposed this minimal change on the basis that 'this new ruling has had the effect of taking the control of good labour utilization out of the hands of the overlookers and managers' (F.9, R.107; see also R.20 and 22).

Thus the archive material shows clearly that Bedaux conceived of the employment relationship in terms of the minimum interaction relationship. The organization should strive for the maximum flexibility and interchangeability of personnel (see Chapter 5).[7]

The sources of resistance at Wolsey

(1) Supervisory resistance   The overlookers and supervisors were a major source of resistance to the implementation of the Bedaux system of control at Wolsey. Despite some attempts at persuasion and education (e.g. see F.9, R.45), supervisors remained sceptical, non-cooperative and downright obstructive. This shows up in the archive material in terms of continual pressure on supervisors and repeated complaints that they do not take the system seriously (e.g. see F.9, R.16, 21, 22, 27, 28, 33, 38, 41, 42, 50, 56, 60, 64, 97, 110, 115, 118, 119, 123, 132, 133, 140, 149, 150, 154, 206, 210). This pattern of attitudes is confirmed by the union secretary who remembers that a number of supervisors were as hostile to the introduction of the system as the workers (Moulden interview, 1979).

One result of this supervisory resistance was a mutual pattern of protection between workers and supervisors. For example, the Bedaux system of control partly depended upon the workers filling in daily work sheets, and the monitoring function of these was often blocked by a general feeling amongst workers that if they showed up certain conditions on their allowed time sheets they would be getting the foreman into 'serious trouble' (F.9, R.47; also R.115). Equally foremen protected workers: for example the foreman in the fancy department cutting room refused to allow Bedaux to be applied to his best workers in the specials room as they were doing difficult, skilled work (F.9, R.206; see also R.149). In general, supervisors were concerned to get the work out and this, for them, meant protecting their best workers and 'star performers' from the depredations of higher management and interfering change-agents (Moulden interview, 1979; F.9, unnumbered report written by Wolsey management, dated 16 January 1932).

Faced with this continuing opposition, Bedaux attempted to get several supervisors dismissed or moved sideways. Thus, in the underwear cutting room, a major source of difficulty, the supervisor was replaced *twice* in two years (F.9, R.149). Similarly, given that the supervisor in the men's cut lockstitch department did not understand the Bedaux system, nor apparently want to, Bedaux demanded that she be replaced. The report continues: 'On the first day of supervision by Bradshaw [the new supervisor] the operatives [because of a misunderstanding] cut off the power' (F.9, R.154)!

Secondly, Bedaux attempted to 'bureaucratize away' the problem by demanding that a list of the duties of all supervisors be issued on the authority of the directors (F.9, R.150 and 154). Indeed, Bedaux even suggested the idea of functional foremanship, such that it would be 'the duty of every supervisor to instruct, advise and encourage the operatives under their control' whilst the Planning Department would be responsible for production and work-flow (F.9, R.118 and 133; cf. Chapter 5).

(2) Worker resistance[8] The responses of the workers to Bedaux are complex. The initial response after the implementation of Bedaux in one department (the underwear cutting department) was an accelerated turnover of employees and reduced output. By November 1930, two months after Bedaux had started work studies, the situation blew up into the first strike. On 10 November the flatlocking operatives decided not to start work, and this example was quickly followed by all the other sections on the same floor. Representatives of the flatlocking department met management and Bedaux. After a long discussion the representatives agreed to give Bedaux a week's trial. When the representatives, however, returned to the department the decision was not upheld, and the whole group of departments remained idle. By 26 November, the whole of the mill was involved in a sympathetic strike, which was also a sit-in. On 28 November there was a meeting called between Leicester Hosiery Union and the workers to discuss the issue and make recommendations, despite the fact that the majority of workers were not in the union. A resolution was passed that the workers should restart work and 'that the union should investigate Bedaux methods and make a report at a later date'. This was accepted and work restarted on 1 December 1930.

By May 1931, after an uneasy period which included go-slows and short stoppages, the Hosiery Union took a ballot of all employees and found an overwhelming majority against Bedaux. Despite the ballot, the installation of the Bedaux system continued amidst extensive short-time working, grumbling discontent, and union inaction.

A year after the first Wolsey strike the introduction of Bedaux system into Wolsey's Coalville plant was strongly resisted by a sit-in strike. As a result of this action, Moulden says that 'the union has been compelled to face the question of whether or not it is prepared to accept the Bedaux system . . . or whether it is going to take active and official opposition to the system'. The union instructed the Coalville workers not to start work under the Bedaux system. As a result management posted a notice giving all workers one week's notice, and reaffirming their belief in Bedaux. The notice read as follows:

It will be remembered that in May last the Union took a ballot of all the operatives employed in the whole of the Wolsey works and when, under the Presidency of the Ministry of Labour, we met the Union officials, they informed us that the result of the ballot was an overwhelming majority against the application of Bedaux. In the clearest language we replied that if this was an ultimatum from the Union that they were prepared to fight on this issue, we accepted their challenge.

The action of the Union . . . in definitely telling our Coalville workers not to start work under the Bedaux system, we can only construe in one way. We feel that we have no alternative but to accept the issue and accordingly, we are posting notices tomorrow in all works under the jurisdiction of the Leicester Hosiery Union, giving our workers a week's notice.

Our belief in the Bedaux principle is as strong now as ever it was. We are convinced that it produces the greatest efficiency; that it will improve our organization by the elimination of waste, the improved methods and the economics which can be effected. We definitely believe and intend that under this system we can pay our workers more money than ever we paid before and we confidently hope, also, that we can give them more consistent and regular employment, and all this without creating any undue strain upon them.

We have no knowledge as to how many of our workers are in the Union; we have never put any restraint upon them nor have we made any enquiries. We realize that our action in issuing the notices will impose a severe hardship on many of our employees; there may be many who are not in sympathy with the action taken by the Union; we have therefore decided to keep open our mills for those who are prepared to work with us in our endeavours.

During mid-December 1931 a series of mass meetings were held by the Union at all Wolsey factories. The workers unanimously resolved to support the Union and fight the Bedaux system. On 16 December there was a second ballot of the workers at the Abbey Park Mills factory only which showed an overwhelming majority (912 to 66) for ceasing work. With this support, the main strike began on Monday, 21 December 1931. On that day a crowd of approximately a thousand assembled outside Abbey Park Mills, and a mass meeting was held by the union. Two days before Christmas 150 workers at the Abbey Meadow Mills Extension came out in sympathy. The strike continued over Christmas and Bedaux withdrew from the works. After Christmas the strike remained solid. The girl pickets were working in half-hour relays because of the snow and intense cold.

By mid-January both sides were presenting faces of intransigence (Moulden, the union secretary, was reported as saying that 'He hoped the last breath would go out of his body before he was prepared to negotiate on the Bedaux system') whilst preparing the ground for negotiation. On 16 January Wolsey senior management issued a confidential report critical of some aspects of Bedaux, especially the over-complex wage sheets which were understood by neither workers nor supervisors.

Between 2 and 9 February 1932 there were Wolsey peace negotiations presided over by the Lord Mayor of Leicester. The major points of the eventual settlement were that management was prepared to re-test any

B-values if queried by a majority of workers in a department. Second, Wolsey would give direct operatives 95% of the premium earned instead of 75%. Indirect operatives would now get 5% matched by another 5% from Wolsey. Third, when new departments were put on Bedaux, Wolsey agreed to pay operatives previous average hourly earnings for three months. Moreover, management agreed to set up a consultative works council in each factory and wage sheets were to be simplified by means of composite allowances. On 12 February 1932 the workers started back after an eight weeks' strike, and so did Bedaux.

The 1931/32 strike at Wolsey was the first major dispute in the company's history: it surprised everyone. The degree of enthusiasm and solidarity was also remarkable. The General Council's report to the 1932 Trades Union Congress commented that 'the effort made by the union was notable for the remarkable solidarity displayed by the employees, the majority of whom were girls. The General Council feel that the wonderful loyalty displayed is a tribute to the union and the employees concerned.' (TUC, 1932, p. 84). What lay behind this consistent solidarity? What was the basis of the workers' resistance to Bedaux?

There is no simple, single answer to this question. Perhaps the most important factor was the increased effort standards. Horace Moulden, the General Secretary of the Hosiery Union at the time, certainly saw the situation in this light. As he puts it:

The individual operative quite naturally measured the value of the system against the return in wages of work done. To tell a girl who week by week was taking home 50s for . . . completing her operation on 80 dozens of garments that in future she had to complete 110 dozens for the same wages, without any great or obvious change in the method of doing her work, was, to say the least, asking her to swallow a bitter pill.

(letter from Moulden, 17 November 1979)

This view was clearly voiced at the time. For example, one letter in the *Leicester Mercury* from a Wolsey worker asserts that under Bedaux:

For shaping men's trousers, cut department, one is allowed 8.1 B-value, for shaping men's shirts 6.3 B-value etc. For one days work one must do either $7\frac{1}{2}$ dozens of trousers *every hour* of $9\frac{3}{4}$ dozens shirts. When one has stood up from 8.0 a.m.–7 p.m. one gets tired and can't keep up this speed – hence a red mark on the posting sheet.
(*Leicester Mercury* 21 December 1931; see also letter from J.P. Fletcher, 18 December 1931)

Nevertheless, the increased effort-norms are only half the story. People often swallow bitter pills. Two factors crucially affected the attempted shift in wage/effort exchange, such that even young, non-unionized girls felt sufficiently indignant to stay on the picket-lines for eight weeks. First, the speed-up was introduced amidst the shadow of unemployment, short-term working and lay-offs. For example, in the week ending 22 October 1931, the percentage of short-time working relative to possible working hours was as shown in Table 9.2 Amidst this context of economic depression and low job security, the logic of capital accumulation seemed manifestly illogical.[9]

Moreover, resentment could be buttressed by self-righteousness because the workers' immediate superiors, overlookers and supervisors regarded the Bedaux 'schedules of performance' as being in conflict with customary effort-norms. And many supervisors themselves were anxious to resist the encroachment and pressures of centralized, bureaucratic controls. Thus the two strands of resistance could combine to form a concerted bloc of shopfloor opposition.

The role of the union in the Wolsey dispute was a contradictory one. This is shown up most clearly by the fact that in May 1931 there was an overwhelming ballot against Bedaux and yet no organized action of any kind occurred until *December* 1931. The intervening six months was an uneasy period without a clear collective agreement and with considerable shopfloor opposition. Moulden himself recognized the ambiguities of his role as union secretary in a speech on 15 December 1931: 'If there is any wavering on the part of anyone at Abbey Park Mills, I am responsible for it. I am responsible because I have helped them to patch up their damned system.' (*Leicester Mercury*, 16 December 1931).

In fact Moulden was subject to considerable pressures from the employers (he knew the managing director quite well) and from Bedaux who made concentrated efforts to convince union officials of the efficiency and fairness of the system. And the first application of Bedaux affected Abbey Park Mill where most of the girls were not in the union. Moreover, the ideology of technocracy and 'scientific management' had some effect and Moulden considered that there was nothing

Table 9.2 *Percentage of short-time working in some departments of Wolsey, 1931*

Department	Section	% of short-time working
Seaming	Flatlock	2
Seaming	Overlock	18
Making-up	Flatlock	23
Making-up	Fancy stitching	47
Cutting room	Rib-cutters	15
Finishing room	Mending	22
Finishing room	Ironing	26

Source: Bedaux archives, F.9, R.109.

intrinsically wrong with the system: 'Taylor's work was full of common sense' and 'if it had been put in right there would have been no trouble at all.' (Moulden interview, 1979). Therefore, he wished to avoid an open dispute until the Coalville girls forced the union 'to face the question of whether or not it is prepared to accept the Bedaux system'.

In general, there are several points to be underlined about the role of the union in the Wolsey affair in the 1930s. First, Moulden, like most union officials in the inter-war period, accepted the given framework of capitalist and managerial power, and had little conception that neo-Taylorite schemes would alter the structure of control over the labour process. Control issues never came into focus, and the policies of the union ignored issues of work organization and job design. It could be argued that the nature of the labour force, unskilled and female, implied that the role of the union would be confined to wages and welfare. We will return to this point in a consideration of Richard Johnson and Nephew which had a skilled labour force.

Nevertheless, despite the above, the outcome of union and worker reaction to Taylorism was a shift from unilaterial 'scientific' systems to negotiated systems (see Chapter 5). And in this process union officials and union representatives could and did become *active* participants in creating and stabilizing effort norms. For example, six months after the strike Moulden spent at least one day a week at Wolsey's 'ironing out problems as they arose', and sometimes this entailed telling Bedaux that some of the performance standards were *too* low – 'You got girls getting 95 B-hours – it was just bloody silly.' (Moulden interview, 1979 and letter, 17 November 1979).

But whatever the role of the union in the Wolsey dispute, the overall outcome was the modified installation of the Bedaux, neo-Taylorite system which survived through until at least the Second World War.

Richard Johnson and Nephew, 1932–7

Richard Johnson and Nephew's industrial situation is a contrast to that of Wolsey. As part of the metalworking sector they were capital-intensive with a highly-unionized, skilled male workforce. It was a medium-sized company employing approximately 1500 people in 1932, with 834 manual workers at the main works, Bradford Iron Mills in Manchester.[10]

From the end of the First World War until 1933, R.J. & N. had continually reorganized the production process, mainly by the introduction of new machinery. In June 1932 R.J. & N. wrote to Bedaux asking if they would visit the works and do a pilot report on a relatively labour-intensive department, with a view to introducing the Bedaux system throughout the works. In July Bedaux visited the factory, and produced a report on the stranding department which made the usual Bedaux claims for reductions in labour costs and increases in worker productivity (see Jenkins, 1974, pp. 5–6). Thus, on 9 November 1932, the Bedaux consultant, P.R. Wace, started work in the stranding shop (F.16, R.15 November 1932).[11]

The structural pressures of Bedaux

Wace, in conjunction with others, worked at R.J. & N. until May 1937. During this long period of shopfloor reorganization, what pressures did Bedaux exert; what type of recommendations were made? First, Bedaux advocated and pushed through a policy of job fragmentation. Bedaux followed a general principle of maximum fragmentation which entailed the divorce of planning and doing and the divorce of direct and indirect labour (especially see F.16, R.1 February 1933). In particular, there was an advocacy of 'stretch-out' – i.e. increasing the machine/man ratio, such that each worker was responsible for operating more machines (e.g. F.16, R.16 January, 1 February, 30 March 1933; 24 May, 8 August 1935). Beyond the obvious effort intensification, such stretching-out broke up work-teams and removed helpers and assistants from skilled and indeed semi-skilled workers. For example, in the stranding department, the work task was based on two operators per machine for some machines, namely a strander and a guider. The strander was semi-skilled and the guider was an unskilled helper. Bedaux's change to each machine being operated by one operator only had the effect of breaking up these long standing work teams (F.16, R.16 January and 30 March 1933).

However, the pattern and process of deskilling was not straightforward. R.J. & N. was selected as a case study because it represented the best potential test of the argument advanced in Chapter 5 that Taylorism was the destroyer of craft skills and craft knowledge. If we look at the division of labour at R.J. & N. transposed onto union organization, then there were fifteen unions at R.J. & N. in the mid-1930s. These unions were almost entirely skilled – there were skilled maintenance unions, the copper workers' union and the main craft union of the Amalgamated Society of Wire Drawers. This union, which had been established in 1840, catered initially only for the skilled wiredrawers. Moreover, the skilled workers employed their own assistants and apprentices and had a strong tradition of autonomy (see Seth-Smith, 1973, p. 22). As Jenkins puts it: 'As with most craftsmen of this period, the skilled wiredrawers were proud of their craft, their apprenticeship and their skills. They tended to be contemptuous towards the ancillary workers. In some factories there was a marked hostility towards the unskilled workers.' (Jenkins, 1974, p. 18). However, the position of the skilled wiredrawers as craftsmen and as employers was eroded from the 1870s onwards. In 1873 cast-iron dies were introduced from America and in 1877 the first barbed-wire machine crossed the Atlantic into the Manchester works (Seth-Smith, 1973, pp. 73 and 76). The slow spread of continuous wire-drawing machines occurred from the 1890s to the 1920s, and these machines were often manned by untrained workers.

Despite the anxieties of the Amalgamated Society, shortly before the First World War the unskilled were admitted into the union, where they formed a separate section as Grade 3 men, paying lower contributions and drawing lower benefits (Jenkins, 1974, p. 18; F.16, R.2 April 1933). And the title of the union was changed to the Amalgamated Socety of Wiredrawers and Kindred Workers, organizing workers in all sections of the wire and wire rope industries (Marsh, 1979, p. 336). Despite this offer of secondary status within the craft union, some sections of the R.J. & N. Manchester factory stayed outside the union. In particular, the men in the stranding department were not unionized (see F.16, R.8 February 1934). The residues of hostility between skilled and semi-skilled were not removed by a change of name.[12]

Like most companies, R.J. & N. suffered badly from the 1921 depression and the economic burdens were shifted onto the wiredrawers in the form of lay-offs and short-time working. Wire production continued at a sluggish rate during the early 1920s until 1925 when the fears of further unemployment mingled with fears of deskilling to eventuate in a significant strike in October of that year. In July 1925 the union of wiredrawers complained to management about the continued introduction of new machines given the high rates of unemployment of their members. The company chairman, Ernest Johnson, replied to the society in a direct manner:

the difference between wages paid to unskilled labour and those engaged in drawing wire on ordinary blocks is far greater in this country than in those countries with which we are in active competition.

It appeared, therefore, necessary that either your Society should reduce their rates to somewhat similar extras over unskilled labour, or that some new form of machinery to produce wire must be found, in which the skill and craftsmanship were not required, and whereby production could be cheaper, and a higher production obtained per man, and at the same time, the worker could earn a reasonable wage and one well above the lowest paid labour.

Realizing your reluctance to reduce wages rates on the old system, the directors decided to spend a large amount of capital on experimenting with continuing machines and die setting, which they claim to have developed with satisfactory results.

(Letter from Ernest Johnson to the Amalgamated Society of Wire Drawers, July 1925. Quoted in Seth-Smith, 1973, pp. 130–1).

Here then, is a clear statement of the employer's conscious desire to eliminate craft-working, and their awareness that this process is already under way.

With their backs to the wall, and with rank and file fears of mass unemployment, the Wiredrawers' Society was pushed into an un-winnable rearguard fight against deskilling. On Thursday, 15 October 1925 the union secretary informed the directors of R.J. & N. that unless they agreed to divide all available work equally between machines and blocks they would cease work on the following Saturday. In response the management posted a notice in the works which claimed that the unrestricted use of machine drawing had never been questioned before, that machine work cut costs and enabled the company to compete in world markets and thereby provide employment (Seth-Smith, 1973, pp. 133–5).

The strike duly took place, but with limited strike funds and fighting a battle which alienated the semi-skilled workers, the union quickly caved-in. By mid-November 1925 a settlement was reached which was a clear defeat for the union. It was agreed that the continuous wire-drawing machines would be used to their fullest capacity, and the only employer concession was a form of words in relation to wire being drawn for stock. In this stuttering struggle the wiredrawers finally shifted from a craft group to a mixed group of machine-minders and operatives with varying levels of skill; and from a craft union to an industrial union.

The significance of the changes in the wiredrawing labour process from the 1870s to 1925 from our point of view is that Taylorism had very little to do with the process of deskilling and the re-division of labour that took place, such that by the time Bedaux appeared on the factory floor in November 1932, the inheritors of the Taylorian principles were not faced with a craft-based work process.

However, at this point in the argument we need to be careful of confusions caused by the fact that the notion of 'skill' has several meanings as was discussed in Chapter 2. By the 1930s, the wiredrawers had lost much of their former technical skill (i.e. skill as work routines) with the spread of machine setting and continuous machine drawing, but they still clung to conceptions of themselves as craftsmen and were often treated as such by foremen and middle management. The events of 1932–7 were to rip away these remaining status shrouds.

We will return to the question of deskilling below. However, at this juncture it is important to note a second set of Bedaux-inspired influences on the shopfloor of R.J. & N.

Central to the Bedaux systematization was a consistent advocacy of shopfloor bureaucratization. This entailed several processes: firstly there was the development of extensive written records. For example, Bedaux instituted a detailed system of recording the use of each die, because 'too often one has to rely on somebody's memory for what the performance of a certain die may have been. This information should now be in writing and up-to-date.' Relatedly, there was the substitution of written formal instructions for verbal orders and the advocacy of work performance governed by explicit rules, i.e. the standardization of procedures. It should be noted that standardized procedures increase the substitutability of workers and work-teams, because job-knowledge is removed from a custom and practice mould and locked into management controlled tables and charts (F.16, R.1 February 1932, 25 August 1933, 6 March 1935, 12 July 1935 and 24 May 1936). In addition Bedaux advocated clear job descriptions such that positions like that of foreman have clearly defined powers. For example, Bedaux complains that in the galvanizing department 'the foremen could take considerably more responsibility than they do at present if they were given clear lines to work on. One real difficulty in the department . . . is the indefiniteness of the instructions they are given.' (F.16, R.14 June, 1934).

Finally, as was said in Chapter 8, the Bedaux system spins a structure of routine data collection over the shopfloor and the worker. The B-values, set for each and every task, 'must show accurately and in detail what each man is doing daily, and what part is really an excess cost. . . . (F.16, R.24 May 1935). In consequence, the employer can see clearly and quickly what is happening throughout the works (F.16, R.24 May 1935).

In general, then, the Bedaux systematization at R.J. & N. entailed bureaucratization of the structure of control. The third aspect of Taylorism analysed in Chapter 5 related to the employment relationship. This leads us on to look for the effects of the Bedaux application on employer/employee relations at R.J. & N.

Like Wolsey, R.J. & N. was a traditional family firm tracing its origins back to 1773. It remained firmly in the hands of the Johnson and the Thewlis families (Thewlis being *the* nephew), right through the inter-war period, and is a good example of an owner-dominated company. It was not until 1928 that R.J. & N. became a public company (Seth-Smith, 1973, pp. 144–6). Like many family firms, R.J. & N. had built up a local, long-serving labour force, most of whom lived in the surrounding streets of East Manchester (Jenkins, 1974, p. 15). Moreover, there were some strands of paternalism linking worker and employer, especially as the Bradford works was a part of the local community. For example, when R.J. & N. went public in 1928, a trust of 5000 shares was set up as a nucleus of a benevolent fund for employees (Seth-Smith, p. 145). Nevertheless, compared to Japanese corporate paternalism (see Chapter 10), these paternalistic links were tenuous indeed: they have an air of vague, distant benevolence.

But, however tenuous, these diffuse employer/employee linkages were quickly shattered under the impact of Bedaux. In brief, the tradition of cooperation and service linked to a vague benevolence was severed in a savage strike which resulted in a relationship much more akin to a minimum interaction relation. Labour became interchangeable – a sea of unknown faces attending to the wants of continuous-running machines. The details of this break with the past are discussed below.

The sources of resistance at Richard Johnson & Nephew

(1) Supervisory resistance Unlike Wolsey, there is little sign that foremen and middle management were a potent source of resistance to the Bedaux system at R.J. & N. It is not really possible to say from the available archive material why this was the case. Bedaux moved quickly to institute the payment of bonus to foremen and chargehands and this, as actual or potential money in the pocket, may have forestalled some opposition (see F.16, R.1 May, 1933). In addition, Bedaux managed to obtain strong support from the Johnson family and this fact undoubtedly percolated down the management hierarchy and may have influenced some minds (see F.16 R.7 December 1936). However, this is largely speculation: the only archival fact is that in this particular instance there is no clear record of supervisory resistance.

(2) Worker resistance: February 1933 – June 1934 The first signs of worker resistance to the Bedaux system of control were channelled through the Wiredrawers' Union. In February 1933, there were employee meetings complaining about Bedaux's intrusions and as a result, Seed, the Society's full-time official, wrote three letters to R.J. & N. complaining about the situation.

The source of the workers' resistance to the Bedaux control system was the fear of increased 'observability' which task-measurement entailed. This had been felt and expressed before the First World War with the beginnings of systematic management (see Chapter 7), but in the inter-war period such fears were intensified and mingled with fears of deskilling. As Seed wrote to the company in his first letter: 'there is a general discontent and unrest among the workpeople in your employ as a result of being beset and watched *for the purpose of procuring their trade secrets and methods of working*, which normally and . . . legally belong to themselves' (Jenkins, 1974, p. 6, emphasis added).

The outcome of the first union protests about Bedaux and reorganization was a period of six months of negotiation between the Wiredrawers and R.J. & N., during which time Bedaux largely confined their activities to the non-unionized stranding shop which continued on

Bedaux (see F.16, R.23 March, 30 March, 10 April, 12 April, 22 April, 1 May, 16 May, 16 June 1933). Moreover, unbeknown to the union, the Board of R.J. & N. had already decided to adopt the Bedaux system *throughout* the works. Thus the minutes of the Board meeting held on 2 March 1933 reveals that:

> The Board unanimously decided that particularly in view of the export trade, a new system of wage payment and shop control, based on a specialized time system, should be put into operation. That the Works General Manager is authorized to negotiate with the employees for the introduction of the system. Failing the negotiations being brought to a satisfactory solution, the necessary steps should be taken to enforce the adoption of the system, even if this course involves a stoppage of work.

(Quoted in Jenkins, 1974, p. 9)

Apart from the shopfloor fears of increased managerial control and deskilling, there were intense fears of unemployment. The rank and file had seen enough unemployment and lay-offs since 1921, and the Wiredrawers' Union was anxious about the solvency of its unemployment fund. R.J. & N., in conjunction with Bedaux, attempted to reassure the men by guaranteeing there would be no dismissals, and that the company would make payments to men laid off at the rate of 5s per week. The state that negotiations had reached by April 1933 is well illustrated by a Bedaux Report dated 22 April 1933 and written by E.E. Butten, Chief Engineer. This report documented the financial weakness of the union as indicated by the insolvency of the unskilled employment fund. Therefore 'The firm's offer of a payment of 5 shillings per week for every week during which a member is laid off owing to the reorganization may therefore prove the turning point. At the most the cost to the firm would be £3000 during the first year after all departments are applied.' Given the perceived weakness of the union, the plan of campaign was to attempt to achieve an agreement with Seed, the union secretary. If agreement could not be reached, the intention was to send Wace, the main Bedaux engineer, into one of the militant departments in order to force the issue, provided the Bedaux strikes at Venesta and Henery Hope had been settled beforehand.

Three things are interesting about this report. First, the extent of collusion between Bedaux and the company. Bedaux clearly took an active part in the negotiations and manoeuvrings between employer and unions. Related to this point, the document indicates that we are seeing the historical emergence of professional industrial relations as a staff function. Third, it is clear that the wireworkers had good cause to fear redundancy. On their own figures (£3000 p.a.) Bedaux was planning for 120 *man/years* of lay-offs out of a total labour force of 833.

R.J. & N. made a last major effort at persuasion on the 22 July 1933, when the Chairman, Sir Walter Campbell, addressed a mass meeting of the men at Fairlie Hall. In his speech he argued from the problem of costs and emphasized that R.J. & N. were at present making losses, not profits. Therefore they needed outside assistance to reorganize the works. Campbell tried to deal with the workers' fears of unemployment:

We realize that, at first, there may be some increase of unemployment until the effect of our work can be felt. This difficulty we propose to meet by guaranteeing that, as a result of this reorganization, no one will be dismissed, and that we will subscribe to the unemployment fund of your Society in order to assist the Society to make its usual unemployment payments.

He went on to assert that the objections to use of a stopwatch and deskilling were unreasonable. The advantages of Bedaux – the increased earnings and the pension fund – were dangled as financial carrots, before ending on a harsher note:

As Chairman of the Company, I feel it would not be right if I did not tell you clearly that the Board of Directors intend to continue this reorganization. We are prepared to face a stoppage if you insist on it.

(Bedaux archives, F.16, R.22 July 1933).

Clearly, then, the company was determined to push through with the shopfloor re-organization, and had taken steps to prepare for a strike.

Given this employer strategy, the response of the union was surprising. After Sir Walter Campbell had withdrawn, the assembled workers passed a resolution which included the statement:

In the event of the Company carrying out their declared intention of terminating present contracts of service with a view to bringing in the Bedaux expert to watch and beset us, such new terms of employment shall be refused on the ground that the conditions of re-engagement are contrary to the best interests of the state and in conflict with the law governing the rights and liberties of British subjects resident in this country.

(Minutes of Special Executive Meeting of ASWDKW, 22 June 1933)

In line with this resolution, the Executive at a further meeting on 12 August 1933, decided:

That the strike weapon shall not be resorted to until all other methods have failed, and that Mr Seed be requested to communicate with the Solicitors with a view to Counsel's opinion being obtained as to the legality of the Bedaux system.

Thus the union put its trust in British justice. Meanwhile, the employers put their trust in property rights.

R.J. & N. decided to push through their works reorganization despite any opposition, and Bedaux proceeded to take time studies on 14 August 1933. As the Bedaux Report puts it:

it was decided to make a start in the Wire Drawing Mill, so that if the Union wished to bring legal action against the firm, they should be given every facility of obtaining evidence while studies were being made of the work of their most skilled No. 1 grade members.

However, Bedaux did not have the situation all their own way:

The threatened stoppage of the works did not take place, but there was considerable disturbance among all the Union men throughout the works and this resulted in a slow-timing and various other retaliatory measures on their part.

(F.16, R.26 September 1933)

From August 1933, until June 1934, the story of worker resistance is a story of informal rank and file resistance with the Wiredrawers' Union desperately attempting to contain and head off strike action until their court case against Bedaux came up. In every department that Bedaux entered collective resistance occurred. For example, on 28 August, time studies started in the barb department and on Monday, 20 November, the department started working under the Bedaux system. But it only did so after the union had advised the men to accept the situation until they could obtain 'the protection of the Courts' (F.16, R.26 September, 27 November 1933 and Jenkins, 1974, p. 12). Faced with the employers and Bedaux on one side and a blind trade union leadership on the other the workers in the barb shop took the only action open to them and purposely restricted their output 25% below their customary norm as a collective act of protest (F.16, R.27 November 1933). R.J. & N. reacted sharply and sacked them at the end of November. What did the Wiredrawers' Society do in response? According to Jenkins, 'The Union pursuing its general policy of trying to avoid a stoppage, got the agreement of the rest of the men to make weekly contributions to keep the barb men out without taking any retaliatory action and without the men suffering financially.' (Jenkins, 1974, p. 12). Negotiations between the union and R.J. & N. avoided a total walk-out, and by mid-December the barb men were reinstated but at a lower wage (48s. instead of 52s/6d.). The barb machinists continued to act as a group and continued to restrict their output as before. Neither the loss of wages, nor the restoration of wages two months' later, seemed to change this collective tactic (F.16, R.8 January, 6 February, 19 February and 28 February 1934. Contrast the accounts in Seth-Smith, 1973, p. 170 and Jenkins, 1974, p. 12).

With this background – individual departments restricting output in reaction to Bedaux and the threat of a mass walk-out – Bedaux next attempted to systematize the cleaning department and the wire drawing mill. The pattern of response in both departments was very similar, and the eventual strike could have been sparked off by either department.

Bedaux approached the cleaning department with the expectation of trouble, and when they started time studies on Monday morning, 19

February 1934, they got it. When Bedaux entered the cleaning department all the men in the shop stopped work, and despite being threatened with dismissal, they completely refused to re-start the acid vats if
work studies continued. With a strike hanging in the air along with the
acid fumes, the union entered the situation:

The Union delegates then asked very strongly to be given time in which to
persuade the men to work. They stated that the Union instructions were still
that there should be no stoppage, and it is understood that the reason given by
the Union is that a stoppage would prejudice the legal case. They were finally
given until Wednesday morning.
   It is reported that Mr Seed, the Union Secretary, addressed the men concerned at a long meeting on Tuesday telling them that they must work, but that
he left the meeting without being able to get a decision on this point.
   When studies were started on 6 o'clock on Wednesday morning, the men did
not stop working, and they have continued to work without any demonstration
during the week, *but they have reduced their output by approximately 25%*.
                            (F.16, R.28 February 1934, emphasis added)

Thus, by the end of February 1934, Bedaux had entered two
departments – the barb department and the cleaning department – and
the employers were faced with continuing output restrictions by both
groups of workers. In mid-March, work studies started in the wire-
drawing department and on the fourth day one operator being studied
switched off his machine, to be followed by all the other men in the
department. Once again, the union stepped in and asked to be allowed
to control the situation, and the potential flashpoint was pushed into
the future (F.16, R.17 March 1934).

(3) Worker resistance: June 1934 – March 1935 The immediate cause of
the strike at R.J. & N. was the situation in the cleaning shop. Despite
its name, this was a key department, where the work required long
experience if not formal skill. At the start of the process of wire
manufacture it is crucial that the steel rods are removed of all impurities
and contaminants because this affects their tensile strength. Thus the
cleaning department passed the steel rods through acid tanks, water,
lime and then loaded them onto trucks to run through ovens heated to
200°C – a process known as 'blueing'. The work was hot and messy and
often required the men to walk through the ovens under temperatures
of 120° or 130°C (F.16, R. 9 March, 4 April, 13 April, 1934; 6 March
1935; Jenkins, 1974, p. 13; Seth-Smith, 1973, p. 164).
   By June 1934 the R.J. & N. directors were faced with continual
output restrictions by the barb men and the cleaning department over
Bedaux. Feeling forced to act, the company sacked nearly all the men in
the cleaning department, and this time the union could not contain the
stifled resentments and anxieties and 450 men walked out in support.

During the summer of 1934, there were no serious attempts at negotiation. There were exchanges of letters between the Wiredrawers' Society and the company which only served to define the positions of both sides – namely 'reorganization of works including Bedaux' versus 'no Bedaux' (F.16, R.20 July 1934). Faced with the reality of the strike the union backed its rank and file. The only serious attempt at negotiation occurred in September at two secret meetings under the chairmanship of the Lord Mayor of Manchester. The following exchange between Johnson's chairman and Tom Seed, the union's national organizer, sums up the position:

LT GEN, SIR W. CAMPBELL. Reorganization was necessary to meet competition from abroad.

MR SEED. Let the firm apply Bedaux to their plant, and machinery and materials but leave the men alone.

LT GEN, SIR W. CAMPBELL. Reorganization must be complete, each aspect was dependent on the other.

MR SEED. I am allowing the firm to apply Bedaux to machinery and their own property, but not to the men.

LT GEN, SIR W. CAMPBELL. Mr Seed had no rights in the matter of the firm's reorganization of machinery.

MR SEED. Could the men have an adviser to inspect the firm's books and ascertain particulars of salaries, selling prices, profits, etc?

LT GEN, SIR W. CAMPBELL. Certainly not!

MR SEED. The firm was ready to take but not to give.

(Quoted in Jenkins, 1974, pp. 20–1)

As this exchange indicates the conferences were not a success and no negotiating progress was made.

Meanwhile, R.J. & N., actively supported by Bedaux, was busy. Firstly, they contacted other wire firms and asked for help. A central depot was organized to which wire from competitors was delivered and relabelled and then despatched (Seth-Smith, 1973, p. 170). In addition, the copper departments continued to work and so did R.J. & N.s Ambergate works in Derbyshire. All this kept R.J. & N. in business.

Right from the start of the strike Bedaux advocated the use of scab labour in order to bypass the problems of worker resistance (F.16, R.6 January and 20 July 1934). In August 1934 'Operation Streamline' was initiated, and Wace, the Bedaux consultant was placed in charge. The company acquired a large, old house as a hostel for the new workers, and advertisements for workers were placed in newspapers throughout the country. The local Chief Constable was informed of the company's plans, which were ready by early October. On 2 October, the Board of Directors announced that the works would re-open on Wednesday, 10 October 1934 with imported labour. Jenkins recounts that:

On Wednesday morning, long before the normal starting time, Forge Lane contained a seething mass of men and women strikers, their families, workers from nearby factories and places of employment, sympathisers and others. All seven entrances were mass picketed. Soon a large force of police arrived and proceeded to move the strikers and everyone else out of Forge Lane; Trade Union officials, leaders of the strikers and individual strikers protested without effect.

The firm, obviously in collaboration with the police, prepared their tactics to the last detail. Led by police motor cycle patrols, two motor coaches, moving swiftly, drove the scabs right into the works.

(Jenkins, 1974, p. 15; cf. Seth-Smith, 1973, pp. 175–6)

The main effect of this was to drive out the workers in the copper departments, swelling the numbers on strike to 600. Nevertheless, the company continued their policy of bringing in labour, and managed to keep the plant running despite the mass picketing and the frustrated violence of some of the strikers.

In November 1934, in the Chancery Division of the Law Courts, the union's case against the legality of the Bedaux system appeared. Five Bradford Mill workers claimed that

it was an implied term of their contract of employment with Richard Johnson & Nephew that the latter would not do, or cause to be done, anything to hinder them in the performance of their contract, and that while employed on piece-work they were entitled to work free from any hindrance or other interference by either of the defending companies

(Seth-Smith, 1975, p. 183)

Encapsulated in this claim was the last cry of the semi-autonomous craftsman-cum-contractor appealing against the control implications of centralized, bureaucratic management. The Judge was not sympathetic and concluded that he was 'satisfied that what was done by way of observation was well within the legal rights of Richard Johnson & Nephew as employers' and the action was dismissed with costs.

Whether Seed lost his faith in British justice is not recorded; nevertheless, the result of the action did nothing to bring the strike to a close. The pickets remained outside the factory gates; the scabs remained inside. By November 1934 the door was firmly closed on any settlement. Six hundred men, many of whom had spent their working lives at Richard Johnson & Nephew had lost their jobs for ever – only ten men ever went back to the works (Jenkins, 1974, p. 27).

The outcome of the Bedaux dispute at R.J. & N.
On 30 March 1935, R.J. & N. issued a statement that the works were now fully manned and that no more men could be taken on. Nearly three months earlier Bedaux had re-started the systematization of the shopfloor. (F.16, R.8 January 1935). However, teaching groups of unskilled and semi-skilled men the techniques of wiredrawing did not prove easy – the new men were not able to step into the vacant jobs and work effectively. Eight months after the imported labour had been brought into the plant, it was still not possible to standardize working techniques and conditions (F.16, R. 24 May 1935). The reason for this was that the standardization of conditions rests on a base of the worker's experience and skill. Remove this at a stroke, and 'scientific management' stumbles along before discovering the obvious (e.g. see F.16, R.7 May 1935).

The interesting point here, which returns the argument to the initial point concerning skill, is that it proved *more* difficult to teach the new men how to run the cleaning and blueing departments than it did to teach men to draw wire. Bedaux and management were forced to make extensive experiments on the acid vats and temperature control in the ovens, before it was possible to acquire the custom and practice job-knowledge of the dismissed workers and encapsulate it in standard procedures and regulations (see F.16, R.6 March, 7 May, 24 May 1935). If job-learning time is an accurate indicator of the technical aspects of skill, then many of the traditional craft jobs in the wire works had become semi-skilled, whilst the traditional non-craft department, the cleaning department, manned by Irishmen, was the one repository of skill!

The combined result of the processes of job-learning, ineffective working and increased scrap became evident at the Board meeting on 8 November 1935, when it was disclosed that most departments had made losses in the six months April–September 1935 (F.16, R.11 November 1935). Richard Johnson & Nephew *were* able to defeat the Wiredrawers' Union, bring in replacement labour, fracture the relations with the local community, systematize the plant on a neo-Taylorite basis, and ultimately increase output per man, but they did so at a considerable cost to themselves.

Summary and conclusions
We started this chapter with a set of questions. If we turn back to those questions, then the significance of the mass of facts and events which have been presented in the case studies becomes apparent.

Firstly, it is clear that the structural pressures exerted by the Bedaux engineers from 1926 to 1939 did result in a divorce of 'direct' and 'indirect' labour and job simplification. The worker who worked within the framework of the Bedaux system lost a large part of his autonomy and initiative, and the latter was concentrated in the hands of the planning department.[13] However, the patterns of job-change do not fit into a simple Braverman model of craft deskilling. In order to make some historical sense of the changes in the labour process it is necessary to distinguish between job fragmentation from a craft-base and from a non-craft base. In addition, we can distinguish between confrontational and non-confrontational transformations as different modes of change. These two dimensions enable us to locate the significance of Bedaux in the inter-war period (see Figure 9.1). It is clear that scientific management was not, at least in the inter-war years, used as a direct confrontational means of craft deskilling. It was largely used in industries with pre-planned or semi-planned production processes or by employers with a low dependence on worker skill and job knowledge. In general the processes of craft deskilling have occurred within a non-confrontational framework of occupational redistribution in terms of the growth of new industries, new geographical locations, the emergence of new firms and the development of new production processes (Lee, 1981).

The second effect of Bedaux in the inter-war period was the increasing bureaucratization of the shopfloor. The elements of this process – the principle of task control, the establishment of a monitoring system, the creation of formal effort norms under the threat of dismissal, the creation of rigid job boundaries – are illustrated throughout the Bedaux archives.

The third effect of Bedaux was the fracturing of traditional diffuse employment relationships and the advocacy and imposition of a re-

Figure 9.1 Types of re-division of labour

Existing labour process	Mode of re-division of labour	
	Confrontational	Non-confrontational
Craft base	British engineering 1890s	Shift from woodworking production process to plastic-based production processes
Non-craft base	Bedaux in the 1920s and 1930s	Re-location of textile industry in Far East, Hong Kong, etc.

lationship more akin to the minimum interaction relationship proposed by Taylor. Given, then, that these neo-Taylorian pressures were the effect of Bedaux, what were the sources and bases of resistance?

It is of course possible that senior management themselves discovered that Taylorism and bureaucratic control strategies generated severe problems and contradictions, such that the Bedaux system was a passing phase, a brief moment of a dialectical process. Ideally then, we would like to conduct a survey of employers in, say, 1938, to test this. Fortunately for us somebody did just that. On 14 May 1938, the Management Research Group No 1, sent out a general enquiry concerning employers' attitudes to the Bedaux system.[14] Extracts from some of the replies of employers who had installed the Bedaux system are reproduced below:

FIRST EMPLOYER. From an administrative point of view, the system is of real and permanent value and even if looked upon as nothing more or less than a system of fixing piece-rates, it is more likely to be accurate and fair than the old and primitive methods. We have found the system of value in connection with the introduction of our Production Control department.

SECOND EMPLOYER. Our experience of the Bedaux system is definitely satisfactory. We agreed that the clerical cost of running the system is high, but this is far outweighed by the savings in direct labour. We do not think that the actual system of calculation causes any difficulty with operators, and the success of the application of the system depends entirely on the relationship between the company and the employees, and the way in which the application of the system is handled. It should not be overlooked that the Bedaux time-study is excellent; it is probably the best in the world.

THIRD EMPLOYER. This company had a three months' strike at their works. They could not possibly admit to the trade unions or to their shareholders that the Bedaux system was not a success but they think that the results are not in any sense proportional to the cost to which it has put them. In reviewing the matter over some years, the company is not by any means satisfied. They have only applied it to one sixth of the operatives at one of their mills.
(Management Research Group Archives, W/11/29–38/19; also W/8/29–34/12)

The number of replies are too small to quantify, and can be taken only as indicative. Nevertheless it is clear from the comments and other evidence (e.g. Standring, 1934) that though there were doubts, hesitances and resistance, senior managers saw the Bedaux system as a useful and lasting mechanism of control. What, then, were the main sources of resistance to bureaucratic managerial control systems?

One of the earliest British companies seriously to introduce job-analysis and systematic time-study, essential ingredients of Taylorism, was W. & T. Avery in Birmingham in 1921. Though its introduction seems to have aroused little overt resistance from the workers, the interesting point is that it aroused considerable opposition from the *foremen*. The foremen insisted on controlling the scheme and the time-study techniques, so that instead of a central time-study office, each department had a time-study man under the foreman. Even sixteen years later an observer comments that the 'chargehands are in effect running the shop as a collection of almost independent small factories . . . each man making what he thinks is required, or what happens to be an easy job for any machine' (Bedaux archives, F.22, 1937). Clearly the supervisors in this factory were insisting on retaining their traditional shopfloor control. This proved to be a common pattern in the inter-war period. The Bedaux consultants consistently found foremen and supervisors a major source of resistance to managerial centralization and control.[15]

Theoretically, the basis of supervisory resistance relates to the dynamics of bureaucracy. The natural tendency in all bureaucratic systems of organization is that the bargaining power of the supervisor dwindles. Circles of autonomy are compressed and freedom for man-oeuvre is reduced (Devinat, 1921, p. 145; Crozier, 1964, p. 194; Lupton, 1957, p. 47). There is a conflict between an established informal pattern of control and Bedaux's bureaucratic system of control. Despite supervisory scepticism and obstruction there were surprisingly few attempts to incorporate foremen into neo-Taylorite systems of the 1920s and 1930s. Instead there was a propaganda campaign against the traditional foreman (see Child, 1975, p. 73) and foremen were often dismissed if uncooperative, or moved to other departments, or demoted. This pattern of conflict is an interesting contrast to Japan, as we shall see.

Despite these measures the effect of middle management and supervisory resistance was often a restricted application of Bedaux's principles, especially in small and medium-sized companies, though as Bedaux became more aware of British practices it was more able to override potential opposition (e.g. British Goodrich Rubber Company Limited, F.3; Rayon Crepes Limited, F.21; The Leeds Fireclay Company Limited, F.21; Trepur Paper Tube Company Limited, F.22; Ferranti Limited, F.21; W. & T. Avery Limited, F.22; and Powell Duffryn Associated Collieries, F.22).

But not only foremen resisted the encroachments and pressures of new control systems, so did many shopfloor workers. It is clear from the Bedaux archives and other source material that there was considerable worker opposition to the rationalizations of Bedaux. As the system penetrated into British firms it met with a good deal of rank and file hostility and unrest. There were numerous strikes against Bedaux schemes in the 1920s and 1930s, of which the most famous was the nine-month strike at Richard Johnson & Nephew's wiredrawing works in Manchester in 1934/35, and the eight-week strike at Wolsey's in 1931/32.

The primary cause of these disputes was the fear of unemployment. This was a period when national unemployment rose above 20%, whilst in certain communities in Wales and the North East it reached the appalling figure of 70%. The last walk through the factory gates was a walk into real, and probably sustained, poverty. Fears of unemployment and poverty were mingled with fears of deskilling and resentment at being 'spied upon' (see Jenkins, 1974, p. 6). Moreover, the workers 'felt that in the name of science they were having unlimited speed-up and rate-cutting imposed upon them without negotiations, and they could neither calculate nor control their own earnings' (Branson and Heinemann, 1973, p. 96).

Rank-and-file resistance certainly had its effects upon Bedaux and the employers. During the worst years of 1931 and 1932, when there were a number of strikes (ICI Metals Group; Joseph Lucas; Wolsey; Salt Union Ltd; Amalgamated Carburettors), much of the systematizing work was conducted under conditions of great secrecy and the Bedaux Company, faced with widespread opposition, gave considerable thought 'to the development of consultancy services in other [less inflammatory] directions, such as plant layout, control of material utilization, quality control, method study, costing, budgetary control, personnel management and the training and selection of operators and staff' (Brownlow, p. 39). Thus worker resistance widened out the work and focus of the systematizers (cf. TUC, 1933, pp. 15–16). Nevertheless, the concerted opposition of the workers to the neo-Taylorite systems of the inter-war period should not be over-emphasized. As Brown (1977, p. 241) points out, the spread of Bedaux schemes was frequently unchecked, and this lack of worker opposition was often influenced by the relative acceptance of Taylorism by the trade union officials of the 1930s. It is only necessary to compare the outright and wholesale condemnation of premium bonus systems by the TUC committee in 1910 with the relative acceptance of the Bedaux system in the 1933 TUC report (p. 16) to realize that the official trade union movement had shifted from opposition to collaboration and compromise over centralized management systems.

This move towards compromise arose from several causes, but it is important to realize that Taylorism was institutionalized in Britain during a period of economic depression with mass unemployment and declining trade union membership. Clearly this weakened working-class bargaining power. On the other hand the economic context influenced the attitudes to and acceptability of neo-Taylorite schemes, with their shadow of redundancy, to the rank and file. Taylorism came to Britain amidst the stench of unemployment.

The eventual organizational outcome of the struggles and compromises over the new control systems was a form of neo-Taylorite organization in Britain, which we have analysed in Chapter 5. Thus the transition process in Britain to direct systems of employment and control was carried through slowly in most industries, and though eventually able to override most collective opposition, it failed to integrate oppositional groups. Partly this was because the institution-alization of Taylorism occurred in Britain without ideological re-inforcement. Once it is realized that the crucial period for Taylorism in Britain was the inter-war period, then the ideological context becomes clearer. Taylorism, rationalization and the American model rang hollow with the blows of the depression years. As C.S. Maier points out:

. . . the conditions of the Depression necessarily undermined all Americanist industrial utopias. Economic contraction destroyed the postulates for class collaboration and discredited the managers of the system. At least until the Second World War and its aftermath America's model of industrial product-ivity lost its catalytic inspiration . . . the supreme confidence in technology and production, in engineering as social redemption, perished with the other dreams of the twenties.

(Maier, 1970, p. 61)

Against this background the employers were utterly unable to integrate ideologically the workers and foremen on British shopfloors.

Part Three   Comparative Perspectives

10   The Japanese Transition Process: from Oyakata to Corporate Paternalism

Up to now we have been examining the evolution of modern work systems in one society and culture, namely Britain. In this chapter and Chapter 11 we will broaden our perspective beyond industry/industry comparisons and look at the development of the labour process in different societies.

Japanese industrialization: capital and the state

The process of industrialization in Japan got under way a hundred years later than in Britain. After the Meiji revolution of 1868 there was a concentrated effort by the new Japanese rulers to achieve economic equality with the West as soon as possible. Thus, between 1868 and 1880 the primary initiative in promoting industrialization was taken by the state: most factories were set up and run by the government. For example, in 1872 the government established a model factory for silk recycling and imported a French expert to teach 200 girls the techniques. Similarly, the government purchased two cotton spinning machines, each with 2000 spindles, from England in order to establish model factories in Aichi and Hiroshima. This was the start of a factory-based cotton industry in Japan (Harada, 1928, p. 25). Managerial positions in these model factories were filled by officials who were usually ex-samurai, and who later became known as 'shoku-in'. However, since these officials lacked the technical competence to train and supervise factory workers, this task was done by the foreign experts brought in for the purpose and by supervisors chosen from among the workman themselves (Yoshino, 1968, pp. 68 and 69; Brugger, 1976, p. 31).

During the initial period of rapid industrialization there were few signs of the paternalistic practices with which Japan is now associated.[1] However, one marked difference from Western practice was in the position of the shoku-in. The shoku-in inherited much of the status of the former samurai class; they were granted permanent job tenure, a salary, and special living accommodation. In general the social position of the shoku-in was modelled on that of the government officials.

In 1880 the government decided to sell off all but a few of its factories to private interests, but they were not sold on the basis of public shareholdings; instead a few selected families were allowed to buy the model factories and mines, often at only a fraction of the cost. These favoured few were the origin of the zaibatsu groups in Japan (Norman, 1940).

The zaibatsu were a unique form of structure and economic power, and provide an interesting contrast to British organizational conglomerates. Essentially the zaibatsu had three characteristics:

(1) Centralized control by a zaibatsu family which extended its power through strategically-arranged marriages and personal patronage relationships;
(2) Well-knit, tightly-controlled relations among the affiliated firms by means of holding companies, interlocking directorships and mutual stockholdings;
(3) Great financial power based on commercial banks which were the hub of the system and were used as the leverage to extend control across several industries.
(Based on Yamamura, 1964, pp. 539–40)

The zaibatsu received subsidies and encouragement from the government. Indeed the extent of the link between government and industry can be indicated by the fact that Mitsui – one of the four big zaibatsu – was appointed the official handler of the government's revenue! This meant that Mitsui had access to all government money, interest-free, until the Bank of Japan was founded in 1882. With government support the zaibatsu groups grew through the First World War boom and even the recession of the 1920s. Thus by 1933 the Mitsui empire consisted of 150 firms, and Mitsubishi controlled nearly 200 companies (Yamamura, 1975, pp. 167 and 169).

Nevertheless, the zaibatsu did not dominate the economy until the 1930s, and the second phase of industrialization, from 1880 to the First World War, was a period in which the competitive pressure in both the domestic and international markets increased, and there was an unfettered, unrestrained pursuit of short-term profit, often associated with widespread ill-treatment of workers. These exploitations were not checked by the government – there were no protective labour laws of any kind until 1916 – nor by significant working-class resistance.[2] The workforce was pre-proletarian. There was little class consciousness, little organization of the workers and protests were usually sporadic and often violent.

Nearly all industrializing societies suffer from shortages of capital. This general problem was exacerbated in Japan by the fact that most of the wealth sufficiently liquid to be channelled into industrial investment was initially in the hands of conservative merchants, merchants who were ignorant of factory-based industry and foreign trade (T.C. Smith, 1955, pp. 114–15).

The upshot was that the Japanese commercial class was marginal to the early industrialization process. It was the *state* which mobilized capital for industrial investment, and the government share of investment activity continued to be predominant through to the 1930s. Overall the government's share of investment activity was larger in Japan than in any other industrializing society in Europe or North America (Rosovsky, 1961). The vigorous mobilization of investment funds meant that Japan was able to resist foreign domination: as Brugger says, 'the Meiji government was able to finance her early industrialization without recourse to overseas aid and without allowing her industries to fall under foreign control' (Brugger, 1976, p. 31).

Early work organization in Japan: the oyakata and the factory dormitory system

Throughout the early industrialization of Japan there were severe problems of labour supply. During the last quarter of the nineteenth century, and indeed well beyond it, the economy was one of family firms, family workshops, and family stores. This had two important effects. Firstly, less than 10% of its labour force was available on the labour market at all, and, secondly, there was a widespread cultural antipathy to paid employment: 'People would offer themselves on the market only as a last resort and would get out of it as soon as prospects improved for proprietorship.' (Taira, 1970, p. 3). Additionally, many rural migrants shunned factory work because of low wages, poor conditions and coercive methods.[3]

Low-wage policies, long hours and antipathy to factory labour was a major factor in creating both severe labour shortages for the Japanese factory-owners and a very high rate of labour turnover, 100% or more per year in some factories. Many of the unskilled men floated back and forth between farm and factory – the so-called *dekasegi* workers – whilst the skilled workers were often on a perpetual journey from one workshop to another (Levine, 1965, p. 642; Yoshino, 1968, p. 71; Karsh, 1976, p. 879). Yoshino records one textile mill which employed about 4000 people. During the year 1900 the mill recruited 6085 new employees, but 7071 left, of which 82% 'escaped': 14% were dismissed, and 1% died! (p. 73)[4] Many factory deserters and absentees took advantage of the Japanese values concerning respect and care for parents. Such considerations took precedence over all contractual obligations, and one establishment finally ruled that an employee could not be granted leave of absence because their mother had died more than twice in any one year! (Foxwell, 1901, p. 110, footnote 1)

The problems of labour recruitment were perpetuated during the first phase of industrialization because employers were slow to adapt and learn the rules of the market. Indeed neither the employers collectively nor the state sought to develop, nor seemed very conscious of the concept of well-organized external labour markets (Levine and Kawada, 1980, pp. 127 and 300). In the absence of such markets employer responses to the persistent problems of recruitment, turnover and labour control took two forms, particularly after the failure of coercive measures. First, employers evolved the factory dormitory system, especially in textiles. Second, many employers, like some British employers, were forced to rely on independent labour contractors, or master workmen, called *oyakata*.

What then was the specific role of the oyakata in the labour process? In general, employers would make lump-sum contracts with oyakata, who would then find the labour, determine methods of work, supervise the work process, provide payment to the workers, and meet any production deadlines. (This definition of the oyakata's role is taken from S.B. Levine, 1965, p. 642; see also Bennett and Ishino, 1963, pp. 45–6; Yoshino, 1968, p. 71). In order to maintain their role oyakata built up bands of followers called *kokata*. One of the most powerful oyakata in the 1890s controlled over 300 kokata and apprentices. (Tsuda, 1979, p. 35).

The oyakata system in some form was important amongst the unskilled and skilled workers, but especially amongst the latter. It was widespread, in engineering and metalworking industries, though, unlike Britain, it was not significant in textiles.

Whilst there are clear and striking similarities between the oyakata and the British internal contractors, there are also significant differences. The main difference relates to the internal solidarity of the oyakata gangs, which drew heavily on traditional Japanese patterns of relationship. The most important pattern here is that of the *oyabun-kobun* relation. This is a simulated kinship tie based on the father (*oya*)/child (*ko*) relation. Thus it entailed patriarchal authority exercised by the oyabun combined with personal loyalty and devotion displayed by the subordinates or followers. The oyabun's power is restrained by customary norms such as *jingi*, the obligation of benevolence (Bennett and Ishino, 1963, pp. 40–2; Nakane, 1970, pp. 44–6). An additional difference was that within the retinue of the oyakata there usually developed a strict status hierarchy based on the length of time of the oyakata–kokata attachment, rather than upon the value or nature of the work performed.

The internal contract system in Japan could be and usually was exploitative. The oyakata extracted between 10–30% of wages due to workers (Bennett and Ishino, 1963, p. 46) but it is difficult to put a figure on the rate of exploitation. Wages were based on the oyakata–kokata status hierarchy; that is, they depended on length of attachment, and wage payments were often irregular and consisted of payment in kind. Moreover, the social relations of the oyakata–kokata were not simply exploitative. The low direct wages which the oyakata often paid were supplemented by financial help at times of crisis, by interest-free loans etc. The deliberate limitation of wages helped to foster a state of economic dependence of the kokata, which in turn enabled the oyakata both to maintain social control and to act out his symbolic role of 'father' to his subordinates (Bennett and Ishino, 1963, p. 75).

The other employer response to the problems of labour recruitment was the development of the factory dormitory system. It is important to describe briefly this system because it constituted a parallel system of employment to the oyakata system, and it influenced the eventual organizational outcome after the decline of internal contract systems in Japan.

During the early period of industrialization in Japan at least half of the labour force were women. Indeed it was not until 1920 that the proportion of women in the factory labour force first fell below 50%, and then it hovered around this mark until 1933 (Whitehill and Takezawa, 1968, pp. 73 and 417). The majority of these women workers were aged between 14 and 25, i.e. they were young and unmarried and they were expected to leave after marriage. These girls were usually employed on the basis of the factory dormitory system. In 1925 as many as 52% of all Japanese factories had dormitories attached, where 60% of the women workers and 17% of the male workers were accommodated (Harada, 1928, p. 121).

These factory dormitories arose from several causes:

(1) Most women were short-term employees coming from rural districts and going back there after two years or so. Therefore, there was a continual need for short-term accommodation.

(2) Dormitories and factory walls prevented the girls from escaping! (see Mears, 1976)

(3) Recruiting rural women workers was expensive, and in order to evade the expenses of recruitment and to get a quick and easy supply of labour it was common before the First World War, and during the economic boom of 1917–20, to abduct girls from one factory to another. The dormitory system was thought to be the best means of preventing the abduction of workers (Harada, 1928, pp. 122–3).

Living conditions in the dormitories were far from ideal. Before 1927 there was no government regulation of factory dormitories, and conditions could be atrocious. The food was poor, and indeed there were some strikes by the non-unionized girls over the quality of the food. Moreover, the girls were socially isolated and not allowed out except once or twice per month. For these women workers work was certainly a 'total institution'.

Thus it was in a curious way that the factory dormitory system contributed to the establishment of Japanese management – familyism. As a result of continual bad treatment of the girl workers there were widespread attacks on the textile employers and on the dormitory system itself. This stimulated some attempt at government regulation such as the 1927 regulation of workers' dormitories. And these pressures in turn pushed the employers towards welfare measures and paternalistic practices. Slowly the larger textile factories developed better housing, subsidized shopping facilities, sick pay and welfare funds, and extensive educational schemes for the girl-workers. These innovations were introduced under the 'umbrella' of a familial ideology, which stressed the fictive parent-child relation, and harmony and cooperation.

These ideas and practices spread beyond the textile industry, especially as most industries had some dormitory workers: for example 37% of chemical plants had attached dormitories in 1925 (Harada, 1928, p. 121, Table XVII). But this is to jump ahead of our story. With this background let us turn to look at the decline, and the circumstances of that decline, of the oyakata system in Japan.

The development of corporate paternalism

Oyakata control of the shopfloor survived through to the second decade of the twentieth century in Japan. It was not until 1910–14 that serious efforts were first made to destroy oyakata control in the labour market and on the shopfloor. As far as I can determine, it was the period from 1910 through the First World War to the early 1920s, which was the crucial period for the withering of internal control systems in Japan (Nakase, 1979, p. 178). As in the British case, this transformation of the labour process raises the question of why the process occurred when it did, and what were the mechanisms of transition.

The important point to note in the Japanese context is that it was attacks by employers on the oyakata's position that was the crucial factor in their decline. The period from 1912 to 1919 was a period of economic prosperity for Japan. The First World War in particular opened many new markets to Japanese goods with the temporary cessation of Western supplies. This economic boom was associated with, and helped to maintain, a new spurt in Japanese industrialization.

There was an increase in the scale of industrial plants; an increasing use of advanced technology, and a greater development of heavy industry employing more men than women. This was also the period when the zaibatsu, the large financial combines, extended their control over large areas of industry and commerce.

All these factors combined to produce more stable product markets plus increasing shortages of skilled labour. Slowly the logic of the employer's position shifted: employers became anxious to reduce the high rates of turnover, and to 'tie' employees to one enterprise (Taira, 1970 pp. 119–26; S.B. Levine, 1965, p. 645, Whitehill and Takezawa, 1968, p. 75; Dore, 1973, Chapter 14; Yoshino, 1968, p. 76; Nakane, 1970, p. 16; Cole, 1979, pp. 11 and 18).

The initial objectives of Japanese employers seem to have been limited and *ad hoc*. The main motives for change were first, a desire for more control over recruiting because of labour unrest and militancy. Second, the need for more trained and better trained workers, and, finally, the desire to reduce labour turnover.

The period 1912–20 saw the development of an industrial proletarian class, the beginnings of a labour movement, and the first serious signs of class struggle in Japan. The First World War had created soft labour market conditions and the number of trade unions increased rapidly – 71 unions were organized in the single year of 1918 (Harada, 1928 p. 185; see also Totten, 1966, p. 32). Growing conflict was reflected in the rice riots of 1918 and in the number of strikes, which grew through the war years until the peak was reached in 1919, with 497 strikes, though the post-war economic depression which began in 1920 pushed workers onto the defensive and reduced some of the overt signs of industrial unrest.

Beyond the bare strike figures the political consciousness of the Japanese labour movement had taken several radical turns. In the early 1920s revolutionary anarcho-syndicalism was the pervasive ideology, though the example of the Soviet Union quickly led to the the growth of communist ideas. Neither anarcho-syndicalism nor communism were acceptable to the Japanese government, however, and the government pursued a policy of rigid suppression of 'dangerous groups' and 'dangerous thoughts', with some toleration of reformist organizations. Nevertheless, 'toleration' meant constant police surveillance and spasmodic mass arrests of trade union leaders (see Orchard, 1930, pp. 390–2).

At the level of the firm, the threat of socialist and union activity frightened many employers into a desire for direct recruitment procedures, so that 'troublemakers' could be screened out. But this undermined the internal contract system at a crucial point. For the first time the company entered the oyakata's private domain and interfered with his right to hire and fire. Nor was this all; the acute shortage of skilled labour prompted a shift to formal training schemes. Most large firms established their own centralized training programmes (S.B. Levine, 1965, p. 646; Yoshino, 1968, p. 77; Evans 1970, pp. 116–17).

These shifts to direct recruitment and training, though limited in intent, looked like an employer takeover of some of the main functions of the oyakata. The oyakata of course resisted these threats to their control over the labour process, and according to both Levine and Tsuda top management's attempt to seize control of the shopfloor was a sizeable struggle marked by considerable hostility (S.B. Levine, 1965, p. 646; Tsuda, 1979, p. 40).

The resistance of the oyakata sometimes took a collective form – they responded by forming their own 'unions', utilizing the nexus of relationships in which they were involved. Thus the first substantial growth of trade unions in Japan depended in part on oyakata leadership. This situation parallels the British one, where the first trade unions were largely associations of sub-contractors. The counter-pressures of the oyakata led to a further politicization of shopfloor relationships.

From the employer's point of view this was a dangerous development. Japanese employers, like Western ones, worried about the possibility of the spread of socialist and unionist ideas from the workers upwards. Oyakata plus kokata could constitute a solid bloc of shopfloor opposition. This threat was underlined by the second form of oyakata opposition to managerial centralization. The oyakata had a virtual monopoly of technical expertise: most company officials were university graduates lacking practical shop experience, a situation very different from Britain, and the oyakata refused to pass on their skills and knowledge to mere strangers recruited from the impersonal labour market (S.B. Levine, 1965, pp. 646–7; for an example of a strike where workers and foremen acted together see Nakase, 1979, pp. 183–4).

The continued, organized resistance of the oyakata, and the oyakata's considerable control over technical knowledge, plus the fact that their social position was still seen as partly legitimate meant that the power balance was different from Britain. The Japanese employers could not merely cast the oyakata aside. Instead many employers tried to incorporate the oyakata. Employers offered the oyakata guarantees of lifelong employment, regular salaries, and even management recognition of oyakata-led unions. In sum, the oyakata were offered the preferential treatment and privileges of the managerial or 'shoku-in' class.

In general the employer's concessions, the 'lures of status and financial reward', won over many oyakata, and they became directly employed along with their retinue, who were slotted into organizational positions in line with the pre-existing status hierarchy (S.B. Levine, 1965, p. 647). Thus the oyakata subcontract groups became firmly meshed into the overall work organization.

The reason that the struggles over the transition to direct control systems in Japan were not even more bitter and protracted was because the employers were in a position to provide concessions. The economic thrust of Japanese industries during 1912–19 created a cluster of oligopolistic, large firms with a wake of small, external sub-contractors, often headed by retired employees, which were able to soak up the financial risks of fluctuating product markets. Thus the pay-off to the oyakata was supported by the creation of the dual structure of the Japanese economy.

Out of the incorporation of the oyakata developed some of the basic features of modern Japanese organizations – especially *nenko joretsu* and *shuskin koyo*. The nenko joretsu wage system is one in which length of service and age play a dominant role in determining a worker's take-home pay *rather than job performance or competence* (see Cole, 1971, pp. 75–8). What happened, according to Levine, was that 'once established within a firm, oyakata usually received the highest wages and benefits' which were scaled down for the kokata depending on length of attachment to the oyakata. New recruits 'had to take their place at the bottom of this hierarchy. Progression up the scale depended on demonstration of faithful devotion to work and respect for the status system' (1965, p. 648).

The nenko joretsu system served to attract recruits, to stabilize the labour force and to reduce labour turnover. The system is such (starting wage plus annual increments) that there are in-built financial penalties for moving from firm to firm.

The oyakata and kokata were also offered permanent employment or 'shuskin koyo'. This pattern of employment has continued to the present. Though we should note that the standard description of Japanese organizations, with its emphasis on the permanent employment system, tends to ignore the counter-balancing labour force without secure jobs and a career-commitment. Employers could offer permanent employment to the oyakata and kokata only by surrounding the system with layers of temporary workers, who grew in number throughout the period 1910–30.

Apart from lifetime employment and a seniority-based wage system (collectively known as *nenko seido*), what was happening to the structures of control on the shopfloor as a result of this transition process? In general, work remained organized around the key role of the oyakata. Unlike the British transition process, in which the institutionalization of new systems of control resulted in social fragmentation and the uncoupling of work-groups with an increasing divorce between formal and informal systems of control, the Japanese employers endeavoured to utilize the existing traditions of team working and collective responsibility as a continued element of work organization (see Dore, 1973, pp. 381–2).

In sum, nenko joretsu and shuskin koyo, plus the fact that the oyakata were able to retain some continued influence over recruitment and training overcame the resistance of the established oyakata leaders, and enabled the Japanese employers to maximize the use of the social cohesion of the oyakata-kokata relationships, which was particularly important during a period of labour turbulence.

The incorporation of the oyakata and their work-teams within a wider oraganizational frame was not the only social origin of the development of corporate paternalism in Japan. We have already discussed the factory dormitory system in Japan as a parallel employment system to the oyakata system. The institutionalization of welfare measures in the textile factories integrated by a familial ideology brought another paradigm to swim around in the Japanese cultural pool in the 1920s. Moreover, the ideological element – management familyism – served to spread the innovations of the textile manufacturers. One effect of a successful ideology is to convert existing social processes into something that is cumulative, rather than spasmodic and scattered. In addition there was the prospect for the employer that a revitalized paternalism could head-off labour trouble and increasing radical unionization. Many employers saw paternalism as a panacea for all the ills of industrial capitalism and specifically as an alternative to Western-type class struggle and this managerial strategy received active support from the Japanese government (Harada, 1928, pp. 234 and 275; Crawcour, 1978, p. 237).

Despite the limitations of the available data, it is fairly clear that welfare practices were still in the early 1920s concentrated in the textile industry, but that there was a slow diffusion across to other industries, and a rapid diffusion in the later 1920s and early 1930s. Indeed, so persuasive was the familial ideology, with its cultural resonances, that it succeeded in creating an acceptance of managerial strategies by many workers. Large Japanese firms were singularly successful by the early 1930s in creating a docile labour force (Taira, 1970, p. 160; Hazama and Kaminski, 1979, p. 73).

The end-result, then, of the Japanese transition process was that the paternalistic paradigm of the textile employers merged with the development of nenko seido to create a distinctive Japanese employment system, namely corporate paternalism, in the late 1920s and early 1930s. The best analysis of this organizational form is provided by Hiroshi Hazama. He suggests that corporate paternalism in its pre-war mould essentially consisted of five characteristics:

(1) A hierarchy based upon ascribed status as a principle or organ-
     ization;
(2) The permanent employment system including career progression;
(3) A wage system in which the family allowance is the basic element;
(4) Welfare schemes;
(5) Familial ideology as applied to labour/management relations.
     (Hazama, 1981).[5]

Such were the beginnings of the Japanese transition process from
indirect to direct systems of employment and control. The story of later
developments is more familiar, and has been told, and well told,
elsewhere (see Dore, 1973; Cole, 1971).

The influence of Taylorism in Japan
It is extremely difficult to obtain material on the influence of Taylorism
in Japan. Fortunately Okuda and Nakase have recently done some
pioneering research in this area which enables us to move beyond
guesswork and surmise (Nakase, 1979; Okuda, 1972; Cole, 1979, pp.
108–11).

The conventional wisdom is that Taylorism had no influence on
Japanese industrial development. In fact the historical reality is more
complex: Taylorism *did* attract the attention of Japanese managers and
government officials. Taylor's 'Principles of scientific management'
was quickly translated into Japanese under the title of 'The secret of
saving lost motion', and, when it was published later in pamphlet form
it sold several million copies with some employers giving free copies to
their workers (Cole, 1979, p. 109; Hazama and Kaminski, 1979, p. 99).

In general, there were two waves of interest in Taylorism in Japan.
The first from 1912 to 1920 was partly stimulated by the Kyochokai
(The Conciliation Society). The primary function of this semi-govern-
mental body was to promote corporate paternalism as a means of
reducing labour conflict (Dore, 1973, p. 397). In addition, the
Kyochokai had a section – the Industrial Efficiency Institute – devoted
to the diffusion of scientific management ideas.

The areas of industry that were affected most by the first wave of
enthusiasm for Taylorism, according to Cole, were:

the Navy Arsenals, the National Railway, and the textile industry, with innovations in selected footwear and cosmetic companies. Many of these initial
efforts were directed towards standardizing work procedures rather than
towards undertaking thorough-going time-and-motion studies.

(Cole, 1979, p. 109)

Thus Taylorism was used as a vehicle for job analysis and standardized procedures rather than as a comprehensive managerial control system. Indeed this extended to the incentive aspects of Taylorism as well. In most of the affected industries during this period wage payments were not based on individual output norms, and 'The Taylor principle of high wages for high efficiency was simply ignored.' (Cole, 1979, p. 109).

There was a second wave of enthusiasm for Taylorism in Japan which ran from the mid-1920s to the end of the 1930s. This was associated with the world depression and a wider rationalization movement. As in Britain, scientific management during this period was conceived in broader terms as 'the American type of industrial system', embracing mass production, standardization and the elimination of waste (see Harada, 1928, p. 273). Again the government played a significant role in stimulating an interest in Taylorism. The Japanese Industrial Association was established in 1931 specifically to diffuse scientific management techniques, and part of its role was to train work-study technicians. This active government intervention contrasts sharply to Britain where most work-study engineers were trained by Bedaux and other private consultants. Nevertheless, the overall effect of the Japanese efforts was one of scattered trials, and in many cases Taylorite techniques, especially work-study, were tried and abandoned as the administration costs became apparent. Indeed, individually-based incentive schemes were entirely discarded during the period of war-time control in Japan (Whitehill and Takezawa, 1968, p. 78).

Overall, Japanese industrialization did absorb some Taylorite ideas, especially in relation to job analysis and work procedures; but Taylorism was adapted and diluted according to *existing* work practices and values, and according to the increasing thrust of the institutionalization of paternalism in Japan. On the shopfloor Taylorism was adapted to the fact that work remained organized around fluid job boundaries within work-teams. Secondly, Taylorism in the West involves the rigid separation of planning and doing, resulting in the downgrading of the foreman's role, whereas in Japan the foreman/oyakata retained considerable production planning responsibilities.

These differences between the effect of Taylorism in the West and its much diluted and adapted influence in Japan has led some Japanese industrial sociologists to argue that:

If Japanese operators with advanced knowledge of both technology and culture were obliged to work under the Taylor system without encouragement of voluntary will and creative initiative, they would lose much of their interest in work itself.

The natural outcome would be: labour efficiency would decline markedly; there would be no will to make good products in the labour force; absenteeism would increase; labour turnover would increase critically.

(Kaora Ishikawa, quoted in *Financial Times*, 24 August 1979)

This is salesman's talk as much as anything – Ishikawa is a leading advocate of quality control circles – nevertheless it indicates the perceived opposition between the influence of Taylorism in the West and the historical development of Japanese work systems.[6]

Summary and conclusions

What we have sought to do in this chapter is to emphasize the importance of internal contract systems in Japan, and suggest the utility of this concept for understanding not only the nature of Japanese pre-bureaucratic work organization, but also the dynamics of the transition to direct control over the labour process.

If we recognize the widespread importance of contract systems as forms of co-domination, then it leads us on to ask questions about their demise. The critical period for the decline of such systems in Britain was from the 1870s to 1900, with some 'over-run' up to the First World War; whilst the critical period for Japan was probably from 1910 to the early 1920s. The ultimate organizational outcome in Japan was corporate paternalism, with considerable shopfloor control still exercised by the oyakata and with continued team working. Japanese employers were aware of Taylorism and scientific management in the 1920s, but its influence was diluted to fit in with existing work practices and values. In Britain, the organizational outcome of the transition process was neo-Taylorite forms of industrial organization, compromised by the continued informal power of shopfloor foremen. Also in the British case, work-groups were unanchored into the system, and proved impenetrable obstacles to centralized managerial control.

Many factors entered into these different channels of change. The transition process started from different cultural bases, and occurred under different economic and ideological conditions. Within these different contexts what we have focused on is how the labour process is shaped by the conflicting patterns and struggles of managerial centralization. Too many analyses of Japan tend to adopt a 'cookbook' perspective with the organizational elite acting as cultural chefs building up organizational models with a meaty base borrowed from Krupps and a light garnish from indigenous cultural sources. This supposed cordon bleu mastery ignores the fact that organizational elites are acting within constrained social milieu, facing oppositional threats or perceived threats. As I have emphasized, it is the dialectical inter-play of employer structures of control and forms of resistance which primarily shapes the labour process.

Given the above perspective, it is useful to summarize the factors affecting the power position of the internal contractors and traditional foremen in Britain and Japan:

Britain	*Japan*
1 Opposition by employers to delegated modes of control. Employers wanted more direct control over the total labour process.	1 Opposition of employers to position of oyakata. Employers wanted more direct control over recruitment and training.
2 Opposition by (most) trade unions to internal contractors. During the critical transition period there was the formation and consolidation of the unskilled unions who were virulently opposed to the contract system.	2 Few trade unions, and many of the ones that did exist were formed or used by the oyakata to gain support.
3 Low social legitimacy of the internal contractors. Associated with 'sweating'.	3 Much greater legitimacy of oyakata.
4 Deteriorating internal group relationships. Internal contract was no longer an effective structure of control from the employer's point of view.	4 Internal ties were still strong.

What these differences in the position of the internal contractor imply is that it was much more difficult for the contractors to become a concerted focus of opposition to managerial centralization in Britain than in Japan. Thus it was possible for British employers to sweep the contractors away, but the absence of a systematic theory of management resulted in traditional foremen inheriting many of the powers and privileges of the contractors, and these foremen provided a rumbling resistance to Taylorism and bureaucratization right through the interwar period: a source of opposition which occasionally united with workers' resistance.

In Japan the picture was different. Far from being associated with 'sweating' and exploitation, the oyakata were seen as the inheritors of traditional Japanese virtues. Their power base and leverage over the labour process were such that in many cases it was in the employers' interests to maintain their privileged position within the organizational frame and so utilize the social solidarity of the oyakata/kokata work groups.

In general then, the employers' strategy in Britain and even more in the USA, was based on Taylorism and bureaucratic control which involved superseding the powers of the contractors and traditional foremen, centralizing managerial control, deskilling part of the workforce and often assuming a minimum relationship between the organization and the shopfloor worker. In Japan, the employer strategy was one of incorporation: utilizing existing social relationships for production purposes, and maintaining an ideological control.

Incorporation and ideological control in Japan provided the means for preventing the build-up of a tradition of industrial craftsmanship: commitment to skill dissolved into commitment to organization and organizational status. In the British situation, job fragmentation and Taylorite rationalization were pursued within a context of economic depression, mass unemployment, low job security and ideological poverty. British capitalism has still not succeeded in solving the inheritance of these historical conjunctures.

11 The Development of Work Organization in the USA

Our understanding of the evolution of work organization in Britain is partly shaped by the axes of comparison. The comparison with Japan has served to highlight certain features. The second axis of comparison is between Britain and the USA, which will throw a spotlight onto different processes and trends. The implications of the three-way comparison will be educed in Chapter 12.

Background to American industrialization

In 1840 the United States was predominantly an agricultural society: less than 10% of the labour force were occupied in manufacturing (Lebergott, 1964 p. 510). The process of industrialization took place largely between 1850 and 1880. The conventional criterion for defining a society as industrial is when less than 50% of the labour force is engaged in primary production. Using this index, the USA became an industrialized country about 1880, which makes it a latecomer in comparison with Britain (1841) and France (1866), though the USA cannot be defined as a 'late-developer' in the same category as Japan. The proportion of the US labour force in agriculture and other primary production fell from 53.5 to 31.6% in the forty years between 1870 and 1910. This transformation of economic activity signified the emergence of the USA as a major industrial power. As Rose puts it, 'in less than fifty years an isolationist, agrarian society transformed itself into an internationally aggressive, economically imperialist, industrial nation' (Rose, 1975, p. 55). The rapidity of the US's growth is indicated by the fact that in 1880 the population of the USA was 50.2 million and its national income was $7.2 billion, whilst the population of Britain was 35.1 million with a national income of $5.2 billion. However, by 1900, the American population and national income were almost double that of Britain's (Chandler, 1976, p. 47).

In Japan, as we have seen, the role of the state was crucial in the industrialization process, whereas in the United States the government only took a background, facilitating role. For example, the government supported the building and extension of the railroads – not a negligible factor in American economic growth, as between 10 and 20% of gross domestic investment between 1850 and 1880 was allocated to the railroads (Temin, 1975, p. 43). Nevertheless, the main flows of investment were not determined at government level, but by business firms, as can be seen from Table 11.1.

Table 11.1 US distribution of gross domestic capital formation by category of user (%)

	Government	Business firms	Households
1889–1918	7	74.9	18.1
1899–1928	9.4	71.1	19.6
1909–38	14.3	67.7	17.9
1919–48	15.9	67.3	16.8
1929–55	15.9	66.6	17.5

Source: Kuznets, 1961, Table 21, p. 178

Reliable data for the earlier period are not available, but there is no reason to suppose that the pattern of investment activity was substantially different. Only with the world depression of the 1930s did the government share start to become significant. In general, the US, like Britain, had a large capitalist class who dominated the industrialization process.

American industrialization was also similar to the British process in that it began with many small and medium-sized family firms. However, the distinctive characteristic of American industrialization was the rapidity with which the economy threw off the familial framework of the early firms and shifted to an economy of large corporations.

In relation to that process there were two important merger waves in the American economy: around the turn of the century, peaking in 1898–1902, and 1926–30. The first merger wave was in many respects the most important. It transformed many industries that had formerly been characterized by small and medium-sized clusters of firms, and it laid the foundations for the oligopolistic structure which has marked most of American industry in the twentieth century. The extent of the concentration of capital which occurred during the first US merger wave is indicated by the fact that between 1896 and 1905 the hundred largest American corporations quadrupled in size, controlling 40% of industry by 1905 (R.L. Nelson, 1959).

The development of large, oligopolistic corporations in the USA was reflected at plant level. In 1870 a factory with 500 employees was considered to be a large plant, and only a handful existed. However, by 1900 more than 1500 plants exceeded this size and nearly a third employed more than 1000 people. There were seventy factories employing more than 2000, and fourteen employing more than 6000. By the 1920s, plant sizes had increased by another order of magnitude, with Ford's River Rouge plant acknowledged as the largest with 68,000 employees (D. Nelson, 1975, pp. 4 and 7–9).

The development of huge, managerialist corporations in the USA at an early period should be contrasted to the situation in Britain, where, as we have seen, familial and proprietorial influence remained strong until very late into the inter-war period (see Chapter 8). Secondly, the American picture should be contrasted to that of Japan, where the zaibatsu were the predominant organizational form. The zaibatsu were of course family-dominated conglomerates (see Chapter 10). The USA is a large market, both economically and geographically, whereas in Japan, firms reached the size of the domestic market fairly quickly and the organizational elite were faced with the problem of how to grow further. At that historical juncture it was difficult to compete internationally, so the Japanese capitalists diversified across industries that had domestic markets (Patrick, 1975, pp. 190–1).

The most important and oft-cited characteristic of the development of an industrial labour force in America was the successive waves of immigration, which created a culture of ethnicity and job instability. Though the proportion of foreign-born people in the USA never rose above 15% the gross population figures conceal the fact that large numbers of immigrants and immigrants' children were concentrated in American factories. In 1907–8 the percentage of foreign-born workers varied between 35% per cent in the boot and shoe industry and 85% in sugar refining. Only in the most traditional industries – paper and wood pulp, boots and shoes, tobacco and glass – did the proportion of native-born to native-father outweigh the huge mass of recent immigrant workers (D. Nelson, 1975, Table 5, p. 80).

What were the main effects of the migrant origins of the American working class? There were three important results from our point of view. First, there was often a wide social gulf between employer and employee in comparison with more homogenous cultural ties in Britain and Japan. Thus American employees were more likely to be dehumanized and treated as a commodity (cf. Noble, 1977, p. 58). This showed itself in the widespread use of racial stereotypes for recruitment and promotion decisions. Apart from the well-known views of blacks as lazy and child-like, many other ethnic groups were judged in terms of 'racial efficiency' – the Poles were stupid and suitable only for heavy work; the Italians were untrustworthy and unreliable; the Jews were good at light, repetitive work (see D. Nelson, 1975, pp. 81–2).

The second effect of the mass immigration on the structuration of the American working class was profound and long-lasting. Essentially, community, religious or kinship ties became paramount, surpassing occupational links in many cases. Moreover, these primary, ethnic-based affiliations were often reinforced by secret societies. In many American towns and industrial centres there sprang up a host of secret, fraternal orders. These secret societies were not just social centres, but served as mutual assistance groups, paying out money, for example, in the case of industrial injury. In other words, the secret societies were ethnically and religiously-based functional equivalents of early trade unions, but as such they *segmented* the labour force and stunted the development of real labour unions (Navin, 1950, pp. 165–7; Bodnar, 1977).

Finally, the waves of immigrants created an ethnic turnover of labour as some groups started by filling the worst, lowest-paid jobs and then moved on into better work conditions. This cycle of national groups helped to create a culture of casualism, of rapid job-mobility and transient links with the employing organization.

The result was staggering turnover rates in the period 1900–1920s. In 1919, in the first detailed study of industrial labour turnover, Sumner Slichter concluded that the average factory labour turnover was 100% per year (Slichter, 1919, p. 16). In a survey of 105 factories and mines covering a wide variety of industries, Slichter found the distribution of turnover rates to be as shown in Table 11.2. The size of the labour turnover varied from 348 to 8%. Moreover, this data was largely collected in 1914, which was a depression year when turnover was below normal, and thus the figures understate the extent of inter-firm mobility. Overall then, an employer with a large plant of 5000 employees could expect to have to recruit 5000, perhaps even 15,000 people in a year, in order to maintain his labour force and production.

It should not be assumed that all pre-First World War US employers

Table 11.2 Labour turnover in 105 US establishments, 1914

Size of turnover	Number of establishments	% of establishments
200% +	11	10.5
100–200%	30	28.6
80–100%	9	8.6
60–80%	21	20.0
40–60%	18	17.1
20–40%	11	10.5
Below 20%	5	4.8

Source: Calculated from Slichter, 1919, Table 1, p. 22

were aware of their labour turnover rates. It was only as a few firms began to collect data on recruitment and discharges that the extent of the endless reshuffling of people and jobs became known. The creation of central personnel departments was *both* an answer to the perceived problems of recruitment, turnover and skill shortages, *and* the mechanism by which the extent of the problems were delineated.

However, the instability of the US labour force should not be seen simply as *sui generis*. We have already noted the very high rates of labour turnover in the early Japanese factories (see Chapter 10). American employers, then, like Japanese and European employers were faced with persistent problems of labour shortages and staggering rates of labour turnover. The problems were the same; what turned out to be different were the answers.

Extent and nature of internal contract systems in the USA

The relationship between the employer and the first-line supervisor was rarely defined in the nineteenth century American plant, and this makes all simple definitions of the early work systems hazardous at best. What is clear, however, is that in most industries the nineteenth century US plant was as fragmented and decentralized an organization as its British counterpart. According to Nelson, delegated structures of control were most entrenched in the New England and Mid-Atlantic machine factories where the internal contract system remained an important form of industrial organization until the 1900s (Nelson, 1975, p. 36). Clawson (1980) argues that inside contracting was extensively used and that the system was so prevalent that it was taken for granted.

What, then, was the specific role of the internal contractor in the American context? In general, the structure of relationships and decision-making powers were remarkably similar to the British pattern. Thus Buttrick describes the role of the contractor as follows:

the management of a firm provided floor-space and machinery, supplied raw material and working capital, and arranged for the sale of the finished product. The gap between raw material and finished product, however, was filled not by paid employees arranged in the descending hierarchy . . . but by contractors, to whom the production job was delegated. They hired their own employees, supervised the work process, and received a piece-rate from the company for completed goods. The income of a contractor consisted of the difference between his wage bill and his sales to the company, plus the day pay he earned as an employee himself. The company's largest single expense was the amount paid to the contractors for finished goods.

(Buttrick, 1952, pp. 205–6)

The only significant difference from the British situation was that British contractors often retained more independence: the latter sometimes provided part of the working capital, and often did not receive a day wage. In other words, the British contractor was more of an independent capitalist working for an anticipated profit (see Chapter 6). Nevertheless, American contractors often succeeded in making handsome profits. Thus Buttrick makes the point that internal contractors could earn more than any manager, and that there were contractors who drove 'to work in fine carriages carrying canes and sporting stickpins. Such men it turned out, had delegated all the dirty work in their departments to assistants and were "outmanagering" the managers.'! (Buttrick, 1952, p. 214, footnote 15 and p. 217). As a consequence the contractor enjoyed a high social status both inside and outside the workshop.

Daniel Nelson distinguishes between the internal contract system and the 'helper system'. The helper system consisted of craftsmen hiring, controlling and paying small groups of 'helpers' or unskilled assistants. However, the system involved more restricted managerial functions than internal contract; often the craftsmen worked under a company foreman and were constrained by more developed cost-accounting systems. Nelson summarizes the differences this way:

> In their relations with management, skilled workers in the textile, glass, pottery and iron industries thus occupied a position considerably inferior to contractors of the New England machine shops. Like the contractors they were their own bosses, made high wages, and enjoyed an enviable social position in and out of the shop. But they had fewer helpers, did more of the actual work themselves, and had fewer strictly managerial responsibilities. And they saw themselves as workmen rather than managers. Whereas the contractors considered them-selves important company officials and long remained a bulwark against unionism, the male spinners, glass blowers, potters, puddlers, rollers, and moulders formed the most powerful labour unions of the manufacturing sector.
>
> (D. Nelson, 1975, p. 40)

Nevertheless, Nelson admits that the helper system bore many similarities to internal contract and given the ambiguities and changes through time, it seems better to regard the 'helper system', as a *form* of indirect employment and control (see Chapter 6) analogous to large-scale contracting, especially as there was no clear dividing line between contracting and the helper system.[1] The basic structural arrangements which carried market relations right onto the factory floor are common whatever the size of the contracting unit.

The internal relationships of the American contracted work-groups bore both similarities and differences from the British pattern. It was certainly the case that familial relations were incorporated into many work-teams. For example, several generations of coalminers, iron molders, etc. built work organizations around actual and fictive paternal relationships. More generally, the power of contractors to control access to jobs meant that they filled positions with relatives, friends and sympathizers (Soffer, 1960, pp. 151 and 154; Clawson, 1980, p. 107). However, one striking difference from the British pattern of relations arose from the immigrant origins of the American labour force. The racial and ethnic divisions in American society were reproduced at the level of the work organization and the work-team. English-speaking immigrants were regarded as dominant, and consequently it was considered acceptable for British butty miners to underpay their Italian or Slav helpers, or for iron rollers and puddlers to exploit their 'foreign' assistants. Thus, internal contract, in the USA, was a mechanism for the 'justifiable exploitation' of newer immigrant groups (Soffer, 1960, p. 151; M. Davis, 1980, p. 37).

Internal contract systems in some form were important in the development of American industry, but how widespread were such systems in the nineteenth century? The spread of such systems varied both geographically and by industry. As we have said, fully-fledged internal contract systems tended to be confined to the East Coast, to the more traditional industrial areas in the New England and the Mid-Atlantic states. It should be remembered that the USA, more than other societies, was subject to waves of industrialization. The North-East was the primary industrial area, and was influenced by European, especially British, traditions. The Mid-West was the second area to industrialize, and Detroit and Chicago provided a very different social terrain which led to the development of 'Fordism'. The third and most recent wave of industrialization has been centred in California. Apart from geographical variations, the extent of internal contract systems depended in the USA on industry. Table 11.3 provides a snapshot summary of industrial and occupational areas in which there is clear evidence of internal contracting in the pre-1914 period.

Table 11.3 raises the question of the relation between internal contract as a set of shopfloor relationships and labour unionism. This is not a question which I can deal with in detail here, but a brief discussion provides a fascinating insight into American labour history. As I have pointed out the larger contractors typically were staunch opponents of unionism, but the smaller contractors with their dual status as managers and skilled workers founded many of the pioneer AFL unions, and constituted dominant blocs within these unions. However, it is necessary to bear in mind that the overall union density in the USA was low: about 6% of the potential manufacturing workers in 1900 and 12% in 1915. Thus major parts of the pottery, iron, foundry and glass industries, etc. remained unorganized, despite the bargaining power of the craftsmen-contractors (Wolman, 1924, pp. 137–55; Soffer, 1960, pp. 148 and 149; and Nelson, 1975, p. 47).

From the union perspective, it was necessary to admit internal contractors in order to control wage levels and to maintain influence

Table 11.3 Some examples of internal contract in the USA, pre–1914

Industry	Reinforcing causes of internal contract	Relations to labour unions
Iron and steel industry Puddlers and rollers were the contractors. They were responsible for the operations of parts of the mill. Contract system established throughout industry.	(a) British tradition (b) Sliding-scale system (c) Technical knowledge and skills	Founders of the predecessors of Amalgamated Association of Iron, Steel & Tin Workers (1876). Later constituted powerful groups within the union. Helpers were not members of the union.
Foundaries, esp. stove moulding Craftsmen moulders hired, trained and directed 'bucks', learners and helpers. Known as the 'berkshire' system.	(a) Tradition of self-employment as a side-enterprise to the blast furnace (b) Piece-work	Founded and controlled Molders' Union. Union formally opposed to berkshire system, but ignored and evaded by the contractors.
Coal industry In anthracite mining the piecemaster employed several helpers. Even in bituminous mining the pick-miner was unsupervised.	(a) Traditions of British mining (b) Difficulty of supervision (c) Piece-work tradition (d) Manual skills of miners	Initiated predecessors of Mine Workers' Union. Constituted major part of membership.
Engineering From the 1830s to mid-1890s large and small contractors were common in the New England firms.	(a) British traditions (b) Lack of effective cost-accounting systems	—
Armament industry In armaments plants, such as Winchester and Colt, production was controlled by large contractors who ran entire departments, and small contractors with one or two helpers.	(a) British tradition (b) Skill-base and technical ignorance of early employers	—

Industry	Factors	Union role
Government arsenals Since their origin government arsenals had used master-tool builders and master mechanics as internal contractors.	(a) British tradition (b) Skill-base	—
Potteries Contractors known as jiggermen, kilnmen, etc. The jiggermen usually employed three helpers. Contract system universal in the pottery industry.	(a) British traditions (b) Piece-work (c) Skill-base	Dominant group in the United Brotherhood of Operative Potters. The helpers refused to join the union of the journeymen employers.
Glass industry Both the blowers (glass bottle trade) and the flatteners (window glass trade) employed their own helpers and auxiliary labour.	(a) British tradition (b) Skill-base	Dominated the Glass Bottle Blowers Association, and the Window Glass Workers, though both unions formally opposed to internal contract.
Newspaper printing Compositor-foremen supervised less skilled crafts in small shops and managed composing room.	(a) British tradition (b) Lack of interest of publishers in production management (c) Piece-work (pre-linotype)	Dominated typographical union by secret society and alliance with conservative union leaders.
Clothing Skilled tailors or machine operators in ready-made clothing were often sub-contractors hiring and training less-skilled labour.	(a) Lack of management and fragmentation of production units combined with homework sweating system (b) Piece-work (c) Sub-contracting made easier because of proportion of immigrants (83%) in the labour force	Dominated Journeymen Tailors who were the initiators of the unions that became the United Garment Workers and ILGWU.

Sources: Based on Soffer, 1960, Table 1, p. 142, and pp. 160–3. Additional sources: Ashworth, 1915, pp. 24, 30–1, 67–77, 89–90, 125 and 127; Buttrick, 1952, p. 207 *passim*; Deyrup, 1948, pp. 101–2, 149–50 and 161–2; Navin, 1950, pp. 142 and 142–9; D. Nelson, 1975, pp. 36–40; Stone, 1973, pp. 19–30; Elbaum and Wilkinson, 1979

wherever the employer was hostile to unionism. The contractors in their turn used trade unions as vehicles for developing sets of rules for limiting competition amongst themselves, for restricting entry to the trade, especially of helpers and unskilled assistants, and for maintaining job jurisdiction (Soffer, 1960, pp. 149–50, 152–3 and 156; Ashworth, 1915).

The question of the relation between the contract system and unionism is intertwined with the more general question of the relations between the skilled and unskilled. There were several sources of tension and conflict between the skilled, whether contractors or not, and the unskilled mass of the American labour force during the period 1870–1917.

First, there was the continuing relation of exploitation between the contractors and the unskilled subordinate workers. The skilled contractors typically shunted all dirty and low-grade work onto the helpers, and sometimes even the *total* burden of work. Thus a writer in the *Iron Molders' Journal* in 1873 tells the following story:

> Let us pay a visit to a carwheel shop. What do we find? Two men working together: one is a molder, the other is a helper. Between them they do two days' work. The helper prepares the chill, inserts the pattern, does all the ramming, and the molder finishes the mold: but if it is a blue Monday, the molder lays back on his dignity, and the helper becomes both molder and helper for the day.
>
> (*Iron Molders' Journal*, October, 1873, p. 132)

However, when it came to pay, the skilled contractors would insist on maintaining high differentials in order to generate considerable profits. Thus, in the iron and steel industry, a committee of the United Sons of Vulcan in 1870 considered: 'that a helper should receive more than one-third, no reasonable man would assert, for when we consider that the helper is, as it were, an apprentice learning the business, one-third is ample' (*Vulcan Record*, Vol. 1, no. 6, 1870, p. 20). It is doubtful if the helpers considered one-third to be 'ample'. Moreover, when trade was slack the skilled contractors would often take advantage of their superior bargaining power to pay their helpers even less than the standard norm (see Ashworth, 1915, pp. 38, 69, 75 and 77. cf. Stone, 1973, p. 22).

The second source of conflict between the skilled and the unskilled relates to the control of job opportunities. The craftsmen in most industries continually complained that the helpers were allowed to encroach upon the work of skilled men. In general, American union policies towards helpers and assistants varied with their vulnerability to helpers as agents to deskilling. It is important to appreciate that the unskilled assistants of the skilled men acted as a running threat to their skill status since in practice, many of them were as technically competent as their superior. As Ashworth puts it, 'Helpers are conducive to the disintegration and the overcrowding of a trade'. (1915, pp. 28, 32, 42, 55–8, and 69). Given this standing threat of deskilling, many of the early unions attempted to confine helpers to 'helpers' work' and thus maintain job jurisdictions. In addition, the craftsmen and contractors attempted to bar the entry of the helper into skilled work. There were absolute, or modified, restrictions of entry of the helpers to the trade. Though by 1915 most unions had some provision whereby helpers could be promoted to journeymen, in reality the possibility was so remote that resentment was rife (Ashworth, 1915, pp. 40 and 109; Soffer, 1960, p. 156). The American unions were largely unsuccessful in their long-term efforts to control rigidly job opportunities or to restrict the number and promotion of the helpers and unskilled auxiliaries. Nevertheless, an accelerating division of labour intensified the existing tensions.

At the level of the plant, the skilled contractors often blocked the collective organization of the unskilled and semi-skilled. They would always try to 'minimize and prevent strikes of the less skilled which would cause them to lose wages' (Soffer, 1960, p. 153; cf. Monds, 1976, p. 87). For example, in 1873, the iron workers' helpers in Chicago went on strike against the wishes of the skilled men. The iron workers, despite great inconvenience, continued to work. The helpers, who were thus deprived of jobs, went to Knightsville, Indiana and took the places of the skilled boilers who were on strike at that time! (Ashworth, 1915, pp. 82 and 93–4; also see p. 103).

At the national level, the continuing desire of the contractors to maintain their organizational and occupational position was a significant factor in the limited scope of the early American labour unions. The early unions were built on a craft and status exclusiveness. Thus the influence of the skilled contractors in shaping union policies and the policies of the AFL long prevented the unionization of the many unskilled and semi-skilled groups (Ashworth, 1915, p. 88; Soffer, 1960, pp. 153 and 159).[2]

The demise of internal contract in the USA
The decades from the end of the American Civil War (1865) until the 1890s were a period of enormous growth and development in American industry. The 1890s in particular were a prosperous period, and many of the organizational and managerial changes which were occurring in the USA did so within a context of widening markets and expanding firms. Contemporaries were certainly aware that the period was one of organizational transition. One management commentator in 1899 wrote:

The present is a time of transition under the stimulus of a wave of remarkable prosperity. Old-fashioned methods of administration are beginning to show signs of wearing out and of being no longer equal to the strain and intensity of modern industrial working. Very searching questions are, consequently, frequently asked as to the probable direction in which reorganization is required. (J. Slater Lewis, *Engineering Magazine*, 1899, p. 59. Quoted in Litterer, 1961, p. 469)

In this and the following two sections, we need to look at the signs of 'old-fashioned methods of administration' 'wearing-out'; ask why this was the case; and briefly examine the bureaucratization of American shopfloor relationships under the influence of the systematic management movement and Taylorism.

As in Britain, the critical period for the demise of internal contract systems seems to have been from 1870 to the 1900s, with some overrun up to the First World War. If anything, the decline of contract systems occurred earlier in the USA, but this still remains open to investigation. In addition, the demise of internal contract in the USA seems largely to have been the result of *pressure from above*. When employers were able to develop the capability of managing their labour force and cost systems, they abandoned the internal contractors in the hope that they themselves would realize the profits those contractors had been earning. In the British case the contractors were squeezed from both ends as the unskilled reacted against the petty tyrannies of the butty masters and the gang-bosses (see Chapter 6). In the USA there was some pressure from below on the contract system; for example the potters' helpers and the iron-workers' helpers were usually unwilling to join the unions of their contractor–employers, and were sometimes militant in their protests. But, as we have seen, the unskilled remained largely unorganized until the New Deal era. Consequently, the pressure from below on the contract system was attenuated by the relative docility of the unskilled workers, a passivity which was assisted by the waves of mass immigration, and the communal acceptance of 'justifiable exploitation' (Soffer, 1960, p. 151).

Pressure from above on the contracting system was stimulated by the fact that the larger contractors were so successful that they posed a running threat to the status of company officials in terms of income and social prestige (Clawson, 1980, p. 122). Moreover, in relation to shopfloor control, senior management feared divided and segmented loyalties, and even sent trusted employees to get jobs in some of the departments and act as 'company spies' (Buttrick, 1952, p. 214, footnote 15 and pp. 215–17). Many companies were ignorant of the actual piece-rates paid by the contractors to the workers, and even more ignorant of the actual techniques used in production (Buttrick, 1952, pp. 208, 209 and 211). Despite the top-down bargaining pressures on the contractors it is clear that the monopoly power of the large contractors and their day-to-day control of the labour process threatened capitalist control over production.

The problems of lack of direct capitalist control showed themselves in relation to labour recruitment. The period around 1900 was one of labour unrest, especially amongst the skilled workers of New England. These 'rumblings of trade union activity' affected many metal-working companies, and management became anxious to screen all potential employees. As a result all hiring was ordered to be cleared through the superintendent's office. As in Japan, this step towards central hiring and firing interfered with the contract system in a crucial way. The contractors no longer had sole control over hiring and firing, which undermined their day-to-day authority position (see Chapter 10).

Even without the threat of unionization there were problems of labour recruitment under the contract system. Many US plants were located in company towns or small industrial centres. At the same time the individual contractor had the responsibility of maintaining an adequate labour force in his department in the context of a limited, local labour pool. With gradual expansion the local labour market, plus the use of kinship ties to suck in immigrants, sufficed. But the rapid expansion of the 1880s and 1890s meant that the informal system of recruitment failed to provide adequate skilled workers. The result, as we have seen, was the centralization of hiring in employment departments. By 1920 about 500 corporations had installed employment departments (Eilbert, 1959). However, the centralization of the hiring function vitally weakened the position of the contractors. As Navin puts it, 'Hiring constituted a very small part of their prerogatives, but it was the keystone of their authority. With the loss of the ability to hire went the loss of the ability to set beginning wages, and with that loss went the foundation of the job-work system.' (1950, p. 148).

The resistance by the internal contractors themselves to managerial centralization varied in different industries. In connection with the larger contractors, there is little sign of overt resistance in Navin's account of the transition process at the Whitin Machine works, and Buttrick sees the transition at the Winchester Arms company as an easy one from management's point of view (Navin, 1950, pp. 147–9; Buttrick, 1952, p. 219). In general, opposition in the engineering industries seems to have been bypassed or converted into more passive forms. Nevertheless, we need to set against this the description by several labour historians of the violent events that transformed the labour process in the American iron and steel industry which had involved craft-forms of contracting. In relation to craft-contractors there were three types of transition process. The size of the United States and the mobility of capital permitted new plants to be set up in non-union areas such that new drafts of workers took the organization of work as given. Alternatively, in many of the older industrial areas there was a limited oppositional base because the mobility of labour weakened both commitment and the potential for collective organization. But in some old plants in craft union centres confrontational deskilling occurred as employers struggled to transform shopfloor autonomies.

The rise of systematic management

Several factors facilitated the shift to centralized managerial control during the period 1880–1920, of which the most crucial was the systematic management movement in the USA. This led to a greater awareness of both Taylorism and developments in cost accounting than in Britain, where there was a lack of an integrated theory of organization and shop management such that managerial techniques and practices were scattered, *ad hoc* and opportunistic (see Chapter 7). In contrast, the systematic management movement in the USA attracted a great many adherents.[3]

Systematic management arose in part out of the increasing specialization in American industry. This specialization was of two types – product specialization and process specialization. After the end of the Civil War product specialization, whereby a firm sharply reduced the range and variety of its products, proceeded very rapidly in the USA. In parallel with this went increasing labour specialization and fragmentation combined with specialized machinery and technology. The increasing division of labour linked to systematic management in two ways. First, in order to accomplish an extensive division of labour, sophisticated job analysis was necessary. Second, the increasing division of labour created intensified problems of integration and co-ordination.

In general there were three social sources for the systematic management movement: (i) the formal organization theorists, primarily based on the railroads; (ii) the shop management movement, primarily based on metalworking shops and centred on the mechanical engineers; and (iii) cost-accounting, which is more difficult to locate socially, because it was more widespread and diffuse (Aitken, 1960, pp. 17–18). These disparate origins meant that there was a certain vagueness about the meaning and use of the term 'systematic management':

although many authors wrote about systems, none spelled out what was included in a system. To some, system meant mostly cost accounting systems. To others, it apparently was mainly production control systems. To most, however, the concept seemed to contain more than these highly specific elements. The common idea appeared to involve an overall approach to operating a business. . . .

(Litterer, 1961, p. 474)

In some ways this vagueness is not too surprising; most ideologies have a force beyond their practical import, and systematic management was as much ideology as technique in the USA of the 1890s and early 1900s.

Enough has been said in earlier chapters (Chapters 5 and 7) and by other writers (Litterer, 1961 and 1963; Nelson, 1975 and 1980; Clawson, 1980) to indicate the content and substance of systematic management, such that only three points need to be underlined here.

Firstly, production control systems were developed and elaborated in order to solve the problems of workflow coordination. Over a period of less than fifteen years during the late nineteenth century, production control systems became progressively more detailed in specifying the schedule and methods of work. Consequently, the 'paper replica of production' gradually took shape:

the volume of paper work grew enormously from a single piece for each customer order, to a piece of paper for each part of a product on a customer order, to finally, a *separate written order for each operation performed in making each part of a product*.

(Litterer, 1963, p. 379, emphasis added)

Production control systems were often integrated with new cost accounting systems. There was a major effort to transform cost accounting from an historical record of past performance presented yearly or quarterly, to a current cost management tool. This improved data-gathering systems and provided the basis for centralized managerial control (Aitken, 1960, p. 18; Litterer, 1963, pp. 380–8; Nelson, 1975, p. 50). It is important to realize that one of the advantages of the contract system was that it standardized labour costs. Part of the burden of fluctuating costs was shifted onto the contractors, and management had only to keep an eye on material costs in order to be able to quote, say, machinery prices (Navin, 1950, pp. 146, 149–50; Nelson, 1975, p. 38). Therefore the development of effective cost-accounting was essential with the demise of contracting.[4]

Thirdly, systematic management involved the creation of specialized, central staff departments who took over many of the powers of the old, traditional foremen and the internal contractors. Frequently, the foremen were initially responsible for the operation of some new administrative system, either because they insisted on retaining control, or because management felt it was easier and cheaper to do this. But after a period of time, the responsibilities and decision-making power were shifted to administrative staff such as production control clerks etc. (Litterer, 1963, pp. 385–7). Overall, systematic management with the development of production control systems linked to new cost-accounting procedures and the creation of centralized staff departments can be regarded as the beginning of the bureaucratization of the managerial function.

A vital question to consider is why did the systematic management movement both as an ideology and as a set of techniques take such a hold in the United States in comparison with Britain? The answer is complex, but relates essentially to the American labour market context, the product market and the organizational context including the relation of industrial capital and financial capital. We will consider briefly each of these factors.

In looking at the background of American industrialization we have already emphasized the successive waves of immigration into the USA, the rapid job mobility, and the transient links to the work organization in many cases. The high rates of inter-firm mobility were possible because of the expanding job opportunities and recurring labour shortages, especially of skilled craftsmen. The relative lack of skilled men combined with the influx of immigrants has frequently been cited as a significant factor in prompting the development of systematic management and the widespread use of automatic machinery (e.g. see Hobsbawm, 1969, p. 176; Pollard, 1969, p. 6; cf. Saul, 1970).

The US Immigration Commission was quite explicit on the effects of the immigrant origins of the American working class:

Before coming to the United States the greater proportion [of the more recent immigrants from southern and eastern Europe] were engaged in farming or unskilled labor and had no experience or training in manufacturing or mining. As a consequence their employment in the mines and manufacturing plants of this country has been made possible only by the invention of mechanical devices and processes which have eliminated the skill and experience formerly required in a large number of occupations.
(Abstracts of Reports of the Immigration Commission, Vol. 1, Reports of the Immigration Commission, Vol. 1, 61st Congress, 3rd session, Senate Document no. 747, pp. 499–500. Quoted in Harley, 1979, p. 394)

The shortages of craftsmen led to high wages for skilled workers, which in turn led to an increasing division of labour according to skill. Jobs were analysed in terms of skill content and high-priced workers were restricted to important work, and all surrounding tasks were assigned to cheaper unskilled or semi-skilled and immigrant workers. The increasing fragmentation and specialization in American industry thus provided an essential dynamic for the rise of systematic management because for the system of subdivided work to be successful, new means of integration and coordination became necessary.

However, this is to examine managerial strategies with hindsight. Employers could have pursued a policy of generally reducing wages allied with extensive training schemes. Indeed, as the USA came up against European industry in a struggle for world markets, there were many voices that warned that the American worker would have to face a severe reduction in wages (e.g. the Secretary of State, William Evarts in

1879). The fears of increasing international competition and floods of cheap imports led to investigations of the American industrial situation, and it soon became apparent that the existing greater mechanization, product specialization and fragmentation of labour had already created *lower* unit costs than in many European industries. The classic statement of this economic awareness is J. Schoenhof's work, *The Economy of High Wages* published in 1892. Thus, the notion of a high wage/low cost economy became widely diffused and underpinned the solutions and techniques of the systematizers from Henry Towne to F.W. Taylor.

In Britain, this certainly was *not* the case. Britain long remained a low-wage economy, in which wage-levels were determined by social norms arising from entrenched beliefs in a class hierarchy. Thus the engineering employers' victory in 1897/8 provided the collective strength to pursue a strategy of depressing district wage-rates in the hope of restoring British manufacturers' competitive edge in world markets (Zeitlin, 1981, p. 28). The effect of this on innovation is indicated by the statement of one British industrialist at the close of the First World War: 'Before the War it often happened that it did not pay to introduce labour-saving devices, because, apart from the difficulty of raising fresh capital, the interest charges came to more than the cost of cheap, manual labour.' (Hichens, 1918, pp. 50–1). Indeed, the employer strategy of 'cheap manual labour' continued long after the First World War in Britain. In general there was a rejection of the American model of a high wage/low cost economy.

The US high-wage economy created a large, potential market for mass-produced goods. This combined with the rapid rise in the absolute size of the American population between 1880 and 1900 to create the economic context for the early development of large corporations in the USA. These larger corporations dominated the mass-production, mass-distribution industries, and were also important in transport and communications (Chandler, 1976, pp. 31–2).

From our point of view, the importance of the early development of large corporations in the USA was that it provided the organizational framework for the development of professional management. Thus by the 1880s in railroads, and by the 1900s in manufacturing industry, specialists in several different functional areas had set up their quasi-professional associations (Chandler, 1976, p. 32). The American railroads in particular, were an important institutional base for the systematizers (Aitken, 1960, p. 17; Haber, 1964, p. 20). The most important group to become organized in American industry at this time was the engineers, and they rapidly assumed managerial as well as technical responsibilities. Between 1880 and 1920 the engineering profession in the USA increased from 7000 to 136,000 members

(Nadworny, 1955, p. 2; D. Nelson, 1975, pp. 48–9; Layton, 1971, p. 3). The ability of American engineers to move out of a technical enclave meant that they were the occupational group which 'captured' and dominated systematic management ideas rather than the accountants, as occurred in Britain at a later date.

Thus the engineers in the USA were an emergent group with the perception and experience of the 'organizational uncoupling' and the organizational chaos described by Litterer, a group whose organizational power could be extended by successful solutions to the unpredictabilities thrown up by the increasing size, the increasing organizational complexity, and the increasing division of labour.

The power of the engineers to diagnose a lack of system or a lack of method in existing management structures was enhanced in the USA by the nature of the links between industrial-capital and finance-capital. In Britain, there had been a persistent reluctance by banks, insurance companies and trust funds to become actively involved in industry and industrial management. In contrast, American financial centres showed no such reluctance; indeed financiers such as Morgan and Rockefeller played leading roles in the turn of the century American merger wave.

The activist role of American financial institutions in industry resulted in the earlier emergence of the management consultancy role in the USA. Management consultants were *par excellence* outside experts whom financiers could use to push through certain policies, to 'encourage' the early retirement of some executive, and to promote others. Many early American consultants were engineers and this meant that the systematizers within management ranks could frequently obtain support and encouragement from outside forces. It is interesting to note that Taylor himself got his first major consultancy job at Bethlehem Steel in 1898 because of the influence of the financier Joseph Wharton, who held a large share of the stock (Nadworny, 1955, p. 10).

In sum, systematic management was a more significant force in reshaping work organization in the USA than in Britain because of the greater need to reduce and keep down unit labour costs in the context of a high-wage economy. Employer efforts to reduce unit labour costs led to a rapid transformation of the division of labour and product specialization which, in turn, created the need for new means of coordination and integration. In addition, there is an intersecting line of causality which begins with the fact that the rapid expansion of demand combined with the homogenous market of the USA led to the early development of large, managerialist corporations with the increasing employment of professional managers. Engineers, who were an emergent group at this time, were able to dominate the systematic management movement, partly aided by the early development of management consultants in the USA. Thus, systematic management, as both ideology and a set of techniques, was sustained and promoted by two emergent and overlapping groups – professional engineers and management consultants.

The influence of Taylorism in the USA

As I pointed out in Chapter 5, Taylorism grew out of the systematic management movement in the USA. Taylor was much influenced by the systematizers and accepted their definitions of the problem-context: lack of work-flow coordination, rudimentary cost controls, and the 'labour-problem'. Taylor was an active participant in the American Society of Mechanical Engineers (ASME) discussions and in 1905 became President of ASME. In general, Taylorism can be viewed as an extension of systematic management ideas (D. Nelson, 1974 and 1980).

The influence of Taylorism in the USA has been the subject of recent debate. Writers such as Aitken (1960) and Haber (1964) tended to assume the importance and widespread influence of scientific management ideas. Braverman (1974) followed by Zimbalist (1979) and Clawson (1980) have been the most recent proponents to argue for the central importance of Taylorism, and that the work process is, and continues to be, organized according to Taylorian principles. These views of the extensive influence of Taylorism have been criticized by Palmer (1975), Monds (1976), Edwards (1979) and by Goldman and Van Houten (1980). The latter argue that Braverman's work:

has contributed to some confusions about the nature of scientific management. Taylorism, as a system, was installed in relatively few plants and often for only short periods of time. It proved too rigid, on its own merits, for the majority of managers. The general trend towards mechanization and the fractionation of work developed independently of Taylor. . . . Braverman may have exaggerated the impact of scientific management in identifying it with the larger trend.
(Goldman and Van Houten, 1980, pp. 132–3, footnote 8)

This argument is partly correct, but it is based on a limited view of Taylorism and an over-simplistic interpretation of the available statistics.

According to Nadworny, by 1915, when Taylor died, the scientific managers and their associates had introduced their techniques into 140 establishments. Of these, 120 were 'complete installations', and the rest were confined to cost-accounting and production control. Thus, 63,000 workers were then working under Taylor's methods (1955, pp. 85–6). Though this is not insignificant, it is a tiny proportion of the $9\frac{1}{2}$ million people then working in manufacturing industry.

Another attempt to assess Taylor's direct influence was made by Nelson. He did a survey of firms, sixty years after the event, and was only able to identify 48 establishments that introduced scientific management between 1901 and 1917 and that were reorganized by Taylor's immediate disciples. Of these 48, 19 were impossible to evaluate because of lack of data. The remaining 29 organizations Nelson used in order to try and determine the impact of Taylorism. Using key features of Taylor's system as a checklist, Nelson concludes that 'The results indicate that Taylor's colleagues were generally faithful to his teachings' (D. Nelson, 1974, p. 490). But, however faithful Taylor's disciples and acolytes were, 48 manufacturing establishments is not an impressive number. Moreover, a rough check on the importance and continuity of the early organizations utilizing Taylorite techniques shows that only *one* firm out of Nelson's 29 has survived through to the 1970s (Goldman and Van Houten, 1980, p. 133, footnote 10).

On the face of it, then, Taylorism did have a limited and restricted influence in the USA. However, such a conclusion ignores several crucial points. First, both Nadworny and Nelson's assessments of Taylor's direct influence are based on the views of the small band of Taylorites themselves. The Taylorites tended to be purists, who believed in 'all or nothing' systematization. Even in 1923, they were lamenting that the number of plants which had been fully Taylorized were only a handful. Seeking an explanation, the Taylorites concluded that the cause was 'the pressure of unfair competition from illegitimate relatives' (Nadworny, 1955, p. 142). Efficiency systems, managerial control systems and incentive payment plans were very saleable. In other words, the widespread success of Bedaux, Emerson and others in installing neo-Taylorite control schemes were invoked to explain the limited diffusion of Taylorism! Second and relatedly, all the available American statistics refer to the early period. There is still no thoroughgoing analysis of the influence of Taylorism and Taylor's emulators in the USA in the 1920s and 1930s. This should prompt us at least to be cautious in denying Taylor's influence.

The recent debate about Taylor's influence has the opposite weakness of the earlier writings on Taylorism: it focuses on the structural aspects and ignores the ideological side. Taylorism was *both* a set of techniques and a set of principles. That Taylorism and the efficiency movement were ideologically important in the USA can be seen from the British comparison. The lack of an integrated theory of management in Britain meant that the employer search for effective methods of control and coordination was spasmodic and scattered. British employers lacked the social resources to create effective alternatives to traditional foremanship before the 1920s (see Chapter 7).

Thus it should be recognized that there were different forms of Taylorism, and that Taylorism *in its initial form* probably did fail in the sense of a widespread implementation of a standard body of techniques.

However this did not prevent Taylorism being crucial to the bureau-cratization of American industry on an ideological level. Unlike Britain, there was the influence and demonstration effect of the Taylor system in the USA as contracting and traditional modes of control were overturned. For example at the Winchester Arms Company:

the necessary enthusiasm to make a formal break with the past and install company foremen in place of contractors was generated by Frederick W. Taylor's 'scientific management'. During the early 1900s, a modification of the Taylor system was successfully installed in the government arsenal at Spring-field. . . . With this case history before them, the younger, technically trained officials were able to press with greater assurance for the elimination of the contractors. They could present concrete evidence to the more reluctant officials which showed not only that it was possible to replace the contractors but that the change would result in reduced costs.

(Buttrick, 1952, p. 219)[5]

Though Taylorism was rarely transplanted onto factory floors as a unit, nevertheless the overall principles and many of the specific techniques were widely diffused. Moreover, there is the totally neglected point that systems, such as the Bedaux system, represented later forms of Taylor-ism and were (probably) the means whereby the effect of Taylorism in the USA was profound and long-lasting (see D. Nelson, 1980, pp. 198–202).

The principles of Taylorism have been analysed in Chapter 5, and it only remains in this section to examine briefly the extent and sources of resistance to Taylorism in the US context. The most interesting point here is that in the USA, as in Britain in the inter-war years, foremen and supervisors constituted a major source of resistance to the new forms of managerial control. For example, when Taylor was working at the Simonds Rolling Machine Company, the supervisors were so incensed at the erosion of their decision-making powers that they resigned *en masse*, and Taylor attempted to replace them with 'functional foremen' (D. Nelson, 1974, p. 484). Overall, Nelson concludes from his survey of 29 Taylorized plants that Taylor's followers 'encountered more opposition from the managers than the workers' (1977, p. 496; also Stark, 1980, pp. 91–2).

Given this recurring story of supervisory scepticism and obstruction, there were systematic employer efforts in the USA to integrate foremen into the new managerial structures. Thus Stone records that the American steel companies, having abolished the contract system, gave their foremen special training courses in order to make them an integral part of management. From the employer point of view, it was necessary to ensure that the new foremen did not identify with their subordinate work-teams. This provision of formal supervisory training was not peculiar to the steel industry, but became widespread throughout

American industry (Stone, 1973, pp. 48–9; Slichter, 1919, pp. 380–5). This provision of formal training schemes for foremen contrasted sharply to the British experience. Though some British companies attempted to create a stratum of managerially-minded supervisors, this was surprisingly rare. Most British foremen remained independently-minded men with their own job definitions derived from occupational expertise and long years of practical experience (Thurley and Wirdenius, 1973, pp. 4–6).

Apart from the supervisory stratum, the workers resisted the introduction of skill-breaking machinery and Taylorite techniques. The extent and depth of this resistance is still open to debate. Certainly there were famous strikes, such as the one at Watertown Arsenal which led to the 1912 House of Representatives investigation of Taylorism (Aitken, 1960). There were long-drawn out and violent strikes on the Illinois Central and the Union Pacific Railroads from 1911 to 1915 over the introduction of Taylorite schemes of control (Montgomery, 1974, pp. 52–3). The skilled workers in particular felt themselves threatened by the new managerial methods and union leaders such as J.P. Frey railed against the development of 'fractional mechanics, who could work effectively only under the groups of functional foremen and super-foremen, provided for by the system' (Frey, 1913, p. 409).

This current of opposition reached a peak during the First World War, when there was considerable revolt against skill dilution, the use of the stop-watch and new payment systems. Nevertheless, the First World War was a watershed. The mounting opposition from labour unions to Taylorism led to the emergence of a small, liberal wing of the Taylorites led by such figures as Morris L. Cooke, who were instrumental in cementing a policy of cooperation between the systematizers and the AFL unions. After the War, when organized labour faced increasing employer and government hostility, the AFL wished to demonstrate that the trade unions were 'constructive' (Nadworny, 1955, pp. 144–53; Stark, 1980).

The eventual outcome was a trade-off between union interests in controlling job opportunities and employer desires to bureaucratize the structure of control. Cole describes the political process thus:

> The emergent unions had two basic options. They could struggle to increase the amount of worker discretion on the job, thereby 'enlarging' the job, or even insist on a worker voice in job design. Alternatively the unions could accept the given framework of power and struggle to make quantitative improvements in worker rewards. The first option was clearly a radical one, which the unions eventually rejected in the face of management and government power and lack of worker support.
>
> (R.E. Cole, 1979, pp. 104–5)

Instead, the AFL unions adopted the second solution and accepted changes in the structure of managerial control over task performance in return for formalization of employment and promotion procedures (see Chapter 4). This process of collaboration was helped along by the fact that, as far as we can tell, many of the earlier generation of craft workers found their way into supervision, design and even management (Duggan, 1977, p. 37; Stark, 1980 p. 110).

In relation to the unskilled workers in the USA, the opposition to Taylorism and the increasing subdivision of work were masked by new drafts of workers (immigrants, women) taking over the deskilled, tightly-controlled jobs, for whom such jobs represented promotion (Braverman, 1974, pp. 128–30; cf. Crozier, 1971, pp. 15–19). The International Workers of the World (IWW), founded in 1905, was the only unskilled labour organization which opposed scientific management and this resulted in a minor strike wave between 1909 and 1913. However no linkage between the IWW strikes and the pre-1914 opposition of the craft workers in the AFL was achieved. On the contrary, in some plants the AFL workers provided the employers with the names of suspected IWW sympathizers (M. Davis, 1975, p. 95, footnote 44). Moreover, the majority of the unskilled remained outside the labour unions until the New Deal era (the CIO was founded in 1935) and most unskilled protests remained isolated and sporadic.

Summary and conclusions

In this chapter we have sought to examine the development of modern work organization in the USA, focusing on the 1880s–1920s. Though there were differences among industries, in general there was a two-stage transition process consisting of first, the demise of internal contract systems and traditional modes of management during the 1870s to early 1900s, followed by the bureaucratization of shopfloor relationships between the turn of the century and the 1920s under the influence of the systematic management movement.

The comparisons and contrasts with the British experience are complex: the most important factors have been summarized in Table 11.4.

The first point to underline is that though internal contract systems were important in the development of both British and American industry, this fact does not carry the same social significance in the US context. The reason for this is that Britain, by the turn of the century, was a *national* social and political entity, whereas the USA was not. In the United States, capitalists could, in a way no longer possible in Britain, build new factories in a different social terrain. And this is precisely what did happen as the new industries established themselves in the Detroit and Mid-West areas. The older, British-influenced traditions of factory life could be left 1500 miles behind in New

Table 11.4   Comparison of the bureaucratization of the labour process in Britain and the USA

	Britain	USA
Internal contract systems		
(1) *Extent of Internal Contract*	Extensive	More limited to East Coast and older industrial centres
(2) *Links between Internal Contract and Labour Unions*	Earlier unions were associations of smaller contractors. Later unions opposed to internal contract	Larger contractors opposed to unions. Smaller contractors used unions to buttress their position
(3) *Period of Demise of Internal Contract*	1870–1900s	1870–1900s
Bureaucratization of industry		
(4) *Periodization*	1920–1930s	1900–1920s
(5) *Economic Context*	Occurred during depression years	Occurred during an expansionary period
(6) *Ideological Context*	Lack of consistent integrating ideology	Systematic management and Taylorism acted as a powerful, integrating ideology
(7) *Dominant Occupational Group in Bureaucratization Process*	Accountants	Engineers
Sources of resistance		
(8) *Foremen*	Resistance by foremen and chargehands	Resistance by foremen
(9) *Integration of Foremen*	Only scattered attempts to integrate foremen	Systematic attempts to retrain and integrate foremen
(10) *Worker Resistance*	Worker resistance including the unskilled	Initial, skilled worker resistance changing to AFL cooperation. Little unskilled resistance. Unskilled not organized until 1935–45 period

England, as Ford worked out his ideas of assembly-line production.

The bureaucratization of industry occurred two decades earlier in the US, associated with the earlier rise of large, managerialist corporations. What this difference in timing implies is that bureaucratization as an employer's strategy was pursued in the USA during an expansionary period: a period of widening markets and widening hopes. In contrast, British employers reacted defensively to the economic depression of the 1930s. This economic context both damped down overt resistance in Britain, and increased passive resistance given the fears of redundancy and loss of skill.

It is also important to note that by the 1920s and 1930s in Britain, the unskilled were largely organized into unions,[6] whilst the main period for organizing the unskilled in the USA was 1935–45, by which time the workers were faced with solidified patterns of work organization.

It seems that the basic conditions for the development and institutionalization of systematic management in the USA were the concomitance of staggering labour turnover rates with the development of large, oligopolistic corporations. This concomitance faced employers with the twin problems of costly labour turnover and 'organizational uncoupling'. Taylorism and systematic management appealed on both counts: they offered solutions to the exigencies of managerial control and coordination, and they minimized the economic impact of labour turnover by structuring work organization around a mobile, shifting, immigrant labour force. The impetus behind many bureaucratic innovations was management's attempt to free itself from uncertainty in the labour market.

12 Conclusions

The preceding eleven chapters point towards a number of conclusions and raise many questions. In this final chapter I will attempt to integrate and underline the most important points which fit readily into four broad themes or perspectives.

Craft control and the deskilling debate
The deskilling debate is beset by conceptual confusions. There has been an excessive emphasis on ill-defined notions of 'craft control' which ignores the overall social relations of production and, in particular, that many craftsmen were petty employers themselves within a system of internal contract. The confusions about craft relations of production have arisen partly because of the habit of calling everything 'craft control' which was the state of the labour process prior to the existing one.

In considering skill as work routines, I argued in Chapter 2 that there are two dimensions of job-roles – namely task range and discretionary content. Putting these dimensions together allowed us to distinguish between two different processes of change in the labour process: specialization and fragmentation. It was argued that specialization is not so much a deskilling process as one which concentrates skill onto a smaller task range, though the process of specialization can facilitate a later fragmentation process.

In addition it is necessary to recognize that there are various forms of the transformation of the division of labour. In Chapter 9 I suggested that there are four different forms. Braverman focused on the more dramatic processes of craft deskilling, but some industries and work processes were never craft-based; nevertheless it is still essential to understand the redivision of labour within the framework of these non-craft industries (see Chapter 6). Moreover, both craft and non-craft redivision can occur in either a confrontational or non-confrontational manner (see Figure 9.1).

Given these sets of conceptual categories we need to locate the historical transformations of the labour process within them. According to Braverman, Taylorism was the rabid destroyer of the craft system. Given that there was very little development of Taylorism on British shopfloors in the first two decades of this century, then the timing of the institutionalization of Taylorism is pushed forward to the inter-war years. Is there any evidence that Bedaux, as the inheritor of Taylorian principles, confronted craft workers during these years? The acid test of this was the Richard Johnson and Nephew case study: here was a struggle within a traditional industry with all the signs of craft deskilling. However, the transition to non-craft working had largely occurred before Taylor's disciples set foot on the factory floor. Taylorism 'rationalized' the new industrial system that was evolving, and developed an organizational model which was applied to factories where craft work, contracting and co-domination had already declined or were in a state of decline.

Thus, as I have stressed, the Bedaux systematizers, though the inheritors of Taylorite principles, were not the agents of craft-destruction envisaged by Stone, Montgomery and Braverman. A simple model of craft-deskilling with F.W. Taylor as the devil incarnate is not tenable. Further, it is not at all clear that mechanization, automation and transformations of the labour process can best be understood in terms of 'deskilling'.

Taylorism and rationalization

The seed-bed of systematic management and Taylorism was the end of the nineteenth century in the United States. The transfer of Taylorite ideas to Europe was slow and uneven. Though the First World War was an important stimulus, it was the inter-war years which were crucial and which laid down the pattern of labour/capital relations in Britain.

The above does not imply that there were no earlier waves of rationalization. In examining the changing structures of control in British industry and the imposition of bureaucratic control, it is crucial to recognize that there were periodic waves of rationalization affecting different core industries. The first wave which occurred between 1890 and 1914 primarily affected engineering and metalworking firms and was *not* influenced by Taylorism, but by indigenous ideas. This raises the theoretical point, which was noted in Chapter 5, that it is necessary to make a distinction between Taylorite rationalization and non-Taylorite rationalization. Indeed at later periods the central ideas of the rationalization effort shifted to incorporate notions of flow production, Fordism and automation. The difference between these processes and Taylorism lies in the nature of the systematization. Though Taylorism was of course concerned with systematization, it was not intrinsically *systemic*. In principle and in practice it was possible to Taylorize one department and leave the rest of the factory under traditional methods of labour control whereas the later ideas *were* intrinsically systemic.

Just as we must be careful not to identify all processes of labour rationalization (i.e. systematization, job fragmentation, standardization) with Taylorism, it is equally clear that Taylorism changed through time. Taylorism was never introduced as a simple package but was modified by the process and context of diffusion. After the First World War the scientific management movement split into a rump of purists, for whom economic salvation could only lie in the strict application of Taylor's principles and methods, and a more catholic school who attempted to integrate pre-war Taylorism with industrial psychology and fatigue studies. The European absorption of scientific management dates from this coalescence of Taylorism and industrial psycho-physiology (Devinat, 1927). The Bedaux system was one outcome of this integration of ideas and techniques.

If the different forms of scientific management and the link between Taylorism and Bedaux is accepted, then questions of the influence of Taylorism posed by labour process theorists can be carried forward to the inter-war arena. All the existing literature inexplicably tends to halt around 1920, whereas a consideration of the inter-war rationalizations provides a broader and different base for historical conclusions. The diffusion of Taylorism to Europe and Britain also involved a different economic and ideological context. Taylorism was introduced to British shopfloors during a period of high unemployment, short-time working and contracting markets. Moreover in Britain the American model of management involving a high wage/low cost economy with mass consumption had limited appeal. British employers were reluctant to concede as large a share of the productivity gains as US corporations, and the markets aimed at were those comprising of the lower middle class not the working class (Fridenson, 1978a).

Taylorization, as I have persistently argued, represents the bureaucratization of the shopfloor, substituting manager-subordinate relations for those of the independent petty-bourgeois contractor. The fabric of control and coordination is woven afresh out of hierarchy, rules, a systematic division of labour and written records and communications. But though Taylorism was important in Britain at the level of job design and the structure of control, strict Taylorite principles involve the complete substitutability of labour (the minimum interaction employment relation) with the result that there is little sign in the inter-war years of the bureaucratization of the employment relationship. In Britain, the development of institutionalized career systems beyond the traditional areas of post office and railways does not occur until after the Second World War. Edwards (1979) argues strongly that Taylorism in the USA was overlain by the implementation of 'bureaucratic control', in the sense of career systems and internal labour markets. In the British case 'bureaucratic control' is still confined to a very limited segment of the labour market.

As has been noted, the diffusion of Taylorism, the Bedaux system and rationalization generally was uneven. Each industrial sector varied. Generally, the traditional assembly industries, such as building, the gang-work industries and the monopolistic service organizations were not affected by the inter-war wave of rationalization. It was the planned and semi-planned industries (chemicals, food, drink and tobacco), and the industries founded with a domestic background (such as textiles; see Table 6.1) which were most affected by the Bedaux form of Taylorism. This pattern cut across older and newer sectors of industry and the common factor was the orientation to a mass market plus the semi-skilled or unskilled labour force.

In understanding the present shifts in work organization (job enrichment, quality-control circles, etc.) it is vital to note that Taylorite forms of work organization are acceptable to capitalists only within a framework of certain trade or exchange relations. If price ceases to be the exclusive factor in exchange, and non-price factors (for example design, reliability, quality) assume a larger significance, then this is likely to result in a structural shift in work organization and an ideological shift in management theory. The organizational impact of Japanese competition suggests that the velocity of throughput is no longer the sole principle of the capitalist production process which it was in the new dawn of Detroit in 1914.[1]

Patterns of resistance

Employer strategies of control must be seen in relation to conflict and the sources and patterns of resistance. In relation to the debate about the nature and effects of trade unionism, it is pertinent to ask whether trade unions are the incorporated managers of discontent or have they consistently pursued control objectives entailing the maximization of control over the production process? In particular, did the trade union movement in Britain form a solid bloc of opposition to managerial centralization and bureaucratic forms of control in the inter-war years? The evidence available clearly points to the opposite conclusion. As we said in Chapter 9, most union officials accepted the given framework of capitalist and managerial power and, moreover, had little conception that neo-Taylorite schemes would alter the structure of control over the labour process. This position was paralleled in France, where in 1927 'the French trade unions, whether reformist or communist, declared their acceptance of "equitable" rationalization for the sake of economic growth' (Fridenson, 1978b, p. 7).

In general, trade union influence over the content of jobs and the hierarchy of the workplace has been insignificant. Even today the study of, and experiments in, work organization arouse little interest among British trade unions. Western and Japanese trade unions have been concerned with, firstly, union security, i.e. the maintenance of the union and the right to belong to it and, secondly, the bureaucratization of the employment relationship, which has often stretched to include job ownership or institutional tenure. These objectives leave jobs unchanged in content whilst regulating access to them. The consequence of this set of trade union objectives (and the lack of concern over control of the production process) was that the official trade union movement in Britain did not pick up and resonate the fears and resentments of the shopfloor. However, beyond the limiting position of the trade union movement we discovered that there were other sources of resistance to centralized, bureaucratic control. In all three societies, though to a lesser extent in the USA, the internal contractor and traditional foreman constituted a significant focus of opposition. Indeed this pattern of foremen, and even middle-management, resistance is a more common pattern than is generally realized, and changes in the labour process need to be reinterpreted in terms of this fact.[2]

The basis of supervisory resistance relates to the dynamics of bureaucracy. The natural tendency in all bureaucratic systems of organization is that the bargaining power of the supervisor dwindles such that circles of autonomy are compressed and freedom for manoeuvre is reduced (Lupton, 1957; Crozier, 1964). The effects of this foremen and middle-management resistance were that it limited the diffusion of Taylorism within firms and factories. Moreover the two strands of resistance – worker opposition and foreman obstruction – could unite to form a concerted bloc of shopfloor opposition (see Chapter 9). The effects of this hierarchical resistance varied among the three societies: in Japan a structural and ideological integration was achieved, and in the USA supervisors became more integrated into the system, whilst in Britain they continued as a sceptical corrosive of shopfloor bureaucratization.

Comparative perspectives

I have attempted in this book to compare and contrast the development of modern work organizations in Britain, Japan and the USA. In Chapters 10 and 11 I have systematically compared Japan and the USA with Britain respectively. Implicit in these two-way comparisons has been a three-way comparison. This is best dealt with in tabular form (see Table 12.1).

In relation to Table 12.1, our main concern is with the second stage of industrial change. In the British case 1880–1939 should be seen as the second stage of the development of industrial work: a protracted

Table 12.1   Development of work organizations in Britain, Japan and the USA

	Period of primary industrial-ization	Nature of industrial elite and role of state	Employer ideology	Means of recruiting industrial labour force	Extent of internal contract	Period of bureau-cratization	Economic context	Organizational outcomes
Britain	1780–1840	Commercial class; minimal state role	Capitalist; laissez-faire	Labour market overlain by internal contract	Widespread	1920s–1930s	Occurred during depression years	Neo-Taylorite forms of work organization
Japan	1880–1915	Samurai class; weak middle class; state crucial; state/zaibatsu links later	Nationalistic; paternalistic later	Oyakata system and factory dormitory system; lack of organized external labour markets	Widespread apart from textiles	1915–1930s	Largely occurred during an expansionary period	Dual-sector economy; corporate paternalism in the larger firms and shudanshugi
USA	1850–1880	Commercial class	Capitalist; laissez-faire; efficiency movement later	Labour market overlain by internal contract and mass immigration	More limited to East Coast and older industrial centres	1900–1920s	Occurred during an expansionary period	Neo-Taylorite forms of work organization

organizational or administrative revolution associated with the increasing size of the units of employment and new technologies. At the shopfloor level the overall shape of this revolution was a transition from systems of co-domination to large-scale bureaucratized or 'Taylorized' organization.

If we widen our focus to look at all three capitalist societies, then the first point to underline is the widespread importance of systems of internal contract and indirect employment and control (see Chapters 6, 10 and 11). This fact constitutes the basis for a common historical thread; namely the transition to forms of direct employment and control which must underlie any form of bureaucracy. The common capitalist problem entailed by this transition process was the transference of the loyalty and accepted subordination from the traditional work-group to a wider collectivity and a larger social frame. Bureaucratization was not just a technical process associated with increasing size and complexity, but a sociological transformation.

Looking now at the end point of the transition process (the 'organizational outcomes'), the cross-cultural comparisons link up with another major issue in the labour process debate, an issue which has been opened up by Friedman. Is it the case that capitalist employers are constrained to use Taylor's methods, or is it necessary to introduce some notion of employer strategy in order to draw attention to the fact that there are a variety of forms of control within capitalism? Is Braverman right to take Taylorism as *the* logic of capitalism? The comparison with Japan enables us to see clearly that there *are* different forms of control within capitalism; there are different employer strategies. In Chapter 5 I outlined and defined the polarities of these different forms of control: Taylorism versus ideological control. Ideological control seeks to solve the problem of commitment to large work organizations by infusing 'existing levels of group solidarity with commitment to the same values as the formal organization' (Brugger, 1976, p. 268). This was largely achieved in Japan by the ideologies of familialism and nationalism. However, the notion of ideological control is not the complete equivalent of Taylorite forms of work organization: at this point we can complete the argument of Chapter 5.

The first step in fully conceptualizing the different employer strategies in Britain and Japan is to recall the three general categories that have been consistently used throughout this book: namely the division of labour, the structure of control and the employment relationship. Thus in Table 12.2 we can describe two alternative ideal types.

Let us look at the two aspects of Table 12.2 – deskilling and paternalism. The interesting point in relation to the division of labour is that *both* capitalist employer strategies appear to involve deskilling. We

Table 12.2   *Capitalist employer strategies*

	Taylorism	Shudanshugi*
Division of labour	A dynamic of deskilling; formalized job boundaries	Development of generalized semi-skilled workers; continued job flexibility and lack of job boundaries
Structure of control	Task control; formal monitoring system; de-collectivization, including (possible) incentive payment system	Ideological control; collectivity-orientation promoted by small-group cooperation and pressure leading to such devices as quality control circles
Employment relationship	Complete substitutability of workers and work teams; minimum interaction relationship	Paternalism, internal labour markets and job security

Note: For the details of Taylorism see Chapter 5; for the details of shudanshugi see Chapter 10).

* It is very difficult to find an adequate English term to express this form of work organization. Several possibilities express only one aspect. Nor is it clear to me that Japanese scholars have yet found an adequate Japanese term. I have used here an inadequate concept 'shudanshugi' which literally means 'groupism'.

have noted already the substantial qualifications which need to be made to a simple deskilling hypothesis in the British case, and in Japan there are conceptual and historical difficulties in talking about craft deskilling, because no extensive tradition of industrial craftsmanship was ever established. Though the position of the oyakata changed as we have seen in Chapter 10, nevertheless their privileged position was based as much on labour market functions (hiring and firing) and authority at the workplace as on their technical functions. Often the correlation between skill labels and types of job was low in Japan. In principle the level of skill changed with experience on the job so that 'fitters, for example, were considered unskilled for the first few years, then semi-skilled after five or six years and finally skilled after more than ten years' (Hazama, 1981, p. 10). The end result of these principles of work-experience, is the cumulative training programmes of large Japanese companies, in which

Skill . . . connotes too much of personalized manual proficiency to be useful for the kind of ability and work habit needed for efficient mass production in modern firms. In other words, a worker is now an amorphous pool of ability from which 'skills' for specific tasks may be drawn from time to time according to the exigencies of evolving technology.

(Taira, 1970, p. 85)

This view of a generalized semi-skilled worker may be a far cry from any craft-conception of skill, but equally, it bears no resemblance to the deskilled worker of Braverman's thesis, and, in contrast, bears some resemblance to the Marxian notion of the multi-skilled worker (Marx, 1976, p. 618).

If we turn to examine the employment relationship, then the differences between the employer strategies and paths of change are more stark. The crucial historical point of choice in Britain was probably 1906–1920, and a few employers and management intellectuals showed themselves aware of an historical turning-point. Thus in 1914 G.D.H. Cole argued that there was a choice between the Quaker paternalism of Cadbury's and Taylorism, but that

> under the present system, 'enlightened' employment is [not] possible for more than a small minority of employers [and] It is therefore to be feared that, in industry generally, scientific management will take rather the opposite line of development, and will make the worker's life more monotonous. It will increase his efficiency, and attempt to compensate him for speeding-up and wear and tear by premium bonus systems and the like. It will be very difficult for the unions to resist the new processes.
>
> (G.D.H. Cole in Cadbury, 1914a. p. 120)

In general Cole prophesied that British capitalism would take the easy and profitable road of Taylorism, involving an accelerating division of labour, and that paternalism ('Cadbury's Chocolate Box') would be left in the interstices of British industrial history.

This was a remarkably accurate sociological prediction. Child details the changes in attitude of the Quaker employers, including Edward Cadbury, in the inter-war years. The diffusion of 'scientific management' practices and shopfloor rationalizations began to obscure welfarism in the 1930s and the economic pressures pushed Quaker industrialists into an acceptance of Taylorism and the unrestrained pursuit of maximum business efficiency (Child, 1964).

The submergence of Quakerism as a set of practices in the 1930s was clearly associated with the widespread consolidation of neo-Taylorite forms of work organization in Britain. However, we have seen in Chapter 9 that this process occurred without a context of ideological underpinning. In the British context Taylorism was indeed a failed *ideology*. In Japan though paternalism developed later than the limited examples in the West, when it finally spread it did so much more definitively. Moreover it is crucial to note that the spread of institutionalized paternalism in large Japanese companies coincided with the diffusion of scientific management ideas to Japan such that Taylorism was filtered through the sieve of prevailing ideology.

In Britain the institutionalization of Taylorism in a depressed economy combined with a culture of casualism and job insecurity to lead to entrenched job regulation by trade unions, surrounded by pools of continued casualism. The bureaucratization of the employment relationship has (partly) been a union attempt to exercise leverage on hiring, firing and promotions, and to fight off the commodification of labour.

In the USA the diffusion of Taylorism and systematic management was also accompanied by the spread of welfare capitalism in many large corporations between 1900 and the First World War. This managerial strategy reached a peak in the early 1920s and Brody has argued that it was the inter-war depression which prevented its survival and the continuation of American capitalism on a paternalistic course (Brody, 1968). However it would seem that the continuing high rates of labour turnover, which only momentarily moderated in the 1920s, shattered any notion of worker commitment which would be the pay-off to the employers for the costs of welfare programmes. In general, then, the employers' strategy in Britain and the USA was based on forms of Taylorism and systematic management whilst in Japan the strategy was one of paternalism, ideological control and 'groupism'.

However, though paternalism may not have triumphed in the US economic and labour market context, American shopfloor rationalizations were nevertheless underpinned by the ideology of the systematic management movement and Taylorism, whereas by the 1930s in Britain rationalization was a weak glimmer flickering in the consciousness of a few (see Chapter 8). The context of the diffusion of Taylorism and of bureaucratization is crucial. In particular it should be stressed that Taylorism and the efficiency movement occurred in the USA during an expansionary period; similarly the development of institutionalized paternalism in Japan largely occurred during an expansionary period. In Britain the neo-Taylorism of Bedaux coincided with the worst depression of the twentieth century. This affected the pattern of resistance, and British capitalism still carries the scars of this historical conjuncture.

Notes

Chapter 1

1. The problems of determining and classifying labour strategies are demonstrated forcefully in Brecher *et al.* (1978) who list *fourteen* largely disparate items as potential employer strategies.
2. Clearly not all the issues can be dealt with in detail and depth in one book. In particular, the questions of class analysis and the relations between waged and non-waged labour are considered in other publications. See, for example, Littler and Salaman, *Work and Society*, forthcoming.

Chapter 2

1. Though Marx repeatedly argued that capitalism tended to replace skilled work with unskilled labour, he was aware of the limits of this process. This point is developed in Chapter 3.
2. The 'agnostic' position in relation to the deskilling hypothesis has been put forward by Cutler. According to him, it is only in relation to a given production process that one can talk about 'conception', 'execution' and 'skill'. The terms do not have the same meanings across different production processes, in terms of which they are incommensurable (Cutler, 1978, pp. 79, 84 and 86).

Chapter 3

1. In fact Marx says that manufacture originates in only two ways; see Marx, 1976, pp. 455–7. However it is possible to glean an additional route from Marx's work; e.g. see ibid, p. 485.
2. In fact there are ambiguities in Marx's treatment of intensification. Contrast Gartman, 1978, pp. 101–2 and Elger, 1978, p. 44, footnote 3.
3. This is a serious weakness in Burawoy's recent work. He concludes that there are only two types of capitalist labour process – despotic and hegemonic: 'Anarchy in the market leads to despotism in the factory' and 'Subordination of the market leads to hegemony in the factory.' (Burawoy, 1979, p. 194). As Stinchcombe long ago pointed out, anarchy in the market *can* lead to the survival of craft controls. (Stinchcombe, 1959). This conclusion is echoed by Lee (1981).

Chapter 4

1. Mouzelis (1967) lists eight modern uses of bureaucracy, whilst Albrow (1970) lists seven basic meanings.
2. An influential example is Blau who lists: (i) Specialization of tasks; (ii) A hierarchy of authority; (iii) A system of rules; (iv) Impersonality; (v) Employment based on technical qualifications, and constituting a career; (vi) Efficiency (1956, pp. 28–31).

3. It is this double origin which has led to the debate concerning formal authority and functional authority (see Parsons's Introduction to Weber, 1947, p. 59; Gouldner, 1954, pp. 21–4). Udy, 1959, split the two up again into 'rationality' and 'bureaucracy' when he discovered that his indicators of each were strongly *intra*-related, but negatively *inter*-related.

Chapter 5

1. Both Bendix (1974) and Braverman (1974) commandeer the early industrial history of Britain and then conjoin it with developments in the USA in the post-war period without much awareness of crossing the Atlantic.

2. Or at least *some* analysis. In practice, manufacturers pressured the early Taylorites, as consultants, to speed-up the initial research and process of standardization in order to produce quick results (Nelson, 1975, pp. 61 and 65; Hoxie, 1915, p. 93).

3. Brugger, 1976, pp. 57–8, 184–5, and 274. The functional type of organization was considered by some Chinese theorists to be the most progressive type of organization.

4. The concept of 'observability' refers to the information conception of power. 'Observability' depends on three factors: (i) physical separation; (ii) congruence of superior/subordinate skills; and (iii) social insulation based on institutions of privacy.

5. For instance, see Taylor, 1903, pp. 191–4 on how to break the resistance of unionized workers. Cf. Stone, 1973, esp. pp. 38, 41 and 56.

6. For example see Mayntz, 1964, p. 96; Etzioni, 1964, Chapter 3; Mouzelis, 1967, Chapter 4.

7. This raises a crucial organizational question in relation to Britain which has never been asked: Why did the railways and the other public service organizations not act, as they did in many societies, as models for large-scale, industrial organizations between 1880 and 1920? After all, the railways, the police, and the post-office were the major organizational innovations of Victorian England. At the turn of the century, unlike now, they still exuded considerable status. I shall suggest some answers to this question in later chapters, but not approach it directly (see Chapter 7). For the influence of the railways on the early systematizers in the USA, see Aitken, 1960; Jenks, 1960; Haber, 1964, p. 20; Chandler, 1965.

8. See Taylor, 1903, p. 58; Taylor, 1912, p. 6; Nadworny, 1955, p. 5; Haber, 1964, p. 16. For the early European over-emphasis on this aspect of Taylorism, see Devinat, 1927, p. 24.

Chapter 6

1. The distinction is not always clear-cut. For example, in the Sheffield cutlery trade, many of the so-called factories consisted of a maze of separate workshops, rented out to the independent masters who hired the power which the 'factory' provided (Dobb, 1963, p. 264).

2. See Emanual Lovekin's account of his career as a butty master between 1840s and 1899. His autobiographical account revolves around his personal relationships with colliery owners (Lovekin, in Burnett, 1977, pp. 289–96).

3. One result of this non-skill basis was that democratic forms of sub-contract, or co-partnership, could develop under exceptional circumstances. For example, Schloss describes a co-partnership system operated by a Scottish group of dockers. This consisted of an association of 61 men: a foreman and 5 squads of 12 men, each with a ganger. All the gangers and the foreman were elected once a year. Pay was equal shares to all, and the foreman plus gangers constituted an executive committee which met once a fortnight. The employer exercised no direct control over the members of the association at all (Schloss, 1898, pp. 163–5).

4. Stedman-Jones argues that the use of the idea of a 'labour aristocracy' has been vague and ambiguous . . . . 'Its status is uncertain and it has been employed at will, descriptively, polemically or theoretically without ever finding a firm anchorage . . . the term has often been used as if it provided an explanation. But it would be more

accurate to say that it pointed towards a vacant area where an explanation should be' (Stedman-Jones, 1975, p. 65). If anything useful emerges out of the recent labour aristocracy debate, it is that authority at work is crucial in understanding any such postulated stratum. See Foster, 1974; Gray, 1976; Moorhouse, 1978; Crossick, 1978.

5. There was some internal contract within the 'sweated trades', but typically they were based on small workshops whose very size precluded extensive internal contract.

6. Shift-working, another form of the extensive use of labour, was not widely used in Britain in the nineteenth century, except in a few continuous process industries. See Bienefeld, pp. 210–11.

Chapter 7

1. It should be noted however that Cole goes on to qualify his description by stating that there were still in force many systems analogous to sub-contract, and, to take a specific example, R.E. Goffee in a detailed study of the Kent Coalfield discovered that the butty system did not finally disappear there until around 1936 (1977, pp. 48–9). Thus in some industries, and some specific areas, contract systems still struggled on through the First World War.

2. Though there was some enthusiasm for, and introduction of, piece-work schemes around the middle of the nineteenth century, (Hobsbawm, 1964, p. 357; G. Brown, 1977, p. 83), it was not the case, as Marx suggests, that piece-work was the most common form of industrial payment in the 1850s and 1860s (Marx, 1976, p. 699). The early introduction of piece-work occurred in combination with sub-contracting and piece-mastership. Indeed for most of the nineteenth century the terms 'piece-work' and 'sub-contract' were *synonymous* (Cole, 1918, p. 32). This fact leads to a great deal of confusion and misinterpretation of nineteenth century practices.

3. In relation to the spread of PB schemes, the 1909 TUC investigation surveyed 23 unions; of these 10 reported experience of PBSs, 9 denied that their members worked under such systems, and 4 said that they had had to fight off such systems and had lost members as a result (TUC, 1910, pp. 7–15). In general it was the *non*-metal working trades (e.g. the cabinet-makers, painters, and french polishers) that reported no experience of PBSs. Eight unions tacitly recognized PBS in 1909, though only the ASE officially recognized and accepted it.

4. Williams, 1915, pp. 274–7; Gospel, 1978, pp. 11–12. One of the main advocates for centralized employment departments was Charles Carpenter, e.g. see Carpenter, 1903. Cf. Edwards, 1979, p. 104.

5. Both legislation (e.g. the 1901 Factory Act) and national agreements (e.g. the 1898 and 1901 engineering agreements) tended to push employers away from the maintenance of or condoning of these practices. See Phelps Brown, 1959, p. 71.

6. See TUC, 1910 *passim*; Cole, 1918, p. 74; and Watson, 1935, p. 92. Of the 58 witnesses who made substantial statements to the TUC committee investigating PBS, 36% complained of glaring errors in rate-fixing, and the percentage is much higher if the government establishments are excluded.

7. Frequently job times arrived *after* the work had been finished. At the Armstrong Whitworth plant in Newcastle there was one 'case of a turner who performed one operation on some forged steel top plates for friction discs in $3\frac{1}{2}$ hours, no time being given until the job was finished, and it was then issued at $11\frac{1}{2}$ hours basis. The ticket was at once taken back and $3\frac{1}{2}$ hours made the estimate time.' (TUC, 1910, p. 39; see also pp. 36, 37 and 38).

8. The nearest we have to a contemporary survey of paternalistic practices and companies is Budgett Meakin's work *Model Factories and Villages*, published in 1905. This looks at firms in Britain, USA and Western Europe. Meakin described 239 companies, and the interesting point is that *only 21% are British*, and of the 52 British companies referred to, including two American subsidiaries, it is difficult on Meakin's evidence to argue that more than one-fifth had a well-developed paternalistic system. If this is indicative, then welfarism had only permeated a tiny minority

of companies – perhaps a dozen – by 1905. This 'guesstimate' fits in with the fact that there were about a dozen welfare secretaries by 1906. By 1914 this number had only grown to 60 or 70 at the most (see Niven, 1967, p. 21). Child also concludes that the majority of firms remained indifferent to working conditions and labour management in the years up to 1914 (1969, p. 35).

9. With this background we must be cautious about interpreting an increase of casualism in the period 1890–1914. It may have been that the skilled workers suffered greater anxieties about unemployment which had afflicted the unskilled army of labour for many years; i.e. casualism became more *visible*, not more frequent. The unemployment statistics for this period are unreliable anyway, but the annual rates of unemployment do not tell us much about job turnover. The 4.3% average unemployment rate between 1891 and 1913 could represent a hard core of long-term unemployed, or it could represent lengthy periods of joblessness for 20% or more of the labour force. In general Stearns concludes that the latter was the case. See Stearns, 1975, pp. 92–3 and 94. Also Phelps Brown 1959, p. 86.

   The casualism of large areas of British industry created a sub-culture of casualism. An excellent account of such a sub-culture is provided by Watson's (1935) autobiography, *Machines and Men: the Autobiography of an Itinerant Mechanic*, covering the period from 1900 to the 1930s. It is clear from this that the institutions of labour mobility – the union, the pub, and the grapevine – were more important than the employing organization, which would change week by week.

10. There are various indications of the lack of response to Taylorism in Britain at the ideological level. Firstly, the technical journals, such as *The Engineer* and *Engineering*, took little notice of Taylor's first two papers. The crucial paper on *Shop Management* in 1903 was totally ignored by all four engineering journals (Urwick and Brech, 1948, p. 93; Levine, 1967, p. 61). Only Taylor's more technical paper on 'The art of cutting metals' in 1906 aroused much interest in the British journals; and this interest was a narrow technical one unrelated to broader organizational problems. Secondly, it cannot be said that there was a plethora of managerial books on Taylorism in Britain before 1914. On the contrary, only *one* book on scientific management was published in the UK before the First World War (H.N. Casson, *Factory Efficiency*, 1917), and as Brown points out, 'The one or two home-produced manuals on factory administration and management methods published before 1914 were given a good deal more attention and praise than any work of Taylor's or his disciples.' (Brown, 1977, p. 158). Thirdly, Taylorism was not much discussed at the meetings of professional institutions (Urwick and Brech, 1948, p. 99; Levine, 1967, p. 61).

11. Child, 1964; Child, 1969, Chapter 2; Fox, 1974, pp. 195–201. See also the reactions to Cadbury's 'philanthropic management' by J.A. Hobson and G.D.H. Cole in Cadbury, 1914a, pp. 117–20.

Chapter 8

1. This quote is particularly interesting because it is the public view of a right-wing engineering employer concerned to resist the claims of the trade unions at the end of the war (see Richmond, 1917).

2. It should be clear that the term 'rationalization' here has no *direct* link to the Weberian use whereby 'rationalization' referred to three inter-connected processes, namely the development of modern industrial capitalism, the spread of bureaucratic domination and the development and application of scientific knowledge. Though clearly there is an overlap of meaning.

3. Despite the development of corporate capitalism in the inter-war years this did *not* mean the end of proprietorial control. Neither the bureaucratization of management nor the professionalization of management proceeded very far, with one or two oft-quoted exceptions such as ICI and Unilever. Instead, there were two common organizational forms. In many small and medium-sized firms owners still managed,

whilst other firms had grown large enough to develop a stratum of salaried and middle managers, but the owners still made the key, strategic decisions. The second, common structure was loose, organizational conglomerations nestling under a holding company umbrella, often permeated by the continued influence of the founding families or the owner-entrepreneurs and invariably operating by means of informal practices and procedures. Such confederations were typically held apart by a desire to preserve circles of autonomy and a continued miasma of distrust (see P.S. Florence in A.C. Pigou (Chairman) 1930, p. 365).

4. This section is based on Janet Flanner, 'Annals of collaboration: equivalism' in the *New Yorker*, 22 September, 6 October and 13 October 1945; plus *Time*, 15 November 1937 and 19 January 1942; Edwin Layton, 1974; Bernard Franks, 1970.

5. Letter to the writer from Edwin Layton, 10 September 1979; interview with V.M.A. Brownlow, 6 March 1979 and J. Pleming, 20 March 1974.

6. The only first-hand, detailed account of Bedaux's system is in *The Bedaux Efficiency Course for Industrial Application* (Bedaux Industrial Institute, 1917). As far as I can discover, there is only *one* copy of this publicly available in the world. It is not surprising then if Bedaux's system is not well understood.

7. It is important to note that, by making the 'B' a minute made up of work-time and rest-time, no *actual* periods of rest are specified (TUC, 1933 p. 11). The 'B' is not referred to in Bedaux's only book published in 1917. The article by Morrow, which appeared in the *American Machinist* in 1922, was probably written by and for the Bedaux Company and 'planted' as a form of advertisement (letter to the writer from Professor Edwin Layton, 10 September 1979). Thus Bedaux worked out his idea of the 'B' between 1917 and 1922.

8. For the parallel development in the USA, see 'Bedaux Reformed', *Time*, 19 January 1942, p. 70.

9. For example, in May 1929 when the Southern textile workers were striking against 'efficiency systems', largely Bedaux, the Taylor Society postponed a meeting in order to avoid any identification with Bedaux (Nadworny, 1955, p. 134).

Chapter 9

1. In 1928 one of the Americans brought over to start up the British Bedaux company was surprised by the total lack of a management consultancy role in Britain:

   First, industrial engineering consultancy had become an accepted fact in the US, while in Great Britain it was most unusual for top management to permit an outside group to examine the inner working of their business. . . . Competition between consultancy firms in the UK at this time was virtually unknown. There was some work being done by the National Institute of Industrial Psychology . . . otherwise the area was entirely open.

   (C.J. Carney, quoted in V.M.A. Brownlow, pp. 1.7 and 1.8)

   Despite this starting point, by the 1940s there were four large consultancy companies in Britain, plus numerous small firms. The basis of this transformation and the origins of all four large companies can be traced back to Bedaux. J.L. Orr worked for Bedaux and left in 1932 to help found Urwick Orr and Partners; R. Bryson and W.H. Craven left Bedaux to form the P.E. Group and E. E. Butten left in 1943 to set up Personnel Administration Ltd, which later became the P.A. Group (Brownlow, pp. 2 and 1.8; also G. Turner, 1969, p. 460).

2. For the history and structure of the hosiery industry, see Friedman, 1977; Gurnham, unpublished, undated history; Head, unpublished Ph.d. 1961; Holmes, 1891; *The Hosiery* Trade Journal 1900 to date; National Economic Development Office, 1970; E.G. Nelson, 1930; Pool and Llewellyn, 1955–8; Walton, unpublished M.A. thesis, 1952; Wells, 1972.

3. Interview with Horace Moulden, 6 November 1979. Horace Moulden was the General Secretary and later President of the Union of Hosiery Workers from 1931 to

1965, and was centrally involved in the Bedaux dispute at Wolsey in the 1930s.

4. Given the lack of a convention about referencing microfilms, I have referred to them by a number (F.1–27) and wherever possible by the number of the report on the specific microfilm, e.g. F.1, R. 2. The Wolsey material is spread over two microfilms, F.9 and F.17. Most of the material on F.17 relates to a different Wolsey plant, namely Bruin Street. Nearly all the reports are clearly numbered and are, therefore, referenced in terms of their numbers. This results in two sequences, the F.9 sequence and the F.17 sequence. A few reports are unnumbered. Most of the reports are written by four Bedaux engineers: H. Cavanagh, W.E. Noel-Clark, M.W. Brown and G.W. Charley.

5. I have attempted to strip away many of the details of the changes in the labour process in order to concentrate on essentials. In fact Bedaux proposed, and Wolsey implemented, a package of changes consisting of (i) the introduction of faster machines and the scrapping of many older machines; (ii) a shift from female operatives to male workers in order to increase machine utilization. The men worked 55 hours per week compared to the woman's 48 hours; (iii) associated with (ii), the introduction of shift working, which again only men were allowed to do; (iv) stretch-out; (v) wage reductions, at least for the new workers brought into the plant (F.17, R.1–9).

6. One facet of the changes in the structure of control was the advocacy of conscious management strategies to socially isolate and fragment workers. For example, Bedaux complains that in the Ironers' Department the lay-out is cramped and tends to produce 'excessive talking'. Therefore they 'strongly urged that ironers should be placed in one long line or in some other way, split in order to obtain a *partial isolation effect*'. (F.9, R.140; see also R.60 and 132; cf. Huntley and Palmers, F.3).

7. At Wolsey there were some pockets of employees – indirect operatives, the workers in the Web Store for instance – who were classified as staff operatives and were paid on a *weekly* basis (as opposed to an hourly basis) and were also paid for holidays. Whenever Bedaux came across this employment situation they opposed it, and argued that the workers should be paid on an hourly rate (e.g. see F.9, R.50 and 216).

8. This account of worker resistance is primarily based on the Bedaux archives, F.9, R.1–138. Other sources are an interview with Horace Moulden 6 November 1979 and letters to the writer from Moulden 17 November 1979 and from R. Gurnham 20 November 1974 plus the *Leicester Mercury*, various issues between 23 August 1930 and 12 February 1932. Gurnham is the historian of the Union of Hosiery Workers and has written an unpublished history, *The Hosiery Worker: A History of Trade Unionism in the Hosiery Industry, 1770–1970*.

9. At an industry level, the proportion of all employed working short time in October 1931 varied between 49.3% in tobacco to 16.3% in brewing. In engineering it was 20.9%. The average hours lost during the working week amounted to one or two days (Cole and Cole, 1937, Table 39, p. 256).

10. The list of departments and the number of operatives is set out below. Some of these departments, and the differences between them, are important in the following story.

Departments of R J & N

	Number of operatives
Wiredrawing Department	95
Straight lengths and staples	24
Cleaning	16
Annealing and Patenting	18
Dies	13
Warehouse	19
Rolling mills	60

Rod mill warehouse	25
Galvanizing	99
Galvanizing warehouse	56*
Barb shop	48
Spinning	12
Copper drawing	52
Copper warehouse	22
Copper rod mill	55
Stranding	70
Maintenance and various	149
	———
Total	833

* This figure may not be correct. Microfilm of manuscript is unclear but it appears to be 56.

Source: Bedaux archives, F.16, Reports 22 February 1932 and 23 February 1933. The departments which will concern us most are in italics.

11. The reports on R.J. & N. are numbered, but there are two different sequences, and confusion is saved by date references. Most of these reports are signed by P.R. Wace, the Field Engineer, though some are signed by E.E. Butten, the Chief Engineer. Butten kept in the background, but is a crucial figure in the events of 1934–7. In addition to the Bedaux Archives, there are two other sources of data available: (i) Mick Jenkins, *Time and Motion Strike, Manchester, 1934–37*, Our History Pamphlet 60, 1974. This account is largely based on union archives (ii) Michael Seth-Smith, *200 Years of Richard Johnson & Nephew*, privately published by R.J. & N. Ltd in 1973. This account is largely based on the company archives. Thus we are in the fortunate position of having *three* separate sources of material on the shopfloor events in 1934–7 at R.J. & N. This must be unique for the inter-war period.

12. This was of course why the stranding department was chosen by Bedaux and R.J. & N. as the first site of reorganization. Mick Jenkins disputes the fact that the stranding shop was not unionized – though it seems an amazing error of fact for P.R. Wace to make after fourteen months in the plant (discussion with Jenkins, 31 March 1979).

13. See Miller, 1938, p. 292 and Laloux, 1951, p. 152. One of the clearest statements of the principle of job simplification as an objective is in Henry Hope Ltd, F.16, R.4, 17 October 1932.

14. The Management Research Groups were a long-running set of seminars and discussions for senior managers and directors founded in 1926. Most large companies were members. The minutes of the meetings, provide an invaluable insight into inter-war management.

15. See Bedaux, 1950, p. 32; Bedaux, 1930a, p. 4, & Devinat, 1927, p. 145. A good case study of supervisory resistance is the British Goodrich Rubber Co. Ltd, F.3, 1926–7. See especially reports dated 16 October, 28 October, 4 November, 5 November, 9 November, 11 November, 12 November, 1 December, 2 December, 3 December, 8 December, 14 December, 15 December, 16 December, 20 December, 21 December 1926; 3 January, 4 January, 18 January and 19 February 1927.

Chapter 10

1. The best evidence on this is provided by a Japanese government official, Kashiro Saito, who was one of the members of the Commission responsible for framing the first draft of the proposed factory legislation in Japan. After an inspection in 1897 of factories and workshops in every part of Japan he writes:

quand j'ai visité les etablissements industriels des diverses provinces, je n'ai jamais constaté en pratique ces relations familières et affectueuses dont on nous parle.

(Quoted in Foxwell, 1901, p. 18)

2. A labour law was passed in 1911, but it did not become operative until 1916 (see Dore, 1969).
3. Indeed it was not until 1960 that the majority of industrial workers for the first time became waged labour (Levine and Kawada, 1980, p. 36).
4. In such industries as cotton textiles the average employment contract was for two or three years. Thus workers 'escaped' in the sense that they evaded the terms of their labour contracts.
5. Though it is important to note that this pattern of employment applied in its totality only to male workers in large firms. The practice of job tenure was not extended to female workers in the textile factories. They were still expected to leave after marriage.
6. Quality-control (QC) circles are small groups of workers usually led by a foreman or senior worker which meet regularly to study and solve production problems. In addition QC circles are intended to stimulate motivation and involvement on the shopfloor. Unlike earlier human relations ideas, QC circles involve systematic training of shopfloor workers.

Chapter 11

1. For one example of change through time, see the career of a contractor in the Whitin Machine Works detailed by Navin, 1950, pp. 143–4. Also see Soffer, 1960, pp. 145–6 on the fact that contractual relations could vary from worker to worker and over time.
2. Montgomery adopts a contrary view of the relations between internal contract and unionism. He emphasizes the formal union rules, such as those of the Iron Molders' Union, against sub-contract and concludes that 'All such regulations secured the group welfare of the workers involved by sharply rejecting society's enticements to become petty entrepreneurs clarifying and intensifying the division of labour at the workplace, and sharpening the line between employer and employee.' (1979, pp. 16–17). This confuses formal rules with actual practices. In general Montgomery makes little attempt to investigate the relations between skilled and unskilled workers (Clawson, 1980, p. 166).
3. Ideas and novel techniques were widely discussed at professional forums, such as those of the American Society of Mechanical Engineers (ASME), and were widely publicized in such journals as the *Transactions* of ASME, the *American Machinist*, and the *Engineering Magazine* (Nadworny, 1955, Chapter 1; D. Nelson, 1975, p. 49).
4. The First World War had an important effect on accounting practices. Before 1914, many companies only kept skeletal, single-entry accounts, but the war-time Excess Profits Tax of 1917 created a sudden need to minimize the government's possible tax-take. As in Britain the need to provide meaningful figures to the government led to the introduction of up-to-date accounting methods for the first time in many organizations (Navin, 1950, pp. 321–4).
5. Another example is provided by the Whitin Machine works. As at Winchester's, the process of managerial centralization at the Whitin works was directly influenced by Taylorism. A New York firm of management consultants – Suffern & Son – were called in the spring of 1912. Though the consultants only stayed for five months, and the experiment in 'efficiency engineering' was judged to be only a qualified success, nevertheless it was retained by the Whitin company and extended to other departments. In 1914, partly stimulated by the war conditions, consultants were again called in to introduce a new shop layout and move from a product organization to a functional organization (Navin, 1950, pp. 318–20 and 607).
6. The Transport and General Workers was founded in 1922, and the General and Municipal in 1924. The basic pattern of British trade union organization was laid down by the 1920s.

Chapter 12

1. The Five Dollar Day was introduced in the year 1914 at Ford's car plants. This

204 Development of the Labour Process

marked a new era of labour management at Fords, and the beginning of Fordism *as an ideology*. The influence on Europe in the inter-war years was such that one German writer saw the solution to the labour problem as 'Ford or Marx' (Walcher, 1925). In a similar vein a British employer wrote in 1932 that 'British industry must nationalize or rationalize' (Sir William Seager, 1932).

2. This pattern was also repeated in France (letter from Fridenson, 13 August 1979).

References

ABERCROMBIE, N. and HILL, S. (1976), 'Paternalism and patronage', *British Journal of Sociology* **27**, pp. 413–29.

ACKROYD, S. (1974), 'Economic rationality and the relevance of Weberian sociology to industrial relations', *British Journal of Industrial Relations*, **12**, pp. 236–48.

AITKEN, H.G.J. (1960), *Taylorism at Watertown Arsenal*, Cambridge, Mass., Harvard University Press.

AKIN, W.E. (1977), *Technocracy and the American Dream: the Technocrat Movement, 1900–41*, University of California Press.

ALBROW, M. (1970), *Bureaucracy*, London Macmillan.

ALFORD, L.P. (1924), *Management's Handbook*, The Ronald Press Co.

ALLEN, V.L. (1977), 'The differentiation of the working class' in HUNT, A. (ed.) *Class and Class Structure*, London, Lawrence and Wishart, pp. 61–80.

AMERICAN FEDERATION of LABOR, (1935), 'AFL report on the Bedaux system', *American Federationist*, **XLII**, pp. 936–43.

ASHWORTH, J.H. (1915) *The Helper and American Trade Unions*, Baltimore, John Hopkins University Press.

ATHENAEUM (1917), 'Industrial reconstruction: an Employer's view', **4615**, March, pp. 134–7.

BABBAGE, C. (1835), 'On the economy of machinery and manufactures', excerpted in DAVIS and TAYLOR (eds.) (1972).

BALDAMUS, W. (1961), *Efficiency and Effort: An Analysis of Industrial Administration*, London, Tavistock.

BARLEY, L.J. (1932), *The Riddle of Rationalization*, London, Allen and Unwin.

BECKER, G. (1964), *Human Capital*, New York, Columbia University Press.

BEDAUX, C.E. (1917), *The Bedaux Efficiency Course for Industrial Application*, Bedaux Industrial Institute.

BEDAUX, C.E. (1928, unpublished), *Code of Standard Practice*.

BEDAUX, C.E. (undated, about 1930a; unpublished), *Code of Application Principles*.

BEDAUX, C.E. Ltd (undated, about 1930b; unpublished), *Training Course for Field Engineers*.

BEDAUX, C.E. Ltd (1933, unpublished) *Standard Bedaux, Weekly Analysis Sheet: Notes on Use*.

BEDAUX, C.E. (unpublished 1950, original version about 1930), *Vade Mecum*.

BEDAUX ARCHIVES, 1926–39, Microfilms 1–27.

BEHREND, H. (1957), 'The effort bargain', *Industrial and Labour Relations Review*, **10**, 503–15.

BEHREND, H. (1961), 'A fair day's work', *Scottish Journal of Political Economy*, **8**, pp. 102–18.

BENDIX, R. (1974 edn.), *Work and Authority in Industry*, University of California Press.

BENN, E.J.P. (1918), *Trade Parliaments and Their Work*, Nisbet.

BENNETT, J.W. and ISHINO, I. (1963), *Paternalism in the Japanese Economy*, University of Minnesota Press.

BENSMAN J. and GERVER, I. (1963), 'Crime and punishment in the factory: the function of deviancy in maintaining the social system', *American Sociological Review* 28, pp. 588–98.

BERG, M. (ed.) (1979), *Technology and Toil in Nineteenth Century Britain*, Conference of Socialist Economics Books.

BEYNON, H. (1973), *Working for Ford*, Harmondsworth, Penguin.

BIENEFELD, M.A. (1972), *Working Hours in British Industry: an Economic History*, London, Weidenfeld and Nicolson.

BLACKBURN, R.M. and MANN, M. (1979), *The Working Class in the Labour Market*, London, Macmillan.

BLAU, P.M. (1956) *Bureaucracy in Modern Society*, New York, Random House.

BODNAR, J. (1977), *Immigrants and Industrialization: Ethnicity in an American Mill Town, 1870–1940*, Pittsburgh, University of Pittsburgh Press.

BRANSON, N. and HEINEMANN, M. (1973) *Britain in the 1930s*, London, Weidenfeld and Nicolson. Refs. to Panther edn.

BRASSEY, T. (1872 edn.), *Work and Wages*, Bell & Daldy.

BRAVERMAN, H. (1974), *Labor and Monopoly Capital*, New York, Monthly Review Press.

BRECHER, J. *et al.* (1978), 'Uncovering the hidden history of the American workplace' *Review of Radical Political Economics*, Winter, pp. 1–23.

BRIGHTON LABOUR PROCESS GROUP (1977), 'The capitalist labour process' *Capital and Class*, 1, pp. 3–26

BRODY, D. (1968), 'The rise and decline of welfare capitalism', in BRAEMAN, J. *et al.* (eds.) *Change and Continuity in Twentieth-Century America: the 1920s*, Columbus, Ohio, Ohio State University Press.

BROWN, G. (1977), *Sabotage: a Study in Industrial Conflict*, Spokesman Books.

BROWNLOW, V.M.A. (undated, unpublished) *A History of the Bedaux Company*.

BRUGGER, W. (1976), *Democracy and Organization in the Chinese Industrial Enterprise, 1948–53*, Cambridge, Cambridge University Press.

BURAWOY, M. (1979), *Manufacturing Consent*, Chicago, University of Chicago Press.

BURCHILL, F. and ROSS, R. (1977), *A History of the Potters' Union, Ceramic and Allied Grades Union*, Stoke-on-Trent, Hanley.

BURGESS, K. (1975), *The Origins of British Industrial Relations*, London, Croom Helm.

BURGESS, K. (1980), *The Challenge of Labour*, London, Croom Helm.

BURNETT, J. (ed.) (1977), *Useful Toil*, Harmondsworth, Penguin.

BUTTRICK, J. (1952), 'The inside contract system', *Journal of Economic History*, 12, pp. 205–21.

CADBURY, E. (1914a), 'Some principles of industrial organization: the case for and against scientific management', *Sociological Review*, First Series 99–125.

CADBURY, E. (1914b), 'Reply to C.B. Thompson', *Sociological Review*, 7, p. 327.

CAPLOW, T. (1954), *The Sociology of Work*, New York, McGraw-Hill.

CARPENTER, C.U. (1903) 'The working of a labour department in industrial establishments', *Engineering Magazine*, XXV, 1, pp. 4–5.

CASSON, H.N. (1917), *Factory Efficiency: How to Increase Output, Wages, Dividends and Good-will*, London, The Efficiency Magazine.

CHANDLER, A.D. (1965), 'The railroads: pioneers in modern corporate management', *Business History Review*, 39, pp. 16–40.

CHANDLER, A.D. (1976), 'The development of modern management structure in the US and UK', in HANNAH (1976b), pp. 23–51.

CHILD, J. (1964), 'Quaker employers and industrial relations', *Sociological Review*, 12, pp. 293–315.

CHILD, J. (1969), *British Management Thought*, London, Allen and Unwin.

CHILD, J. (1975), 'The industrial supervisor', in ESLAND, G. SALAMAN, G. and SPEAKMAN, M, *People and Work*, Holmes McDougall, pp. 70–87.

CLAWSON, D. (1980) *Bureaucracy and the Labor Process*, New York, Monthly Review Press.

CLEGG, H., FOX, A., and THOMPSON, P. (1964), *A History of British Trade Unions since 1889*, Oxford, Oxford University Press

COHEN, J. HAZELRIGG, L.E., and POPE, W. (1975), 'De-parsonizing Weber', *American Sociological Review*, **40**, pp. 417–27.

COLE, G.D.H. (1918), 'The payment of wages', T.U. Series no. 5, Fabian Research Department.

COLE, G.D.H. (1923), *Workshop Organization*, London, Hutchinson.

COLE, G.D.H. and COLE, M.I. (1937), *The Condition of Britain*, London, Gollancz.

COLE, R.E. (1971), *Japanese Blue Collar: The Changing Tradition*, University of California Press.

COLE, R.E. (1979), *Work, Mobility and Participation; A Comparative Study of American and Japanese Industry*, University of California Press.

COOMBS, R. (1978), 'Labour and monopoly capital', *New Left Review*, **107**, January–February, 1978, pp. 79–96.

COPLEY, F.B. (1915), 'Frederick W. Taylor: Revolutionist', *The Outlook*, **III**, September.

CRAWCOUR, S. (1978), 'The Japanese Employment System' in *Journal of Japanese Studies*, **4**, 2, pp. 225–45.

CRESSEY, P. and MACINNES, J. (1980), Voting for Ford: industrial democracy and the control of labour', *Capital and Class*, **11**, pp. 5–33.

CROSSICK, G. (1978), *An Artisan Elite in Victorian Society, Kentish London 1840–80*, London, Croom Helm.

CROZIER, M. (1964), *The Bureaucratic Phenomenon*, Chicago, University of Chicago Press.

CROZIER, M. (1971), *The World of the Office Worker*, Chicago, University of Chicago Press.

CUTLER, T. (1978), 'The romance of labour', *Economy and Society*, **7**, pp. 74–9.

DAVIS, L.E. (1966), 'The design of jobs', in DAVIS and TAYLOR (eds.) (1972), pp. 299–327.

DAVIS, L.E. and TAYLOR, J.C. (eds.) (1972), *Design of Jobs*, Harmondsworth, Penguin.

DAVIS, L.E., CANTER, R.R. and HOFFMAN, J. (1955), 'Current job design criteria', in DAVIS and TAYLOR (eds.) (1972), pp. 65–82.

DAVIS, M. (1975), 'The stop-watch and the wooden shoe: scientific management and the IWW', *Radical America*, **9**, pp. 69–95.

DAVIS, M. (1980) 'Why the US working class is different', *New Left Review*, **123**, September–October, 3–44.

DEKADT, M. (1976) 'The importance of distinguishing between levels of generality', *Review of Radical Political Economy*, **8**, pp. 65–7.

DEVINAT, P. (1927), *Scientific Management in Europe*, ILO, Studies and Reports, Series B, No. 17, Geneva.

DEYRUP, F.J. (1948), *Arms Makers of the Connecticut Valley: a regional study of the small arms industry*, 1798–1890, Vol. 33, Smith College Studies in History, Northampton, Mass. (printed by George Banta Publishing, Menaska, Wisconisin).

DOBB, M. (1928), *Wages*, Cambridge, Cambridge University Press.

DOBB, M. (1963, first edn. 1948), *Studies in the Development of Capitalism*, London, Routledge and Kegan Paul.

DOERINGER, P. and PIORE, M. (1971) *Internal Labour Markets and Manpower Analysis*, Lexington, Mass., Heath Lexington Books.

DORE, R.P. (1969) 'The modernizer as a special case: Japanese factory legislation, 1882–1911', *Comparative Studies in Society and History*, **11**, 4, pp. 433–50.

DORE, R.P. (1973), *British Factory – Japanese Factory*, London, Allen and Unwin.

DUGGAN, E.P. (1977), 'Machines, markets and Labor: the carriage and wagon, industry in nineteenth-century Cincinnati', *Business History Review*, **51**, Autumn, pp. 308–25.

DUNKERLEY, D. (1980), 'Technological change and work: upgrading or deskilling?', in

BOREHAM, P. and DOW, G. (eds.), *Work and Inequality: the Impact of Capitalist Crisis on Work Experience and the Labour Process*, Sydney, Macmillan.

DUNKERLEY, D. and SALAMAN, G., (1980), *The International Yearbook of Organization Studies, 1979*, London, Routledge and Kegan Paul.

DURKHEIM, E. (1933), *The Division of Labour in Society*, New York, Free Press.

EDWARDS, R. (1978), 'Social relations of production at the point of production', *Insurgent Sociologist*, **8**, 2–3, pp. 109–25.

EDWARDS, R. (1979), *Contested Terrain*, London, Heinemann.

EILBERT, H. (1959), The development of personnel management in the United States, *Business History Review*, **33**, Autumn, pp. 345–64.

ELBAUM and WILKINSON, F. (1979), 'Industrial relations and uneven development: a comparative study of the American and British steel industries', *Cambridge Journal of Economics*, **3**, pp. 275–303.

ELGER, A. (1978), 'Valorization and deskilling: a critique of Braverman', paper presented at the Nuffield Deskilling Conference, December 1978. Published in *Capital and Class*, **7**, 1979.

ETZIONI, A. (1964), *Modern Organizations*, Englewood Cliffs, New Jersey, Prentice Hall.

EVANS, R. (1970), 'Evolution of the Japanese Systems of Employer–Employee Relations, 1868–1945', *Business History Review*, **V.XLIV**, 1, pp. 110–125.

FLANNER, J. (1945), 'Annals of collaboration: equivalism', *New Yorker*, 22 September, 6 October and 13 October, 1945.

FOSTER, J. (1974), *Class Struggle and the Industrial Revolution*, London, Methuen.

FOX, A. (1955), 'Industrial relations in nineteenth century Birmingham', *Oxford Economic Papers*, **8**, Part 1, pp. 57–70.

FOX, A. (1971), 'A sociology of work in industry', New York, Collier-Macmillan.

FOX, A. (1974), *Beyond Contract: Work, Power and Trust Relations*, London, Faber & Faber.

FOXWELL, E. (1901), 'The protection of labour in Japan', *The Economic Journal* **11**, March.

FRANCIS, A. (1980), 'Families, firms and finance capital', *Sociology*, **14**, 2, pp. 1–28.

FRANKS, B. (1970) *The Measured Day Work and Productivity Deal Swindle*, an All Trades Union Alliance pamphlet, Workers Press.

FREY, J.P. (1913), 'The relationship of scientific management to labour', *Journal of Political Economy*, **21**, pp. 400–11.

FRIDENSON, P. (1978a) 'The Coming of the Assembly Line to Europe', in KROHN, LAYTON and WEINGART (eds.), *The Dynamics of Science of Technology*: Sociology of the Sciences Vol. II, Dordrecht, Holland, D. Reidel.

FRIDENSON, P. (1978b, mimeo), 'Corporate policy, rationalization and the labour force: French experiences in international comparison, 1900–1929', paper presented at the Nuffield Deskilling Conference, December.

FRIEDMAN, A. (1977), *Industry and Labour*, London, Macmillan.

FRIEDMANN, G. (1955), *Industrial Society: the Emergence of the Human Problems of Automation*, New York, Free Press.

FRIEDMANN, G. (1961), *The Anatomy of Work*, London, Heinemann.

GARTMAN, D. (1978), 'Marx and the Labor process: an interpretation', *Insurgent Sociologist*, **8**, nos. 2 and 3, pp. 97–108.

GINTIS, H. (1976), 'The nature of labour exchange and the theory of capitalist production', *Review of Radical Political Economics*, summer, pp. 36–54.

GOFFEE, R.E. (1977), 'The butty system and the Kent coalfield', *Bulletin of the Society for the Study of Labour History*, spring, no. 34.

GOLDMAN, P. and VAN HOUTEN, D.R. (1980), 'Bureaucracy and domination: managerial strategy in turn-of-the-century American industry' in DUNKERLEY and SALAMAN, 1980.

GOODRICH, C.L. (1921, 1975 edn.), *The Frontier of Control*, London, Pluto Press.

GORDON, D.M. (1972) *Theories of Poverty and Underemployment*, Lexington, Lexington Books.

GOSPEL, H. (1978), 'The development of management organization in industrial relations – an historical perspective', mimeo, University of Kent.

GOULDNER, A.W. (1954), *Patterns of Industrial Bureaucracy*, New York, Free Press.

GRAY, R.Q. (1976), *The Labour Aristocracy in Victorian Edinburgh*, Oxford, Oxford University Press.

GURNHAM, R. (undated, unpublished), *The Hosiery Worker: a History of Trade Unionism in the Hosiery Industry 1770–1970*.

HABER, S. (1964), 'Efficiency and Uplift: Scientific Management in the Progressive Era, 1890–1920', Chicago, University of Chicago Press.

HANNAH, L. (1976a), *The Rise of the Corporate Economy*, London, Methuen.

HANNAH, L. (ed.) (1976b), *Management Strategy and Business Development: an Historical and Comparative Study*, London, Macmillan.

HARADA, S. (1928), *Labor Conditions in Japan*, New York, Columbia University Press.

HARLEY, C.K. (1974), 'Skilled labour and the choice of technique in Edwardian industry', *Explorations in Economic History*, 11, pp. 391–414.

HARRIS, N. (1971 edn.), *Beliefs in Society*, London, Penguin.

HARRIS, N. (1972), *Competition and the Corporate Society: British Conservatives, the State and Industry, 1945–64*, London, Methuen.

HAZAMA, H. (1981), 'Japanese industrialization and labour-management relations, 1860–1930', unpublished paper presented at the SSRC Conference on Business and Labour History March 1981.

HAZAMA, H. and KAMINSKI, J. (1979), 'Japanese Labor–Management Relations', *Journal of Japanese Studies*, 9, 1, pp. 71–106.

HEAD, P. (1961, unpublished), 'Industrial organization in Leicester, 1844–1914: a study in changing technology, innovation and conditions of employment', Ph.D., University of Leicester.

HICHENS, W.L. (1918), *Some Problems of Modern Industry: Being the Watt Anniversary Lecture*, London, Nisbet and Company.

HIMMELWEIT, S. (1982), 'Modern Britain: The Economic Base', Open University Course D.102, Block 2, Unit 5.

HINTON, J. (1973), *The First Shop Stewards Movement*, London, Allen and Unwin.

HOBSBAWM, E.J. (1964), *Labouring Men*, London, Weidenfeld and Nicolson.

HOBSBAWM, E.J. (1969 edn.), *Industry and Empire*, The Pelican Economic History of Britain, Vol. 3.

HOLMES, J. (1981), *The Strike in the Hinckley Hosiery Trade* (pamphlet).

HOXIE, R.F. (1915), 'Scientific management and labour', extracted in KLEIN (1976).

HYMAN, R. (1976), 'Trade Unions, Control and Resistance', Open University Course DE351, Unit 14.

HYMAN, R. and BROUGH, I. (1975), *Social Values and Industrial Relations*, Blackwell.

INDUSTRIAL RECONSTRUCTION COUNCIL (1918), *Reconstruction Handbook*, Nisbet.

JAQUES, E. (1961) *Equitable Payment*, London, Heinemann.

JEFFERYS, J.B. (1945), *The Story of the Engineers*, 1800–1945 London, Lawrence & Wishart.

JENKINS, M. (1974), *Time and Motion Strike, Manchester, 1934–7*, Our History Pamphlet 60, London, autumn.

JENKS, L.H. (1960), 'Early phases of the management movement', *Administrative Science Quarterly*, 5, pp. 421–7.

JOHNSON, T. (1976), 'Work and Power', in Open University Course DE351, Unit 16.

JONES, B. (1978) 'Destruction or redistribution of engineering skills? The case of numerical control', paper presented at the Nuffield Deskilling Conference, December, mimeo.

KARSH, B. (1976), 'Industrial relations in Japan', in DUBIN, R. (ed.) *Handbook of Work, Organization and Society*, Chicago, Rand McNally.

KERR, C., DUNLOP, J.T., HARBISON, E., and MYERS, C.A. (eds.) (1973), *Industrialism and Industrial Man*, Harmondsworth, Penguin.

KLEIN, L. (1976), *New Forms of Work Organization*, Cambridge, Cambridge U.P.

KOCKA, J. (1971), 'Family and bureaucracy in German industrial Management, 1850–1914: Siemens in comparative perspective', *Business History Review*, 45, pp. 133–56.

KUMAR, K. (1978), *Prophecy and Progress: The Sociology of Industrial and Post-Industrial Society*, Harmondsworth, Penguin.

KUZNETS, S. (1961), *Capital in the American Economy*, Princeton, Princeton U.P.

KYNASTON-REEVES, T. and WOODWARD, J. (1970), The study of managerial control' in WOODWARD, J., *Industrial Organization: Behaviour and Control*, Oxford, Oxford University Press, pp. 37–56.

LALOUX, P. (1951), *Le Système Bedaux Calcul Des Salaires*, Paris, Edition Hommes et Techniques.

LANDES, D.S. (1969), *The Unbound Prometheus: Technological Change and Industrial Development in West Europe From 1750 to the Present*, Cambridge, Cambridge University Press.

LAYTON, E. (1971), *The Revolt of the Engineers*, Ohio University Press.

LAYTON, E. (1974), 'The Diffusion of Scientific Management & Mass Production From the United States In The Twentieth Century', Proceedings of the XIVth International Congress in the History of Science, Tokyo, Vol. 4, pp. 377–86.

LAZONICK, W. (1979), 'Industrial relations and technical change: the case of the self-acting mule', *Cambridge Journal of Economics*, 3, pp. 231–62.

LEBERGOTT, S. (1964), *Manpower in Economic Growth: the United States Record since 1800*, New York, McGraw-Hill.

LEE, D.J. (1981), 'Skill, craft and class: a theoretical critique and a critical case', *Sociology*, 15, 1, pp. 56–78.

LEE, J. (1921), *Management: A Study of Industrial Organization*, London, Pitman.

LEVINE, A.L. (1967), *Industrial Retardation in Britain*, London, Weidenfeld and Nicolson.

LEVINE, S.B. (1965), 'Labour markets and collective bargaining in Japan', in W.W. LOCKWOOD (ed.).

LEVINE, S.B. and KAWADA, H. (1980) *Human Resources in Japanese Industrial Development*, Princeton University Press.

LITTERER, J. (1961), 'Systematic management: the search for order and integration', *Business History Review*, 35, pp. 461–76.

LITTERER, J. (1963), 'Systematic management: design for organizational recoupling in American manufacturing firms', *Business History Review*, 37, pp. 369–91.

LITTLER, C.R. (1976, mimeo), Research report on British and American banks.

LITTLER, C.R. (1978), 'Understanding Taylorism', *British Journal of Sociology*, 29, pp. 185–202.

LITTLER, C.R. (1980), 'Internal contract and the transition to modern work systems: Britain and Japan', in DUNKERLEY and SALAMAN, pp. 157–85.

LITTLER, C.R. (1981), 'Power and Ideology in Work Organizations: Britain and Japan', Open University Course D.207, Block 3, Study Section 22.

LITTLER, C.R. and SALAMAN, G. (1982), Bravermania and beyond: recent theories of the labour process', *Sociology*, 16, 2 May.

LIVINGSTON, J., MOORE, J., and OLDFATHER, F. (eds.) (1976 edn.), *The Japan Reader*, Vols. 1 and 2, Harmondsworth, Penguin.

LIVINGSTONE, P. (1969), 'Stop the stopwatch', *New Society*, 10 July, pp. 49–51.

LOCKWOOD, W.W. (ed.) (1965), *The State and Economic Enterprise in Japan*, Princeton, Princeton University Press.

LUPTON, T. (1957), 'A sociologist looks at work study', *Work Study and Industrial Engineering*, 1, February, pp. 43–8.

MAIER, C.S. (1970), 'Between Taylorism and technocracy: European ideologies and the vision of industrial productivity in the 1920s', in *The Journal of Contemporary History*, 5, 2.

MARSH, A.I. (1979), *Trade Union Handbook*, London, Gower Press.

MARX, K. (1973), *Grundisse: Introduction to the Critique of Political Economy*, Harmondsworth, Penguin.

MARX, K. (1976, edn.), *Capital: A Critique of Political Economy*, Vol. *1*, Harmondsworth, Penguin.

MAYNTZ, R. (1964), 'The study of organizations', *Current Sociology*, **XIII**, 3.

MEAKIN, B. (1905), *Model Factories and Villages: Ideal Conditions of Labour and Housing*, Fisher Unwin.

MEARS, H. (1976) 'Year of the wild boar', extracted in LIVINGSTON *et al.*, pp. 413–24.

MELLING, J. (1980) 'Non-commissioned officers: British employers and their supervisory workers, 1880–1920', *Social History*, May, pp. 183–221.

MILLER, S. (1938), 'Labor's attitude toward time and motion study', *Mechanical Engineering*, **LX**, April, pp. 289–338.

MILLER, D.C. and FORM, W.H. (1964), *Industrial Sociology*, New York, Harper and Row.

MILLS, C. WRIGHT (1951), *White Collar*, Oxford, Oxford University Press.

MONDS, J. (1976), 'Workers control and the historians: a new economism', *New Left Review*, May/June, pp. 81–100.

MONTAGNA, P.D. (1977), *Occupations and Society: Towards a Sociology of the Labor Market*, New York, John Wiley.

MONTGOMERY, D. (1974), 'The "new unionism" and the transformation of workers' consciousness in America 1909–22', *The Journal of Social History*, Summer, 1974.

MONTGOMERY, D. (1979), *Workers Control in America*, Cambridge, Cambridge University Press.

MOORHOUSE, H. (1978), 'The Marxist theory of the labour aristocracy', *Social History*, **3**, pp. 61–82.

MORE, C.R.V. (1980) *Skill and the English Working Class 1870–1914*, London, Croom Helm.

MORROW, L.C. (1922), 'The Bedaux principle of human power measurement', *American Machinist*, **56**, 16 February, pp. 241–5.

MOUZELIS, N. (1967), *Organization and Bureaucracy*, London, Routledge and Kegan Paul.

MOWAT, C.L. (1955), *Britain Between the Wars, 1918–40*, London, Methuen.

MYERS, C.S. (1932), *Business Rationalization*, London, Pitman.

NADWORNY, M.J. (1955), *Scientific Management and the Unions, 1900–32*, Cambridge, Harvard University Press.

NAKAGAWA, K. (ed.) (1979), *Labour and Management: Proceedings of the 4th Fuji Conference*, Tokyo, University of Tokyo Press.

NAKANE, C. (1970), *Japanese Society*. Refs. are to 1973 edn., Harmondsworth, Penguin.

NAKASE, T. (1979), 'The introduction of scientific management in Japan and its characteristics', in NAKAGAWA, pp. 171–202.

NAVIN, T.R. (1950), *The Whitin Machine Works since 1831*, Russell & Russell.

NEDO (National Economic Development Office) (1970), *Hosiery and Knitwear in the 1970s*, HMSO.

NELSON, D. (1974), 'Scientific management, systematic management, and labor, 1880–1915', *Business History Review*, **28**, pp. 479–500.

NELSON, D. (1975), *Managers and Workers*, University of Wisconsin Press.

NELSON, D. (1980), *Frederick W. Taylor and the Rise of Scientific Management*, University of Wisconsin Press.

NELSON, E.G. (1930), 'The English framework-knitting industry', *Journal of Economic and Business History*.

NELSON, R.L. (1959), 'Merger Movements in American Industry, 1895–1956', Princeton, Princeton University Press.

NIESR (National Institute of Economic and Social Research) (1980) *Skill, Training and the Machine Tool Industry*.

NIVEN, M.M. (1967), *Personnel Management 1913-63: The Growth of Personnel Management and the Development of the Institute*, Institute of Personnel Management.

NOBLE, D.F. (1977), *America By Design: Science, Technology and the Rise of Corporate Capitalism*, New York, Knopf.

NOBLE, D.F. (1979), 'Social choice in machine design: the case of automatically controlled machine tools', in ZIMBALIST (ed.), pp. 18–50.

NORMAN, E.H. (1940), *Japan's Emergence As a Modern State*, Institute of Pacific Relations.

NORRIS, G.M. (1978), 'Industrial paternalist capitalism and local labour markets', *Sociology*, 12, 3, pp. 469–89.

O'CONNOR, J. (1975), 'Productive and unproductive labor', *Politics and Society*, 5, 3, pp. 297–336.

OKUDA, K. (1972), 'Managerial evolution in Japan', *Management Japan*, 6, 1.

ORCHARD, J. (1930), *Japan's Economic Position: the Progress of Industrialization*, New York, McGraw-Hill

PALLOIX, C. (1976), 'The labour process: from Fordism to neo-Fordism', in CSE Pamphlet no.1, *The Labour Process and Class Strategies*, 1976, pp. 46–67.

PALMER, B. (1975), 'Class conception and conflict: the thrust for efficiency, managerial views of labor and the working class rebellion', in *Review of Radical Political Economics*, 7, pp. 31–49.

PALMER, B. (1976), 'Political economists, historians and generalization', 8, pp. 68–9.

PARSONS, T. (1964), Introduction to Weber (1947), pp. 3–86.

PATRICK, H.T. (1975), 'Comment' on Yamamura (1975), in H.F. Williamson (1975), pp. 186–92.

PAYNE, P.L. (1974), *British entrepreneurship in the nineteenth century*, London, Macmillan.

PEARSON, H.S. (1937), 'The Bedaux System', *The New Republic*, XCIII, Part 17, p. 71.

PERROW, C. (1972), *Complex Organizations: A Critical Essay*, Scott Foresman.

PHELPS-BROWN, E.H. (1959), *The Growth of British Industrial Relations*, London, Macmillan.

PIGOU, A.C. (Chairman) (1930), 'Problems of rationalization: discussion', *Economic Journal*, 40, pp. 351–68.

PIORE, M.J. (1972), 'Notes for a theory of labor market stratification', Working paper no. 95, Department of Economics, MIT.

POLLARD, S. (1968 edn.), *The Genesis of Modern Management*, Harmondsworth, Penguin.

POLLARD, S. (1969 edn.), *The Development of the British Economy, 1914–67*, London, Edward Arnold.

POLLARD, S. and ROBERTSON, P. (1979), *The British Shipbuilding Industry 1870–1914*, Cambridge, Mass, Harvard University Press.

POOL, A.G. and LLEWELLYN, G. (1955–8), *The British Hosiery Industry: A Study in Competition*, Three reports published by Leicester University.

POUNDS, N.J.G. (1952), *The Ruhr: A Study of Historical and Economic Geography*, Bloomington, Indiana University Press.

PUGH, A. (1951), *Men of Steel*, London, Iron and Steel Trades Confederation.

RAMSAY, A. (1977), 'Cycles of control: worker participation in sociological and historical perspective', *Sociology*, September 1977, 11, 3.

RANDALL, P.E. (1969), *Introduction to Work Study and Organization and Methods*, London, Butterworth.

REID, A. (1980), 'The division of labour in the British shipbuilding industry, 1880–1920', unpublished Ph.D. thesis, University of Cambridge.

RICHARDSON, J.H. (1954), 'An introduction to the Study of Industrial Relations', Allen and Unwin.

RICHMOND, J.R. (1917), 'Some aspects of labour and its claims in the engineering industry', Presidential address to the Glasgow University Engineering Society, mimeo.

ROSE, M. (1975), *Industrial Behaviour: Theoretical Developments since Taylor*, London, Allen Lane.

ROSOVSKY, H. (1961), *Capital Formation in Japan*, New York, Free Press.

ROWE, J.W.F. (1928; re-issued 1969), *Wages in Practice and Theory*, London, Routledge and Kegan Paul.

SAMUEL, R. (ed.) (1977), *Miners, Quarrymen and Salt Workers*, London, Routledge and Kegan Paul.

SAUL, S.B. (1969), *The Myth of the Great Depression, 1873–96*, London, Macmillan.
SAUL, S.B. (1970), *Technological Change: the United States and Britain in the Nineteenth Century*, London, Methuen.
SCHLOSS, D.F. (1898 edn.), *Methods of Industrial Remuneration*, London, Williams & Norgate.
SCHOENHOF, J. (1892), *The Economy of High Wages: An Inquiry into the Cause of High Wages and their Effect on Methods and Cost of Production*, New York, G.P. Putnams Sons.
SEAGER, W. (1932), 'British industry must nationalize or rationalize', *Business*, May, pp. 9–10.
SETH-SMITH, M. (1973), *200 Years of Richard Johnson & Nephew*, privately published by R.J. & N.
SHADWELL, A. (1906 edn.), *Industrial Efficiency: A Comparative Study of Industrial Life in England, Germany and America*, 2 vols., London, Longmans.
SHADWELL, A. (1916), 'The welfare of factory workers', *The Edinburgh Review*, October, pp. 375–6.
SHELDON, O. (1923), *The Philosophy of Management* London, Pitman.
SLICHTER, S.H. (1919), *The Turnover of Factory Labor*, New York, D. Appleton & Co.
SMITH, A. (1970 edn.) *The Wealth of Nations*, Harmondsworth, Penguin.
SMITH, H.L. and NASH, V. (1889), *The Story of the Dockers Strike 1889*, London, Cedric Chivers.
SMITH, T.C. (1955) *Political Change & Industrial Development in Japan: Government Enterprise, 1868–1880* Stanford, Stanford University Press.
SOFFER, B. (1960), 'A theory of trade union development: the role of the "autonomous" workman', *Labor History*, 1, pp. 141–63.
SPENCER, E. GLOVKA, (1979), 'Rulers of the Ruhr: leadership and authority in German big business before 1914', *Business History Review*, 53, pp. 40–64.
STANDRING, P.K. (1934), 'The Bedaux system', *Industry Illustrated*, May/June 1934. Report by Standring of ICI to the Manchester Branch of the British Works Management Association, 14 February 1934.
STARK, D. (unpublished 1978), 'Class, Structure, Class Struggle and the Labor Process', Harvard University.
STARK, D. (1980) 'Class struggle and the transformation of the labour process', *Theory and Society*, 9 pp. 89–130.
STEARNS, P.N. (1975), *Lives of Labour*, London, Croom Helm.
STEDMAN-JONES, G. (1975), 'Class struggle and the Industrial Revolution', 90, March/April.
STINCHCOMBE, A. (1959), 'Bureaucratic and craft administration of production', *Administrative Science Quarterly*, 4, pp. 168–87.
STINCHCOMBE, A.L. (1968), *Constructing Social Theories*, New York, Harcourt Brace.
STINCHCOMBE, A.L. (1974), *Creating Efficient Industrial Administrations*, New York, Academic Press.
STONE, K. (1973) 'The origin of job structures in the steel industry', *Radical America*, 7, pp. 19–24.
SWARD, K. (1972), *The Legend of Henry Ford*, New York, Holt, Rinehart and Winston.
TAIRA, K. (1970) *Economic Development and the Labor Market in Japan*, New York, Columbia University Press.
TAYLOR, A.J. (1960) 'The sub-contract system in the British coal industry', in PRESNELL, L.S. (ed.), *Studies in the Industrial Revolution*, Athlone Press, pp. 215–35.
TAYLOR, F.W. (1903), 'Shop management'. Reprinted in Taylor (1964).
TAYLOR, F.W. (1909), 'Why manufacturers dislike college students', Proceedings of the Society for the Promotion of Engineering Education, 1909, 17, 87.
TAYLOR, F.W. (1911), 'The principles of scientific management'. Reprinted in Taylor (1964).
TAYLOR, F.W. (1912), 'Taylor's testimony before the Special House Committee'. Reprinted in Taylor (1964).

TAYLOR, F.W. (1964), *Scientific Management*, New York, Harper and Row.

TEMIN, P. (1975), *Causal Factors in American Economic Growth in the Nineteenth Century*, London, Macmillan.

THOMPSON, C.B. (1913), 'The relations of scientific management to the wage problem', *Journal of Political Economy*, **21**, July, pp. 628–35.

THURLEY, K. and WIRDENIUS, H. (1973), *Supervision: A Reappraisal*, London, Heinemann.

TOTTEN, G.O. (1966), *The Social Democratic Movement in Prewar Japan*, New Haven, Yale University Press.

TOURAINE, A. (1962), 'An historical theory in the evolution of industrial skills', in WALKER, C.R. *Modern Technology and Civilization*, New York, McGraw-Hill, pp. 425–37.

TRIST, E. (1973), 'A socio-technical critique of scientific management', in EDGE, D.O. and WOLFE, J.N., *Meaning and Control*, Tavistock, pp. 95–116.

TSUDA, M. (1979), 'The formation and characteristics of the work group in Japan', in NAKAGAWA, pp. 29–42.

TUC (Trades Union Congress) (1910), *Premium Bonus System Report*.

TUC (Trades Union Congress) (1932) *General Councils Report*.

TUC (Trades Union Congress) (1933), *Bedaux Report*.

TURNER, G. (1969), *Business in Britain*, London, Eyre & Spottiswoode. Refs. to 1971 edn., Harmondsworth, Penguin.

TURNER, H.A. (1962), *Trade Union Growth, Structure and Policy*, London, George Allen and Unwin.

UDY, S.H. (1959), 'Bureaucracy and rationality in Weber's organization theory: an empirical study', *American Sociological Review*, **24**, pp. 791–95.

URWICK, L.F. (1929), *The Meaning of Rationalization*, London, Nisbet.

URWICK, L. and BRECH, E.F.L., (1948), *The Making of Scientific Management*, Vol. II, London, Pitman.

UTTON, M.A. (1972), 'Some features of the early merger movements in British manufacturing industry', *Business History*, **14**, pp. 51–60.

WALCHER, J. (1925), *Ford oder Marx. Die praktische Lösung der sozialen Frage*, Berlin, Nener Dt. Verlag.

WALTON, J. (1952, mimeo), 'A History of Trade Unionism in Leicester to the End of the nineteenth century', M.A. Thesis, University of Sheffield.

WARBURTON, W.H. (1939), *The History of Trade Union Organization in the North Staffordshire Potteries*, London, Allen and Unwin.

WATSON, W.F. (1934), *The Worker and Wage Incentives: the Bedaux and Other Systems*, Day-to-Day Pamphlet no. 20, The Hogarth Press.

WATSON, W.F. (1935), *Machines and Man: An Autobiography of an Itinerant Mechanic*, London, Allen and Unwin.

WEBB, S. and WEBB, B. (1898), *Industrial Democracy*, published by the authors.

WEBB, S. and WEBB, B. (1909), *The Public Organization of the Labour Market*; Being Part II of the Minority Report of the Poor Law Commission. Royal Commission on the Poor Laws and the Relief of Distress, London, Longman.

WEBER, M. (1947), *The Theory of Social & Economic Organization*, Refs. to 1964 edn., New York, Free Press.

WEIGHTS, A. (1978), 'Weber and legitimate domination: a theoretical critique of Weber's conceptualization of relations of domination', *Economy and Society*, 7, 1, pp. 56–73.

WELLS, F.A. (1972), *The British Hosiery and Knitwear Industry: Its History and Organization*, David & Charles (originally published 1935).

WERSKY, G. (1979), 'Review of D. Noble's *America by Design*, in *Radical Science Journal*, 8, pp. 109–18.

WHITEHILL, A.M. and TAKEZAWA, S. (1968), *The Other Worker*, Honolulu, East-West Center Press.

WILLIAMS, A. (1915), *Life in a Railway Factory*, London, Duckworth.

WILLIAMSON, H.F. (1975), *Evolution of International Management Structures*, University of Delaware Press.

WOLMAN, L. (1924), *The Growth of American Trade Unions, 1880–1923*, National Bureau of Economic Research.

WOODWARD, J. (ed.) (1970), *Industrial Organization: Behaviour and Control*, Oxford, Oxford University Press.

WORK IN AMERICA (1973), Report of a Special Task Force to the Secretary of Health, Education and Welfare, M.I.T. Press.

WRIGHT, E.O. (1975), 'Alternative perspectives in Marxist theory of accumulation and crisis', *Insurgent Sociologist*, **6**, 1, pp. 5–39.

YAMAMURA, K. (1964), 'Zaibatsu pre-war and Zaibatsu post-war', *Journal of Asian Studies*, **23**, pp. 539–54.

YAMAMURA, K. (1975), 'A compromise with culture: the historical evolution of the managerial structure of large Japanese firms', in WILLIAMSON (1975), pp. 159–85.

YOSHINO, M.Y. (1968), *Japan's Managerial System*, M.I.T. Press, Refs are to 1971 edn.

ZEITLIN, J. (1979), 'Craft control and the division of labour: engineers and compositors in Britain, 1890–1930', *Cambridge Journal of Economics*, **3**, pp. 263–74.

ZEITLIN, J. (1980), 'The emergence of shop steward organization and job control in the British car industry', *History Workshop Journal*, **10**, pp. 119–37.

ZEITLIN, J. (1981), 'The labour strategies of British engineering employers, 1890–1914', paper presented to the SSRC Conference on Business and Labour History, March, 1981, mimeo.

ZIMBALIST, A. (ed.) (1979) 'Case Studies On the Labor Process', Monthly Review Press.

Index